Note: Any archival images credited in the captions (RW) were personally photographed by Robert Welch

Opposite: Photograph of flowering artichoke head taken by Robert Welch, 1960s. Obviously attracted by its spiky, dramatic form, Robert later used it as a motif for various designs, including the logo for his own manufacturing company, Campden Designs.

LAURENCE KING

Published in 2015 by
Laurence King Publishing Limited
361–373 City Road
London EC1V 1LR

Text: Charlotte & Peter Fiell
Initial Design Concept: Tony Muranka
Graphic Design: Samuel Morley

www.laurenceking.com

A CIP catalogue record for this book is available from the British Library.

ISBN: 9781780676050

Printed in China

The quotation on page 4 is taken from William Blake's 'Exhibition and Catalogue of 1809' (page 550), quoted by Patricia Welch at the opening of the exhibition 'Robert Welch: Inspiration and Innovation' held at Court Barn Museum, Chipping Campden, Gloucestershire in 2014

ROBERT WELCH

Design: Craft & Industry

Charlotte & Peter Fiell

Laurence King Publishing

'The great and golden rule of art, as well as of life, is this:
that the more distinct, sharp and wiry the bounding line,
the more perfect the work of art;
and the less keen and sharp the greater is
the evidence of weak imitation.'

William Blake, 1809

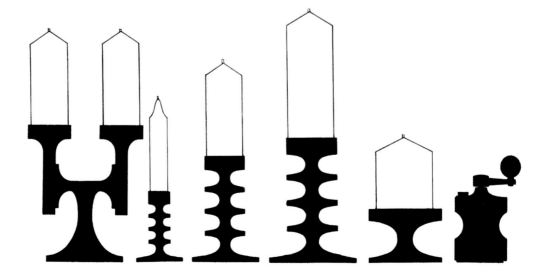

Contents

7	Foreword
8	Robert Welch – Design: Craft & Industry
42	Chronology
46	1950s
78	1960s
128	1970s
148	1980s
166	1990s
178	2000 to present
208	Selected Additional Designs
242	Footnotes
243	Bibliography
244	Index
248	Acknowledgements & Credits

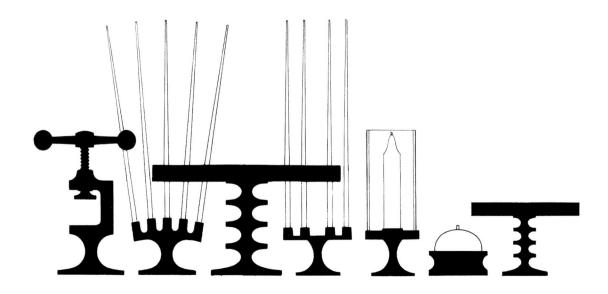

Foreword

It is hoped that this book will give the reader a real insight into the life and work of our father Robert Welch, who was an extraordinarily talented yet very humble man. He really wanted nothing more than to be allowed to draw, design and paint, and rarely a day passed when he was not applying himself to some creative activity or another – for him the pursuit of good design was a lifelong and all-encompassing obsession.

Throughout his career, Robert created beautiful, functional products for the home, which were manufactured and sold through other companies – often highly successfully. Yet the painstaking transformation of his original ideas into finished products was also at times incredibly frustrating for him as ultimately he had little or no control over the production of his designs. The year 2000, however, was truly significant for Robert Welch Designs for, although the company lost its main helmsman, the seeds of change were sown to move the company forward. And while the vision of the company controlling its own manufacture and distribution had seemed implausible to Robert, on the final day of his life he understood and realized that it could and indeed was going to happen, and that his business was entering a new and exciting chapter.

Today we have over 60 talented people working for the company, with the same passion and pride as Robert himself had for reputation, service and manufacturing excellence. And although our father was publicity shy, we hope that he would be quietly proud of this book as a document of his remarkable design legacy.

Alice and Rupert Welch

Robert Welch – Design: Craft & Industry

Robert Welch and the Arts and Crafts Movement

Throughout his illustrious career, Robert Welch – one of the leading designers of his generation – balanced craft-manufacture and industrial production to create an impressively broad range of designs, many of which are now rightly considered icons of modern design. To understand his work fully, however, one has to go back to the late nineteenth century and the origins of the Arts and Crafts Movement. While John Ruskin (1819–1900) laid the philosophical bedrock from which the movement would flourish, it was William Morris (1834–1896) who put theory into practice with his activities at Morris & Co., which subsequently emboldened succeeding generations of designers to pursue the idea of design reform through hands-on action. In addition, it was Morris who showed that it was possible to work as both a designer-maker and a successful retailer of one's wares – a lesson that was certainly not lost on those later designers who possessed an entrepreneurial spirit, such as Robert. It was Morris who also sought Arcadia in the English countryside, leasing the beautiful seventeenth-century Kelmscott Manor near Lechlade, Gloucestershire in 1871 with his friend and love rival the Pre-Raphaelite painter Dante Gabriel Rossetti (1828–1882). This was the first of many associations that the Arts and Crafts Movement had with the Cotswolds – and it was where Robert made the decision to spend his life in pursuit of the better-designed solution.

Another designer who must be mentioned in conjunction with Robert Welch's design activities is Charles Robert Ashbee (1863–1942). Certainly, no architect or designer was more influenced by Ruskin or Morris's socially inspired utopian writings than Ashbee, who founded the Guild of Handicraft in 1888 as a sort of proactive social design experiment. At first the Guild was based at Toynbee Hall, a radical social-reforming educational mission that had been established three years earlier by Samuel and Henrietta Barnett in Commercial Street in Whitechapel, then one of the most squalid areas of London's grimy East End. The guiding aim of Ashbee's new enterprise was to provide practical training in handicraft to the very poorest people living in the surrounding slums, thereby giving them a means by which to earn an honest livelihood. The venture began with just five members, but soon expanded to include already skilled cabinetmakers, silversmiths, metalworkers and woodcarvers. The beautifully executed wares that the guildsmen produced were displayed in shows put on by the Arts & Crafts Exhibition Society, and were either commissions or produced to sell through the later guild-run shop in Brook Street. In 1891 the Guild and school moved to larger premises at Essex House in Mile End Road, and there the community made furniture, fixtures and fittings that were often related to Ashbee's architectural commissions. Bolstered by the early success of the Guild, Ashbee became caught up with the idea of realizing the Arts and Crafts Movement's guiding yet highly romanticized vision of a self-sustaining rural community of artistic craftspeople – a veritable Arcadia where workers could produce meaningful creative work in pleasant and healthful surroundings. After much deliberation and consultation, he and his guildsmen made the momentous decision to relocate the Guild to the countryside. After various reconnaissance trips to different parts of the country, Ashbee eventually settled on Chipping Campden as the perfect town to which to decamp; having been a thriving wool town in bygone days, it boasted a plentiful supply of beautiful yet now largely unoccupied honey-coloured stone buildings. Importantly, although these buildings were in a state of general disrepair, he could see that with a bit of fixing up they could provide suitable working premises for the Guild's activities, as well as provide accommodation for the 50 or so guildsmen and their families. One of these buildings was the Old Silk Mill, which became the Guild's headquarters, and which was where, just over half a century later, Robert Welch would set up his design studio and workshop. Although the Guild was to all intents and purposes a short-lived, socially motivated design experiment, it left a lasting legacy, for it was the powerful moral message behind this design-making-teaching venture that prompted various American designer-makers to establish similar creative communities in the United States, and which also inspired the founding of the various design-reforming associations in Europe that would ultimately lead to the birth of Modernism. Indeed, it was Ashbee's belief in the morality of well-made and well-designed wares that likewise guided Robert Welch's approach to design throughout his prolific career, and which continues to inspire the firm that still bears his name.

Previous spread: Robert Welch working in his workshop (photo: Enzo Ragazzini)
Left: Drawing of the 400-year old Market Hall, Chipping Campden by John Limbrey, ca. 1970s

Opposite, top: The Old Silk Mill in Chipping Campden (photo: Tony Muranka)
Opposite, bottom: Alice and Rupert Welch outside the Robert Welch Studio Shop in Chipping Campden (photo: Tony Muranka)

Childhood and Education

Robert Radford Welch was born in Hereford in 1929 to a respectable middle-class family with artistic leanings. When he was three, his family moved to the small village of Colwall, nestled in the Malvern Hills. As Robert would later recall, these early childhood years were happy ones, full of countryside pursuits. Certainly these 'carefree days brought him in close contact with nature' and engendered 'a deep appreciation of its beauty and a lasting love of the Malverns.'[1] He went, initially, to the boy's school in the village and then later to Lyttelton Grammar School in Malvern.

Even at this early age, Robert showed an aptitude for drawing and working with his hands. His father, Leonard Welch, who had previously served in the Navy[2] worked for an oil-blending firm and was a keen self-taught craftsman who enjoyed making models. Robert firmly believed that his own aptitude for craftsmanship was a direct result of his father's love of craftwork. From his mother, Dorothy (née Perkins), the daughter of a Welsh farmer, Robert inherited his gift for draughtsmanship; she had studied at Hereford Art School, where she became quite an accomplished painter. Even though she did not continue her artistic pursuits after marriage, Robert recalled that, 'the fact that the house was full of canvases, watercolours and

drawings, as well as enticing piles of old *Studio* magazines, added a strange excitement to art for me.'[3] Certainly, *The Studio* magazine, with its careful mix of articles on both the fine and applied arts, must have had a profound influence on Robert, acting as a crucial introduction to the international design scene.

When he was ten years old, Robert's family moved to West Malvern in Worcestershire. Two years later, after passing his eleven-plus exam, he enrolled at the nearby Hanley Castle Grammar School, first as a dayboy and later as a boarder. Although run by the state, the school operated very much along the lines of a traditional English public school and had, according to Robert, a problem with bullying thanks to a recent influx of evacuees from Birmingham. Luckily, however, he escaped such unwanted attention due mainly to his prowess as a fast bowler on the cricket pitch. While at the school he entered and won several art competitions sponsored by the National Savings Movement, which was responsible for such campaigns as 'Wings for Victory' and 'Dig for Victory'.

As an only child, Robert became quite adept at relying 'on his own resources'[4], which included spending hours upon hours in his father's workshop producing sketches and watercolours, and obsessively building 'crystal sets' – simple radio receivers, the construction of which had become a popular hobby among schoolboys in the 1940s. This youthful interest in radios led him to buy second-hand sets and dismantle them, presumably only to rebuild them. This in turn gave him a useful hands-on appreciation of their construction – an early yet valuable lesson in how products were put together for industrial manufacture.

Malvern School of Art and Birmingham College of Art

As his school education came to an end, Robert briefly flirted with the idea of becoming a professional cricketer, but instead opted to study at the Malvern School of Art, run at that time by the painter Victor Hume Moody (1896–1990), who had studied at the Royal College of Art. Under Moody's direction, the art school exacted the highest Renaissance-style standards from its students, who were thoroughly grounded in the use of traditional brush and paint techniques as well as in life drawing. Robert spent two terms there before his two years of – then compulsory – National Service, which he spent working as a wireless operator for the RAF. Frequent night shifts meant that he had quite a bit of time off during the day and that allowed him to keep up his artistic studies by attending various classes at the Cambridge School of Art. When he was eventually demobilized, he was given a much-needed grant to complete his NDD (National Diploma in Design) because his studies had been interrupted by National Service. He returned to

Malvern School of Art, but became rather disconcerted to find that the school had a relatively poor pass rate for the NDD. Nevertheless, he passed the first part of the diploma there, but decided to transfer to Birmingham College of Art for its completion. This proved to be an excellent choice, for it placed a far greater emphasis on the teaching of the applied arts than had been the case at Malvern, the curriculum of which was almost entirely focused on the study of fine art.

Although he had done 'very little craftwork' because of the 'meagre'[5] workshop facilities offered at Malvern, Robert decided to study silversmithing. By his own account, when being interviewed for a place on the course, he was 'completely over-awed' by the 'miraculous' quality of the work being produced by students enrolled at Birmingham's renowned School of Silversmithing and Jewellery. He was duly accepted onto the course, and just before leaving to take up the place in Birmingham, he received a letter from Worcestershire's Director of Education informing him that he had been awarded the Charlotte Jacob Prize for Silversmithing, which was accompanied by a cheque for one pound ten shillings – a modest award that was the first of many he would win during his illustrious career.

On his arrival at Birmingham College of Art, however, Robert must have been somewhat perturbed to find that he was actually one of only three students who had opted to study silversmithing that year.

This was presumably because it was seen as not offering particularly good job prospects; after the war silverware was still deemed to be a luxury item, and therefore incurred an onerous purchase tax of around 100 per cent, which ensured that commissions were scarce. However, it must have been even more alarming when one of these fellow students died during the night following the course's first day, thereby reducing the number of participants to a mere two. While studying at Birmingham, Robert was mainly concerned with design and production, and was taught the technicalities of metalwork to an extremely exacting standard by his tutors, Cyril Shiner and Ralph Baxendale. Reflecting later in life, he felt that he would have benefited enormously had the course focused more on recent design history rather than, as it did, only up to the Georgian era. However, as he would later also note, 'The study of what has gone before has the power to make one feel very humble'[6], and certainly during his career he frequently looked to historical precedents for inspiration and then evolved their forms into his own contemporary design language.

Opposite: The young Robert Welch, 1930s

Above: *Detail from a pen-and-ink drawing of soldiers by Robert Welch, ca. 1948, believed to have been created while he was undertaking his National Service*

The Royal College of Art

After completing his studies at Birmingham, Robert, now 23 years old, made the decision to enrol at the Royal College of Art, London, in 1952 – the year after the Festival of Britain had converted the British public to the idea of modern design. Certainly this resolution was not taken lightly, for it involved delaying his entry into the world of paid employment and committing to another three years of study, as well as a related nine-month industry work placement. Yet Robert was never to regret his choice, for – bolstered by the success of the Festival of Britain – the Royal College of Art was itself, as Fiona MacCarthy puts it, 'in an optimistic phase'[7] thanks to the recent appointment of a new forward-looking rector, Robin Darwin (1910–1974). As Robert was later to observe, 'The marvellous thing about the RCA is that it is an amalgam of artists and craftsmen from many different backgrounds',[8] and certainly he was stimulated as a designer by the creative synergies that this mix of talented young individuals produced

at this remarkable institution. At this point the RCA was being swept along creatively on a tide of confidence about the key role contemporary modern design could play in shaping a better society. And although Robert was the only student in his year to study silversmithing, he could not have failed to have been inspired by the creative buzz of the RCA. As he later noted, 'Everyone was doing their own thing, and the freedom was phenomenal. You worked as much or as little as you chose, and for that reason you worked like a lunatic.'[9] Robert also undoubtedly benefited from the dedicated one-to-one tuition he received from his tutors, including Professor Robert Goodden (1909–2002), who is generally credited with playing a pivotal role in the emergence of a new and innovatively modern style of British metalwork. Robert's decision to study silversmithing marked him out as somewhat of an individualist, and, like such types, he possessed a resolute determination to succeed. Over subsequent years, therefore, he ploughed his own very individual design furrow, guided by a firmly held conviction about what good design really constituted.

While at the RCA, Robert met two slightly older and similarly gifted silversmiths who were in the year above him, Gerald Benney (1930–2008) and David Mellor (1930–2009). The former went on to become one of the most influential British goldsmiths and silversmiths of the second half of the twentieth century. Benney had previously studied at Brighton College of Art; his work epitomized the rather flamboyant 'Brighton' style and was often attractively adorned with his signature bark-effect finish. In contrast, Mellor, who had previously studied at Sheffield College of Art, pursued a more uncluttered, functionalist approach associated with that town's cutlery tradition. On leaving the RCA, both Benney and Mellor established independent silversmithing workshops, which must have influenced Robert's decision to do the same a couple of years later. Robert was more attracted to, as he put it, the 'sheer austerity'[10] of Mellor's designs, although he did for a while share student digs with Benney in Gunter Grove – a notoriously busy and rather grubby thoroughfare in Chelsea. Importantly, together with Mellor and Benney, Welch would over the coming years lead a postwar silversmithing revival that infused this age-old craft with a striking contemporary modernity. Another of his housemates from this time was the architect Patrick Guest, who would later design a thoroughly modern family home for Robert in Alveston, Warwickshire, as well as David Mellor's original studio–workshop in Sheffield (1960).[11]

Above: *Study of an antique Georgian cruet set, 1952, executed on a visit to the Victoria and Albert Museum, during Robert's first term at the Royal College of Art*

Opposite, top: *Fish silver sugar sifter, 1952, executed at the Royal College of Art*

Opposite, right: *Skylon silver sugar sifter, 1952, first piece executed at the Royal College of Art and with the form of its handle directly inspired by the Skylon sculpture at the Festival of Britain in 1951*

Opposite, middle left: *Scallop Shell silver salt cellar, 1952, executed at Birmingham College of Art; this was Robert's examination piece for the National Diploma in Design*

Opposite, bottom left: *Silver hot water pot, 1953, executed at the Royal College of Art. Originally part of a tea set, but the tea pot is only known from photographs.*

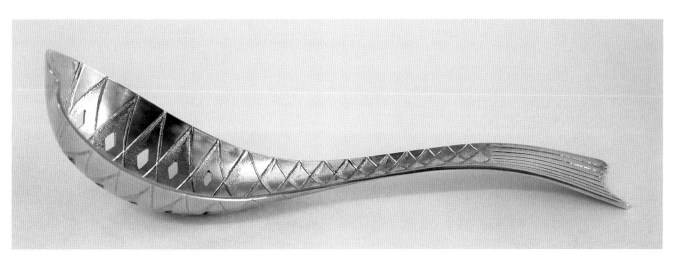

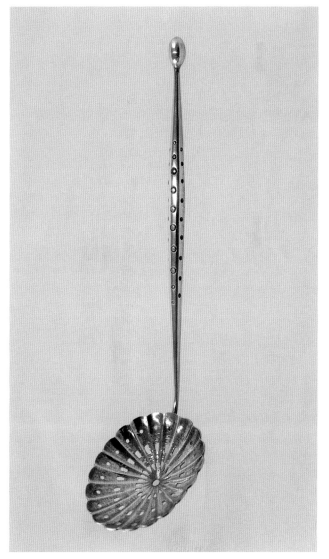

The Scandinavian Connection

While studying at the RCA, Robert was strongly inspired by the contemporary metalwork designs then coming out of Scandinavia. One of the reasons for this was that on leaving Birmingham he had been awarded the H. Samuel Travelling Scholarship, worth the princely sum of £50. This cash he had put to good use by paying for his attendance at a summer design course in Sweden. He had found out about this course for 'Anglo Swedish Designers and Architects' run by the Svenska Slöjdföreningen[12], from an advertisement in *Design* magazine. Its cost of £50 meant that he was putting, 'all his eggs in one basket'[13], and in order to fund the additional travelling and living costs he worked temporarily as a seasonal fruit-picker. The course proved to be worth every penny, with its round of useful fact-finding factory visits. It was on this trip that Robert encountered for the very first time stainless steel, a then seemingly new material that would open his eyes to interesting design opportunities within the field of metalwork. He later recalled a moment of revelation when he came across a display of modern stainless-steel wares by Sigurd Persson (1914–2003) in the front window of a bank. So impressed was he with the quality of the work on show that right then and there he made the career-defining decision to concentrate on stainless-steel design during his final year at the RCA. Robert had immediately realized through this chance encounter that this seemingly state-of-the-art material offered exciting formal possibilities.

In fact, stainless or 'rustless' steel had actually been first developed by the English metallurgist Harry Brearley (1871–1948) at Firth Brown's research laboratory in Sheffield in 1913, in an attempt to find a better and harder alloy for the manufacture of gun barrels. During World War I it had also been used for aircraft engines, services cutlery and surgical instruments. It was not until after the war, however, that it managed to shed its utilitarian associations and began to be used for homewares, and it was not until World War II was over that its remarkable properties – hardness, brilliance, durability – were fully exploited to create truly modern-looking designs for the home. One of the reasons Sweden led the way in the design of contemporary stainless-steel wares during the postwar years was that, unlike other countries in Europe, which had seen their factories destroyed during the conflict, it had maintained a policy of neutrality throughout, which meant that research and development had continued unabated as there had been no switch to armament production. Thus, Sweden's metalworking factories remained intact and were able to quickly ratchet up export production once the war had ended. The long-held social ethos of Scandinavian design also came into its own during these postwar years. As Robert recalled, 'the philosophy of the Scandinavians, so popular at that time, designing simple everyday objects that were functional and beautiful and which most people could afford, greatly appealed to me.'[14]

The Swedish trip of 1953 also provided Robert with various invaluable contacts, the most notable being Stig Lindberg (1916–1982), who left a 'tremendous impression'[15] on Robert. One of the most influential and exciting Swedish designers of the postwar generation, Lindberg demonstrated through example that it was possible to design successfully across a broad range of disciplines, from studio ceramics and textiles to mass-produced dinnerware, glassware and more industrial products, including the stylish television sets he created for Luma. In fact, Lindberg became a design hero for Robert, and must surely have helped to motivate his later diversification from silversmithing into other areas of design.

Above: *Bergen vase, 1954, executed at the workshops of Theodor Olsen in Bergen and later purchased by the Vestlandske Kunstindustrimuseum in Bergen (photo: KODE Art Museums of Bergen)*

Opposite: *Vegetable/entrée dish prototype, 1954–5, executed towards the end of Robert's studies at the Royal College of Art, London, and later purchased by J. & J. Wiggin*

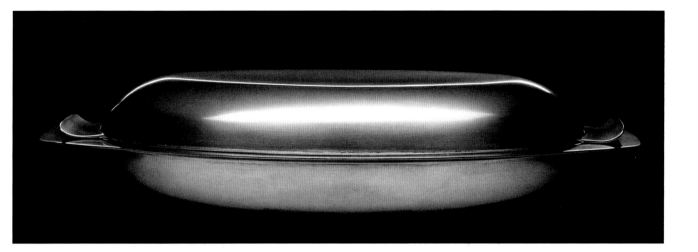

During the summer of 1954 Robert returned to Scandinavia, this time travelling to Norway as one of a group of students from different British art colleges who had been invited on a goodwill mission to work in various Norwegian factories. The intention was that an exhibition of the work generated by the students would be held in Bergen at the end of this trip. Robert with his silversmithing skill was assigned to the workshop of Theodor Olsen of Bergen, a renowned silversmithing company that had been established in 1868 and that was well known for its Nordic-style silver and enamelled pieces. While he was there, Robert made a silver vase that he intended to enamel but never actually did because he ran out of time, nevertheless it was subsequently acquired from the exhibition by the Vestlandske Kunstindustrimuseum (Museum of Applied Arts) in Bergen. He also produced a candleholder that he sold through the show. The museum's acquisition completely 'bowled him over',[16] and such was the favourable impression he left on Theodor Olsen that the workshop offered him a permanent position on the completion of his studies at the RCA. This must have been a tempting proposition, as work for silversmiths in Britain was still very thin on the ground, to say the least.

New Stainless Steel and Old Hall

Returning to Britain after the summer to begin his final year at the RCA, Robert was so inspired by the stainless-steel designs he had seen being produced by the Norwegian manufacturer Gense and other Scandinavian firms that he was determined to broaden his own design remit to encompass the development of such wares. Accordingly, Robert created a prototype stainless-steel vegetable dish with cover and removable three-portion liner as his major project at the RCA. With its sculptural form, this early design was made of gilding metal

that had a chrome-plated satin-finish in order to give the appearance of stainless steel. Around this time, Robert designed a stacking tea set that also speculated on the idea of mass-production in stainless steel. The serving dish so impressed Leslie Wiggin, the chairman of J. & J. Wiggin – then the only British manufacturer of stainless-steel tableware – that he purchased it for the sum of £25. Although this early design was never put into production, it showed a more industrial direction to Robert's work.

The acquisition of this dish in his final year was the first contact Robert had with the Wiggin family, and marked the beginning of a long and fruitful association with their Bloxwich-based firm, which then marketed its products under the 'Olde Hall' brand – a name that made reference to the old Salvation Army hall that the company had occupied as a workshop from the turn of the century. Indeed, Leslie Wiggin was so taken with Robert's student work that he subsequently invited him to visit his factory in the autumn of 1954. Robert had recently purchased a Lancia Lambda open tourer of 1923 from Gerald Benney, which had used up most of his savings but would prove to be a canny purchase. With it, he had 'found an astute short cut to the hearts of British businessmen – a vintage car'.[17] The chief directors of J. & J. Wiggin – Leslie and Wilfred Wiggin – fortuitously happened to be utter devotees of the Lancia marque, and so when Robert drove up to the factory in this rare model he was 'welcomed with outstretched arms'. Whether the car eased the way to his appointment as the firm's design consultant following the completion of his studies is a matter of conjecture, but it cannot have hurt. What is certain, however, is that this young and talented designer arriving on their doorstep must have seemed like a godsend to the Wiggin family, who were facing increasingly stiff competition from Scandinavian manufacturers.

Established in 1893, this family-run firm had – in response

to an initiative sponsored by Firth Brown of Sheffield – pioneered the development of tableware using Firth Brown's 'Staybrite' stainless steel in 1928. These early 'rustless steel' designs were sold under the 'Olde Hall' brand. During the late 1920s and throughout the 1930s there was a popular fashion for 'Ye Olde England', especially in home furnishings, but later J. & J. Wiggin dropped the old-fashioned 'e', changing the brand name to 'Old Hall' in 1959 to reflect the changing times. In 1934 Wiggin had exhibited the world's very first stainless-steel tea set on Firth Brown's Staybrite City display stand at the Daily Mail Ideal Home exhibition, and subsequently the company produced wares designed by family members as well as by Harold Stabler (1872–1945), who had previously trained as a metalworker at the famous Keswick School of Industrial Art. The outbreak of World War II had, however, meant that Wiggin's factory was converted to wartime production for the Admiralty. In the immediate aftermath of the war the firm had struggled

with shortages of materials, and as a consequence had found it difficult to resume its prewar manufacture. There was 'a need to build up export sales as quickly as possible because, by Government direction, supplies of stainless steel were only obtainable under licences directly proportional to the value of finished goods exported. Although the domestic markets overseas were difficult to break into, what did emerge was considerable interest from hotels, hospitals and other catering users. Accordingly, the company quickly developed new designs specifically for the catering trade.'[18] Realizing that it was competing for these crucial export markets with Scandinavian companies producing stylishly modern stainless-steel wares, the firm knew it must revitalize the design of its product line to give it a more contemporary feel, and Robert appeared to be just the right person to do this. Although he had not completed his studies at the RCA, he began designing for Olde Hall during his final year, with the understanding that he would be appointed the firm's design consultant once he had graduated.

Knowing he had a job lined up, Robert threw himself into his last year of study, earnestly immersing himself in the design and production of stainless-steel wares, including the tea set and a condiment set. He did not, however, completely abandon his first love – silversmithing – and during this period he also created a number of silverware designs, including a teapot for the businessman Sir John Charrington. It was, nonetheless, an analysis of stainless steel and its application to homewares that would form the focus of his thesis, 'The Design and Production of Stainless Steel Tableware'. This fascinating document outlined the hundred-year search 'to discover an alloy for retarding corrosion in steel'[19] and described Harry Brearley's role in heralding 'the era of chrome bearing steel' through his development of a new alloy for the manufacture of guns. Brearley was also instrumental, Robert noted, in getting Sheffield manufacturers to find novel applications for this new alloy, most notably F.S. Moseley & Co., which was the first to produce cutlery from it. Although the first advertisement for stainless-steel cutlery appeared as early as 1914, World War I curtailed the alloy's further development and refinement. After the cessation of hostilities, however, the term 'stainless' came to be widely associated with rather poor-quality cutlery, as Sheffield-based manufacturers in a rush to get to market largely abandoned the high standards previously associated with the city's cutlery industry. As Robert noted in his dissertation, 'The legacy of this policy is still very evident in the Sheffield cutlery industry today. The remedy can only lie in a fresh and more imaginative outlook',[20] and certainly he was the young designer who was able to provide this new perspective. Although he did include three designs by Harold Stabler from the mid-1930s for special consideration, by far the vast majority of the designs he extolled as exemplars were

from the Nordic countries. As he explained, 'In Denmark and Sweden in particular, there are great activities in the development of this work [stainless-steel ware], where the most advanced designs are to be seen'.[21] He rigorously assessed the developments within Scandinavian design from 1940, when various Nordic manufacturers began mass-producing a number of contemporary cutlery designs, thereby heralding, as he put it, 'a new era of stainless-steel flatware'. Among the designs he mentioned in this context were Thebe (1944) and Facette (1949) by Folke Arström (1907–1997) for Gense, and Obelisk (1954) by Erik Herløw (1913–1991) for Copenhagen Cutlery (the Danish Universal Steel Company), this latter cutlery pattern being forged rather than stamped and having a remarkable contemporary elegance and delicate refinement. To achieve such designs, Robert noted that it was critically important for designer and manufacturer to collaborate closely, in terms not just of production but also of sales and marketing – with Gense being a case in point. Other contemporary stainless-steel designs he highlighted as exemplars were the Cultura covered serving dish (1953) designed by Sigurd Persson (1914–2003) for Silver & Stål, and cutlery ranges designed by Kay Bojesen (1886–1958) and Jens Quistgaard (1919–2008) for Georg Jensen. In his thesis, Robert contrasted such work with the problems of the British stainless-steel industry, and noted that one of the biggest hindrances to increasing the widespread acceptance of stainless steel was its utilitarian associations – it was seen as a perfectly good material for everyday kitchen cutlery, but not for more formal dining. Robert felt that this perception could be overturned with the application of 'good design' principles. Robert observed:

'From a purist point of view, the definition of good design as that which embodies function, utility and economy is especially applicable to stainless steel...design is the outcome of the nature of the material and fabricating technique, and while the material and technique place certain limitations on the design, in the same way they also make possible unique characteristics, and it is by the special development of these characteristics that an independent and organic style in steel design is being formulated. The development of this style is only part of the outcome of the contemporary trend of the re-assessment of the everyday articles of life.'[22]

Thanks to his fact-finding travels in Sweden and Norway, Robert had been exposed to the Scandinavian countries' 'living tradition of good taste' as well as to the logical development of new production techniques whereby articles made in stainless steel had been afforded, as he put it, a 'fit and rightful character to a degree independent of tradition'.[23] Having seen with his own eyes the design and manufacturing possibilities offered by this extraordinary metal alloy, which was lustrous yet also

incredibly durable, he felt that it was a potent material of the future. But perhaps as importantly, during his travels Robert was exposed to the long-held Scandinavian belief that good design is the birthright of all, and that well-designed objects for everyday use are essentially life enhancing. For Robert, the examples of contemporary stainless-steel wares he had chosen to illustrate in his dissertation were literally shiny exemplars that bore witness to the processes by which they had been fabricated, and as such exuded a 'distinctive character of good stainless-steel design',[24] but also they accorded with the Scandinavian societies' desire for well-made and democratically affordable design. Perhaps what is most interesting about this essay, however, is that for such a young designer Robert had a remarkably good understanding of the interrelationship between design, manufacture and marketing – an insight that can ultimately be seen as the firm foundation upon which he would build his career.

Opposite: Two-part tea-set prototype, 1954–5, designed and made by Robert Welch while still a student at the Royal College of Art

Above: Stainless-steel and yew carving set, 1953, executed on a Royal College of Art visit to the factory of George Wolstenholm in Sheffield

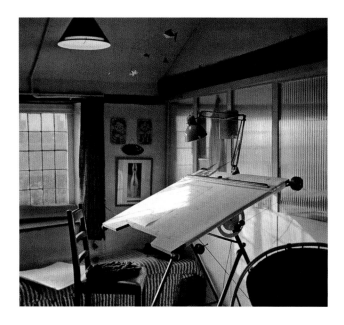

A Workshop in Chipping Campden

Having submitted his thesis, and with his career plans more or less ironed out thanks to the job offer from J. & J. Wiggin, Robert graduated in 1955 with an honours certificate, an RCA Silver Medal and the RCA Prize for Design in Three Dimensions, awarded for his silver and amethyst glass condiment set. After graduating, Robert began earnestly looking for somewhere 'to set up shop'.[25] At first, he looked for a suitable site in London, but given his one-day-a-week commitment to working at the Olde Hall factory in Bloxwich, he soon decided to focus his attention on the environs of Birmingham instead. He then began wondering if the furniture designer and manufacturer Gordon Russell (1892–1980) might have some spare workspace at his factory in Broadway, Worcestershire. The idea of this beautiful historic town must have appealed to Robert, set in the rural idyll of the Cotswolds yet still within relatively easy reach of Birmingham. To this end, his RCA tutor Robert Goodden kindly wrote him a letter of introduction to Russell, who was by now one of the leading and most influential figures in the British design establishment. A meeting was arranged, and at it Russell suggested that a suitable space might be found in the Guild of Handicraft's former workshop, which was still being operated by the silversmith George Hart (1882–1973) and his family in the Old Silk Mill in nearby Chipping Campden. Russell saw that the town's long-held associations with progressive silverware design would be perfectly suited to the needs and development of this young up-and-coming designer and thought the Harts might be able to offer useful assistance to Robert during his start-up phase. Fortuitously, when he drove over to see the premises he found that the second

floor of the mill, which had previously been used as a studio by the woodcarver and sculptor Alec Miller (1879–1961), was available to rent, albeit 'piled with junk and [with] windows [that] were almost opaque'.[26] The mill's owner, Harold Pyment,[27] agreed to lease the space to Robert for a three-year term at ten shillings a week, which was just about the amount he could afford.

At this stage, Robert knew next to nothing about the mill's remarkable history and its central role in the story of modern design thanks to its associations with Charles Robert Ashbee and his influential Guild of Handicraft. Indeed, it was only over the succeeding years, as he became fully immersed in Campden life and lore, that Robert came to realize just how serendipitous his choice of location had been. In order to get the new studio up and running, Olde Hall provided Robert with an interest-free loan to construct a new ceiling and acquire all the tools and equipment he needed. By the end of September 1955, the new workshop was finished and kitted out, and Robert, as well as his design consultancy work for Olde Hall, was already busy with several silverware commissions from the Worshipful Company of Goldsmiths: one was for a pair of double-panned fruit bowls for Imperial College and another was a 'loving mazer' for the Administrative College in Henley-on-Thames. So, even from the very start of his professional career, Robert was balancing bespoke craft design with mass-produced industrial design. As Sir Gordon Russell would later note, 'Don't forget that hand and machine are complementary – an improvement in one leads in time to an improvement in the other.'[28] So it would be with Robert's work: his understanding of craft informed his designs for industrial production, and likewise the techniques he used for his mass-produced wares often inspired the experimental development of his one-off pieces – so much so that when he came to write his autobiography in 1986, he chose the title *Hand and Machine*.

Initially, Robert fitted out the northern end of the top floor of the Old Silk Mill as his workshop and constructed a partitioned area off it, which he used as a studio/office/bedroom. Gradually the workshop expanded to encompass the whole of the top floor, and Robert found rented living accommodation in town. During this process, he discovered traces of the Guild's previous occupancy, including plaster casts by Alec Miller and a portrait medallion of Ashbee. This tangible link, together with first-hand accounts of the Guild's activities from various townsfolk such as the Harts, meant that over time Robert became steeped in its history. His interest was piqued by Ashbee's life and guiding design mission to the extent that he spent time in the Victoria and Albert Museum's library in order to read Ashbee's memoirs. Also, when finances permitted, he began collecting objects – silver, furniture, books, and so on – that related to the Guild. Although in many ways he was following in Ashbee's footsteps, there were marked differences between these two believers in the benefits of good design: while Ashbee was essentially an urbanite incomer with a rose-tinted vision of the countryside, Robert was more or less on home ground, having been born in the neighbouring county of Herefordshire, and at his heart was a true countryman who understood and delighted in nature.

By now thoroughly ensconced in the Old Silk Mill, Robert often stayed with his parents at weekends, and during these visits his father helped him crucially with the management of his fledgling business, such as setting up his book-keeping and showing him how to keep orderly files for each commission. During this early period, his friend and fellow silversmith Donald McFall occasionally helped him, and both his company and his assistance were of great support to Robert.

Having experienced what must have been a period of intense mental and physical duress during the months of setting up and establishing his workshop in Chipping Campden, Robert suddenly fell ill while travelling back home for Christmas. He was subsequently diagnosed with poliomyelitis and hospitalized, even though it was thankfully not the more acute paralytic strain of the virus. Even so, for the next three months he was confined to his bed while he recuperated from this serious illness. During this period, the Wiggin family – despite the fact that up to this point Robert had really done very little design work for them – were hugely supportive, both financially and emotionally, continuing to pay his monthly retainer and sending him weekly letters and parcels of magazines.

By April 1956, Robert had finally recovered enough to resume his professional activities, and – as though making up for lost time – he began an intensely prolific period of designing. Around this time he moved into new and better digs at Little Martins Cottage on the High Street in Chipping Campden, just a short walk from his workshop. In September of that year, at the invitation of Christina Foyle, who had seen his student work in *The Studio* magazine's *Decorative Art* yearbook, he exhibited his work at Foyle's Art Gallery in London. As William Whatley noted, 'he regarded this as a tremendous compliment and although the prospect of it did not dominate his work it certainly added a spur to it.'[29] Among the pieces exhibited were two Scandinavian-style glass vases, his Campden toast rack and two silver reliquaries, one that contained what purported to be a piece of the 'True Cross' and the other encasing a fragment of bone from Saint Thomas à Becket, the twelfth-century martyred Archbishop of Canterbury. One could hardly get a more diverse range of design work than this, and as such it revealed Robert's extraordinary creative adaptability even at this early stage in his career.

Opposite: Early photograph of Robert Welch's first studio/living space in the Old Silk Mill in Chipping Campden, 1955 (RW)

Above: Glass vases designed and made by Robert Welch while on an RCA visit to Stourbridge School of Art, 1953, and later included in the Foyle's exhibition in London

Hand and Machine

As happened often in Robert's life, one event led on to another career-building opportunity. In this case the Foyle's exhibition led to his meeting the eminent graphic designer and design educationalist, Albert Halliwell, who taught at Central School of Arts and Crafts in London. Halliwell subsequently asked Robert to become a visiting lecturer at this august institution, with the remit to teach young industrial-design students the importance of craft values when it came to designing objects for mass production. And in turn, the students to some degree influenced his own approach to design and making. Teaching 'stainless-steel design' one day a week at Central School also provided Robert with a much-needed second income, and the fees he received from teaching he considered a 'princely sum',[30] providing him with greater financial stability.

During this period, one of Robert's greatest influences was Gordon Russell, who as the director of the newly established Council of Industrial Design wielded a huge amount of authority and practical experience in all kinds of design matters. Crucially, Russell understood the vital connection between craft and industry, and sought to revitalize within a postwar context the teachings of Ruskin, who had famously noted: 'Art without industry is guilt, industry without art is brutality.'[31]

Growing up in the early twentieth century, Robert would have also been well aware of the paradoxical legacy of William Morris and his belief in democratic design, summed up in his well-known statement: 'I do not want art for a few; any more than education for a few; or freedom for a few',[32] which he was sadly unable to fulfil owing to his dogmatic rejection of the machine. Having learnt about Morris's tribulations, British pre- and postwar designers, such as Robert, were ambivalent about the use of mechanization, yet – having evolved from an Arts and Crafts tradition – still understood the need for a craft sensibility when it came to the design of goods destined for industrial mass production.

Indeed, Robert's early designs for Olde Hall were just a sign of things to come in terms of his ability to apply craft values to industrial production. His first design for the company was an exercise in restyling, being essentially a modification of an existing condiment set produced by J. & J. Wiggin. The original had a streamlined Art Deco feel to it, especially through the use of three vertical ribs on its carrying handle. In contrast, Robert's redesign had a far more organic and contemporary quality, with a triangular tray with gently curved sides and a carrying handle consisting of a simple ring of stainless steel. Another early design for Olde Hall that revealed Robert's ability to simplify a design to its barest functional bones was his Campden toast rack, which, as

---

Above: Photograph of Robert Welch's first solo exhibition, held at Foyle's Art Gallery in Charing Cross Road, London, 1956

Opposite, top: Record photograph of the Campden four-slice toast rack (RW)

Opposite, bottom: Photograph of J. & J. Wiggin's Old Hall factory in Bloxwich, ca. 1962, showing the manufacture of the later six-slice Campden toast rack

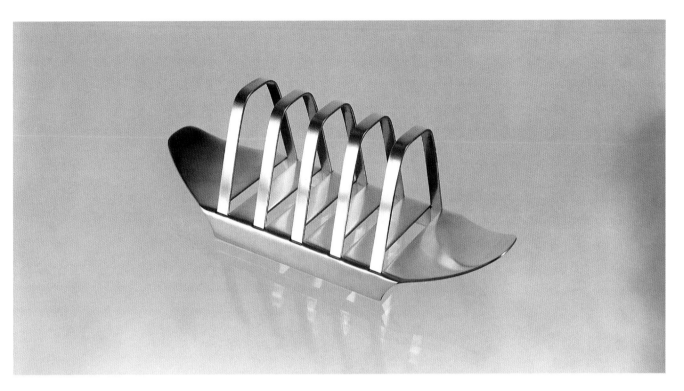

the Council of Industrial Design's *Designs of the Year 1958* exhibition catalogue noted, proved that 'simplest solutions are often the best'. It went on to observe:

'This toast rack is a good example of elegant and ingenious construction in an increasingly popular and eminently suitable material, but one which manufacturers have not been as quick to exploit as its many advantages warrant. The judges welcomed this economical design as a good step forward in an industry in which the imitating of older forms in other materials has been more common than original thinking.'[33]

Indeed, this early award-winning design placed Robert firmly in the vanguard of the stainless-steel revolution – today it is difficult to comprehend just how cutting-edge this design must have seemed, with its gleaming unadorned surfaces. Yet, despite the design's simplicity, it took Robert a considerable time to develop its construction so that its manufacture was reduced to just four operations, with the four arching

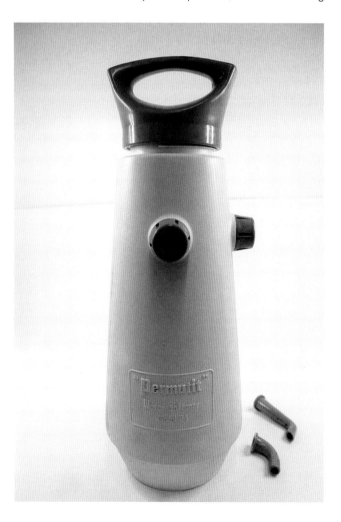

strips of stainless steel being welded to the runner-like base.

Over the succeeding years, Robert became known for his 'single-minded concentration'[34] when it came to problem-solving. Later in his career his personal assistant Lilias Foggin, as well as his other colleagues, knew better than to disturb him when he was locked away in his office attempting to work out the most purposeful solution to a particular design conundrum. Once he had a design concept in mind, he undertook painstaking research and analysis involving numerous sketches, models and prototypes. During the early years, Robert executed most of the models himself, with the ad-hoc help of his friend Donald McFall. When the Birmingham-trained silversmith John Limbrey (1933–2013) joined the studio in the late 1950s, however, he almost exclusively undertook this part of the design process, which freed Robert to spend more time designing new products. During this early part of his career Robert also came to relish the design challenges of working within the constraints of industrial mass production. In 1957 he received via the Council of Industrial Design his first commission for a mass-producible design that was not manufactured in metal: the housing for the Permutit water softener made from moulded polythene (launched in 1959). This early foray into so-called proper industrial design could have been utterly disastrous: a flammable spray paint was employed for a better finish on the prototype, which subsequently caught fire, and in the ensuing chaos Robert was so badly burned while helping to put out the flames that he had to take several days off work.

That same year, the Council of Industrial Design also instigated a manufacturing collaboration between Olde Hall and the silversmith Walker & Hall to develop a new cutlery pattern that could compete with the stylishly modern ranges being produced in Scandinavia by companies such as Gense. The idea was that Olde Hall, with its expertise in the manufacture of stainless-steel designs, and Walker & Hall, being a well-known Sheffield-based cutlery manufacturer, could pool their resources to create the first ever truly modern stainless-steel cutlery range in Britain. It was arranged that Olde Hall would sell the resulting design to the domestic retail trade, while Walker & Hall would distribute it to the contract-catering market. The design of this new cutlery also involved a creative collaboration between Robert and his long-time friend David Mellor, as both designers had associations with the respective manufacturers. Rather confusingly, the pattern was marketed under the name 'Campden' by Olde Hall and under the title 'Spring' by Walker & Hall. The new range was featured prominently in a dedicated article in *Design* magazine in June 1958, which noted that the collaborative manufacturing effort was 'at once apparent in the smooth precision of manufacture and excellence of the finish'.[35] Interestingly, the pattern was manufactured with a satin finish, a treatment that had originated in

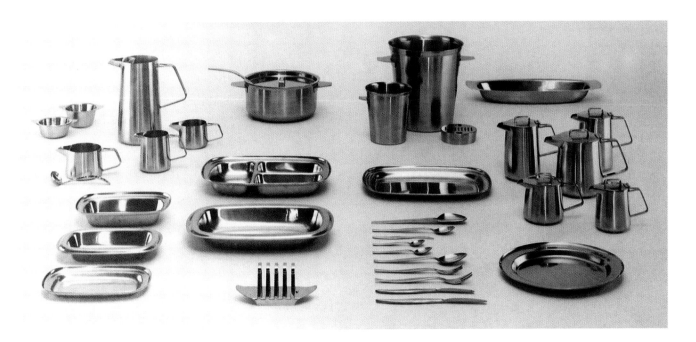

Scandinavia and which, as Robert was later to note, 'was so beautiful and so right for the material and which gave such satisfaction to hand and eye'.[36] Importantly, it was not only the unadorned form of the cutlery, but also this finish that gave it a striking modernity.

Robert also designed an extensive range of tableware to complement the Campden/Spring cutlery, with a similarly contemporary feel. Although Leslie Wiggin described the collection as 'middle of the road'[37] – by which he meant that it possessed a kind of understated ordinariness born out of utilitarian practicality – this new range of tableware was anything but ordinary, especially when compared to the overly decorative and downright fussy historically inspired wares still being produced in Britain at the time. It was, in fact, the first comprehensive range of modern British tableware to be produced, and its sense of practical no-nonsense utility would become a defining hallmark of all the designs created by Robert for Olde Hall over the coming years. Taken as a whole, this impressive body of work revealed his understanding of appropriateness and his desire to find the best solution to a particular brief, for ultimately his Olde Hall wares were for the most part intended to be used within the catering sector, which required wares that were not only hardwearing but also eminently serviceable. Yet despite the utilitarian bias, Robert managed to imbue each piece with an almost elemental beauty born of form following function.

Apart from fostering export-boosting alliances between designers and manufacturers, the Council of Industrial Design was also hugely instrumental in publicizing contemporary British design to the general public, mainly through its opening of the Design Centre in London's Haymarket in the spring of 1956, which acted as a high-profile showcase for homegrown design innovation. And, of course, Robert's designs were frequently included in this 'permanent but constantly changing exhibition of well-designed British goods'.[38] Another council initiative was the introduction in 1958 of its well-known black-and-white kitemark, which functioned as a seal of approval for designs deemed to meet the exacting standards of good design. Robert's homewares were often emblazoned with these distinctive stickers and tags, which helped to bolster their contemporary design credentials in the eyes of the buying public both at home and abroad.

The Council of Industrial Design also boosted Robert's career by recommending him to the Orient Line in 1957, as a suitable designer for a new range of tableware to be used on the company's soon-to-be-launched ocean liner, *Oriana*. The name of the ship was inspired by Queen Elizabeth I's nickname 'Oriana', which was used in madrigals during the seventeenth century, and as such alluded to Elizabeth II's recent coronation and the dawning of a new Elizabethan Age. Oriana would prove to be a career-defining design for Robert, as over 42,000 individual pieces were made for the ship. The commission also brought a considerable upturn to J. & J. Wiggin's profits, although

Opposite: Model P4 Permutit water softener designed by Robert Welch for Permutit Company, 1957

Above: Publicity photograph of the entire Oriana tableware range (including cutlery), ca. 1960

reputedly the factory's tool foreman suffered a nervous breakdown from the stress of completing such an immense order. Happily for Robert, this prestigious commission provided a healthy design fee, and although he never received royalties from Old Hall (as it was renamed in 1959), it ultimately enabled him to build his own house in Alveston a few years later.

In 1958, the year following the Oriana commission, Robert met Patricia Hinksman, five years his junior, who had similarly trained at Birmingham College of Art, although as a commercial artist rather than a silversmith. Introduced by a school friend, they made a rather glamorous couple and were married the following year in St. John's Church in Bromsgrove, Worcestershire. It was definitely a meeting of creative minds, as Pat notes: 'Bob was in another world … we had a lot of shared interests, you couldn't have been married to Bob unless you'd been artistic.'[39] Certainly, she believes he benefited from being an only child who was the focus of his loving parents' undivided attention, and throughout his childhood his creative talents were thoroughly nurtured by them – so much so that his draughtsmanship became highly accomplished. As Pat observes, 'he just didn't make mistakes when drawing…in fact, no matter where he was, he always had a pencil in his hand. In fact they don't come better than Bob when it comes to draughtsmanship and that was thanks to him having quite the best teachers'[40] – both at Birmingham and the Royal College of Art. After their wedding, Pat put her own artistic ambitions on hold, feeling rather intimidated by her husband's prodigious talent, and instead helped practically with the day-to-day running of the workshop by typing his letters, and so on. Around this time, Robert's digs in Campden were sold, and as newlyweds they rented a pretty cottage in Broadway and set up their first home.

In 1958, the year before the Welchs' marriage, John Limbrey, who had trained as a silversmith at Birmingham College of Art a couple of years after Robert had made a tour of the Cotswolds, and dropped in to see Robert at his studio in Chipping Campden. As Robert would later recall, he came into the studio and said: 'This is a nice place to work, do you want any help?'[41] Of course, Robert did, and Limbrey subsequently never left – in fact, from then on he executed most of the models and silverware commissions, enabling Robert to concentrate on what he did best: creating superlative designs for both craft and industrial production. Just a month or so before Limbrey joined the studio, Robert was invited to take part in a high-profile travelling show entitled 'British Artist Craftsmen: An Exhibition of Contemporary Work' (1959-60), organized by the Smithsonian Institution in Washington, DC. It included work by a veritable roster of British artistic talent, including Ben Nicholson (1894–1982), Graham Sutherland (1903–1980), John Piper

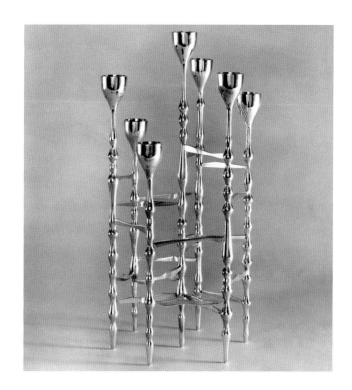

(1903–1992), Henry Moore (1898–1986), Elisabeth Frink (1930–1993), Hans Coper (1920–1981), Lucie Rie (1902–1995) and Gerald Benney, and as a recently graduated silversmith, Robert must have felt himself to be in august company.

For this presentation of British creative endeavour, Graham Hughes (1926–2010), the art director of the Worshipful Company of Goldsmiths, had commissioned a number of silverware designs, including one from Robert. His contribution was an extraordinary seven-branch silver candelabrum, the like of which had never been seen before. It was inspired by the Abstract Expressionism of Jackson Pollock (1912–1956), which he had seen at a recent exhibition at the Whitechapel Art Gallery in London. This beautiful silverware piece was the first design that Robert created using only models (i.e. no sketches), and as a result it has an undeniable free-form freshness born of creative spontaneity. This was a piece that was defiantly Mid-Century Modern in spirit, and with its bold 'New Look' essentially revitalized the centuries-old craft of silversmithing, making it aesthetically relevant to the forward-looking postwar generation. Gordon Russell wrote in his foreword to the exhibition's catalogue:

Opposite: Robert Welch (standing) and John Limbrey working together in the workshop in Chipping Campden, 1960s

Above: Seven-branch candelabrum designed in 1957–58 by Robert Welch for the Smithsonian Institution's 'British Artist Craftsmen' exhibition of 1959

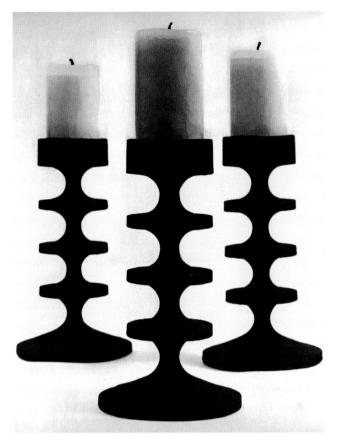

'Before the development of the machine, the artist – as painter, sculptor, and craftsman – was an honored member of the community … I believe there will always be a need for special things, which cannot be produced economically by machine … The craftsman's way of life, where pride in the job takes precedence of all else is something which cannot fail to be a valuable lesson to all who make things by machine.'[42]

This belief certainly accorded with Robert's understanding of design practice – for perhaps more than any other designer of his generation working in Britain at that time – he understood the immense value of craft when applied to industry having seen it first-hand in Scandinavia.

    Also in 1959, Robert created two stridently modern silver coffee services: the five-piece Broadway set and a distinctive three-piece set with a pot that had a strongly attenuated Persian-style swan-necked spout. This venture into experimental form was, however, most radically expressed in three cutlery designs for a competition for a new silver range organized by the International Silver Corporation of Meriden,

based in New England, in 1960. He actually submitted two of these highly sculptural designs to the competition, but then began to feel uncomfortable, for they did not really express his design philosophy. He felt they were too aesthetically extreme, and not functional enough. Feeling as though he had 'perjured' himself as a designer, he vowed to go back to functional basics, and the resulting Alveston range of cutlery designed in 1961 marked a new high point in his design career, for it was based purely on exquisitely refined form following mindfully honed function. As he was to later note in 1963:

'the English contribution to modern cutlery design should not be extremist, but aimed at producing a classic standard of design developed with care, comfortable to use and unselfconscious, and catering for the grip that is so commonly used in this country…This more than anything would establish function as one of the most important aspects of cutlery design as opposed to fashion, because it is bought to last and not languish in a drawer.'[43]

Above, left: Photograph of Alveston cutlery range, taken for inclusion in the Student Yearbook of Decorative Art in Modern Interiors 1964/5. (photo: Dennis Hooker)

Above, right: Photograph of the cast-iron Hobart candlesticks specially taken for inclusion in Robert Welch's first book Design in a Cotswold Workshop published 1973 (photo: Enzo Ragazzini)

Opposite: Alveston tea set designed for Old Hall, 1961–4, and considered by many to be Robert Welch's masterwork

A Period of Creative Productivity

In 1961, Robert's eldest child, Alice, was born, followed two years later by the birth of his son Rupert. As the Welch family grew, so did the amount of work Robert undertook – although as the balance sheets for the fledgling Robert Welch Studio attest, it was still very much a financial struggle, with Robert often taking on silverware commissions that cost more to produce than they earned. As Pat recalls, 'Robert wasn't a businessman but a creative. He really wasn't interested in money, he was only interested in the work.'[44] As a result, throughout the 1960s he was extremely prolific as a designer, juggling one-off silver commissions with designs for industrial production, which ultimately helped to increase his creative breadth as a designer. The period spanning 1961 to 1962 was in many ways a turning point in his career, for it saw the creation of one of his best-loved and most accomplished designs: the Alveston tea set with its distinctive Aladdin-style teapot. It was also when he designed his first cast-iron homewares, which were initially manufactured by Campden Designs – a joint venture between Robert and Wigmore Distributors – before being marketed by Old Hall Tableware from 1968 and then later licensed to Victor Cast Ware of Telford in the mid 1970s. This time also marked a new and exciting chapter in the Welchs' family life, as in 1962 they constructed a brand-new architect-designed home: the White House – designed by Patrick Guest in close consultation with Robert, and built using the proceeds from his Oriana commission.

The White House came about rather fortuitously: Robert had been designing some aluminium kettles for SonA, a manufacturing company based in Stratford-upon-Avon, and the firm's owner N.C. Joseph, had just acquired a largish tract of land nearby with a view to developing it. This land had originally been part of the Alveston Leys Estate situated on the outskirts of the town. The idea was that the land could be used to build a small group of modern homes by different architects. The concept appealed enormously to Robert, as the planning restrictions around Chipping Campden were far too conservative to allow the type of modern home he wanted to live in. The land the Welchs purchased to build their dream home was actually the estate's kitchen garden, which was walled on two sides and planted with trees on another, thereby affording sufficient privacy for them to, as Pat puts it, build 'our glass house'.[45] Flat-roofed and open-plan, the White House was the subject of a multi-page article in *Homes & Gardens* in January 1965, which noted:

'*The whole conception of the house is a series of interrelated shapes, a contrast of solid and space, and the pattern of one texture or tone against*

another. It has strong "bones" and without being over-insistent it is more than a background, rather a showcase, for a collection of furniture, paintings, and objets d'art.'[46]

With underfloor heating, double-glazed louvred windows, and teak-strip and quarry-tiled flooring, it was a stylish, state-of-the-art home that also boasted lighting and kitchen fittings designed by Robert. In 1968 it was extended to accommodate the growing family, providing additional space in the form of a playroom, a study-workshop and another bedroom and bathroom. Alveston Leys Park, as this progressive development of four modernist architect-designed homes became known, was really a little enclave of like-minded modern aesthetes – the architect Barry Kettle designed his own home there, and another of the houses was designed by the renowned Scottish modernist architect, Peter Womersley (1923–1993). Importantly, the White House offered Robert a haven of uncluttered domestic peace, and he would return to it every evening after working hard in the workshop all day to spend his time reading, sketching and listening to his beloved Mozart. Pat Welch understood that he had 'a talent that had to be nurtured and fed' and therefore tried to make home life as easy as possible for him, as 'he just couldn't cope domestically with anything because he was putting absolutely everything he had into his work'.[47] Often he would bring home designs that he was working on at the studio and ask Pat for her critical opinion, which she gave only when she really thought something needed to be changed. He valued this input from a like-minded creative. The family's dining table also became the focus of the Welch children's design education, as new products were often trialled at home before making it into production. Both Rupert and Alice Welch recall that they ultimately learnt about design through a kind of osmosis: well-known

designers would frequently come to stay with their parents, yet as children they did not realize that these people were famous or even that what they did was special.

The White House would remain the epicentre of the Welchs' family life for more than 39 years, and although it was in retrospect a daring exercise in contemporary living, for their children growing up in it and playing cricket with Robert on the lawn every Sunday (including William, who was born in 1973), it just seemed to be a normal family home. But, much like the products Robert was designing in his workshop, the house actually had a strong sense of stripped-down functional simplicity – an aesthetic that is still very much part of Robert Welch Designs' DNA. As Pat observes, 'Bob knew exactly what he was doing and where he was going. Nothing got between him and his work',[48] and it was this single-mindedness that allowed him to create designs that had a remarkable sense of precision – whether it was a tea strainer or a piece of jewellery. Throughout his life he maintained a highly disciplined work ethic that meant he laboured in the workshop not only during the week but also every Saturday morning alongside John Limbrey, his right-hand man. As Pat remarks, Limbrey was 'so quiet, never said a word' and yet he and Robert intuitively understood each other and were able to create really exceptional designs together in the small workshop where 'everything was laid out in a row meticulously'.[49]

Robert's decision to set up his workshop in Chipping Campden started to focus attention once more on this small Cotswold town with

Above: Front elevation of the White House in Alveston Leys Park, designed by Patrick Guest, built 1962 (RW)

Opposite: The interior of the White House with its open-plan living/dining area, ca.1969 (photo: Bretcht-Einzig)

its long design associations, and from 1962 the Society of Industrial Artists and Designers (later the Chartered Society of Designers) held its annual conference there. Each year the highlight of the event was the dance that for many years was held in Robert's top-floor studio, which was cleared out specially. As the architect Ray Leigh remembers, 'Bob was kind enough to make the space available for the party, but every year got increasingly worried about whether the floor of the Old Silk Mill would be able to take the weight of the energetic dancing taking place, until eventually he had to call it a day for fear of the whole lot collapsing.'[50] Crucially, this annual conference helped Robert to maintain contacts with contemporary designers working in London.

By now Robert's work was also garnering considerable attention in the design media both at home and abroad. In 1963, *The Connoisseur* published the first of a series of articles on contemporary British craftsmen written by the art director of the Worshipful Company of Goldsmiths, Graham Hughes, who was firmly committed to contemporary design. Hughes's initiation of commissions made him instrumental in the renaissance of modern silverware design that took place during the mid-to-late 1950s. It is telling that he chose Robert as the subject of this first article, and it shows the high esteem in which Robert was held by this influential and knowledgeable figure, who noted of him:

'all his pieces have the same bold simplicity, a quality entirely expressive of our time, and deriving very little inspiration from before. Many foreigners think of Britain as the home of whimsical Emmett railways filled with absurd objects. The real modern Britain is, of course, much more diverse, and it is designers like Welch whom we have to thank for the strong, sensible end of our artistic reputation. He is a national asset.'[51]

Around this time, silverware commissions from Goldsmiths' Hall had begun to tail off, so Robert started looking for a way to stimulate sales of domestic silverware in order to fill what was effectively a patronage gap. To this end, in 1963 Rolf Falk, the main buyer at Heal's, suggested that Robert should design a modern collection of domestic silverware that could be sold exclusively by the shop. Launched the following year, the range was exhibited in a pair of showcases in the retailer's 'Present Choice' department, the idea being that clients could commission pieces from the collection via Heal's and then the items would be made to order in the Campden workshop. The exhibition of this new range of silverware was opened by Gordon Russell and was well received by customers and press alike. Interviewed by the *Daily Telegraph*, Robert stated:

'Until now there has been no big silver range on the market at all. I feel sure the time has come for it to be appreciated and stainless steel to some degree paved the way for this by conditioning people to modern design.'[52]

It was, however, having his new cast-iron designs featured in *The Studio* magazine's *Decorative Art Yearbook* in 1964 that would bring him international recognition as an up-and-coming designer. Shortly after the publication of the annual, Robert received a letter from Hagbarth Skjalm Petersen (ca. 1922–1995), who owned a high-profile gallery in Copenhagen that sold antiques alongside cutting-edge design, ordering two dozen fruit bowls. Encouraged by this initial order, Robert decided to undertake a sales trip to Scandinavia in 1966. He went first to Norway, then on to Finland, where he met Tapio Wirkkala (1915–1985) and Timo Sarpaneva (1926–2006), both of whom he 'worshipped' according to Pat, and ended up in Denmark, where on walking into Petersen's shop he began a life-long friendship. As Pat recalls, Petersen 'fell for Bob and Bob's work'[53] and subsequently placed a massive order of his designs and began actively to publicize his work. During this visit to Copenhagen, Robert made another very useful contact, the vice-president of Raymor, a New York firm well-known for its import of progressive modern design from Europe and Scandinavia. Raymor placed a similarly large order of Robert's designs, which led to his work being introduced into the United States, where it was later successfully sold by Georg Jensen.

Very taken with Robert's designs, Petersen staged a solo exhibition of his work in Copenhagen in 1967. This led to an important

Above: Coffee and tea set designed by Robert Welch as part of the Heal's silverware range, 1963 (RW)

Opposite, top: Solo exhibition held at Heal's in Tottenham Court Road, London, 1967 (RW)

Opposite, bottom left: Cast-iron fruit bowl designed by Robert Welch, 1961, manufactured initially by Campden Designs. The smaller nut bowl was a slightly later addition to the cast-iron range.

Opposite, bottom right: Merlin alarm clock designed by Robert Welch for Westclox, 1961

30

31

article on Robert's work in *Mobilia* in August, written by the architect Svend Erik Møller (1909–2002), who noted:

'*In some strange ways the English designer Robert Welch forms a bond between the past and the present and the future. Today he is one of the most alive English industrial designers with a very special flair for and interest in the production of articles in metal for everyday use … A modern artist of industry with an interest in the needs of the future … he always makes his own models before they go into production … there is no doubt that it is this close association with the crafts, combined with his intimate knowledge of the requirements of industry, that lends such assurance and balance to the design of his works. Robert Welch is an interesting and intelligent artist who prefers evolution to revolution.*'[54]

Indeed it was Robert's evolutionary approach to design, which is a very Scandinavian ethos, that allowed him to hone his designs to such functional perfection – with only a very few exceptions. Often basing his products initially on successful design antecedents, he would then evolve their forms based on his knowledge of new materials and cutting-edge manufacturing processes to create something utterly modern that nevertheless retained familial echoes of the past. For instance, his Campden Designs range of cast-iron wares, designed from 1962, possessed a curious blend of modernity and nostalgia, and it was this sense of the past being translated into the present that made people find (and they still do) the designs from this range so emotionally compelling.

Coinciding with the Copenhagen exhibition, another one-man show of Robert's work was held at Heal's in Tottenham Court Road in London. In both exhibitions silverware pieces were shown alongside products he had designed for various companies, including his space-age Lumitron lights, his Old Hall stainless-steel wares, his ever-popular Campden Designs cast-iron wares and his Westclox clocks. As Robert was later to note, 'I could see that the idea of mixing domestic silver and product design was a good one, and it was this idea which was the germ of the Studio Shop which I opened in Chipping Campden in 1969.'[55] Fortunately, Robert was able to purchase suitable premises in 1968, on the corner of Sheep Street and Campden's historic Lower High Street. This seventeenth-century stone building had originally been an alehouse, known variously as The Elm and The Plough, and in the 1930s it had been remodelled into a shop and a separate house by the

architect Norman Jewson (1884–1975). The left-hand half of the building had more recently housed the Plough Antiques shop, although having lain vacant for around eighteen months it was in a pretty poor state of repair. The first thing to be done once the keys to the property had been handed over was to remove the plaster to let the ancient stone walls breathe. While stripping the property back to its bare bones, care was taken to preserve any historic features, and the result was a stylish ground-floor 'studio shop' with a small exhibition space, and above it a flat for Robert's recently widowed mother, Dorothy, to live in, to allow

---

Opposite, top: Exterior of the Robert Welch Studio Shop in Chipping Campden, ca. 1970 (RW)

Opposite, bottom: Interior of the Robert Welch Studio Shop in Chipping Campden, post-1972 (RW)

Above: Invitation designed by Robert Welch for the opening of the Robert Welch Studio Shop on 1 December 1969

her to keep an 'eye on' the shop. In fact, as things transpired she would actually run the design-led retailing venture for the next twelve years, and thoroughly enjoyed doing so. The shop was finally opened on 1 December 1969 to great fanfare with a party, and so a new chapter in the Robert Welch story began.

New Horizons and the Craft Revival

Now that the shop was up and running, for a brief time silver commissions once again took centre stage. Customers would come into the shop and place orders for domestic silverware, and Robert also received a number of important commissions, including several for various trophies. This was fortunate, since while the early-to-mid 1960s had been a time of numerous industrial-design commissions, many of which had gone into production, by the late 1960s this line of business had contracted decidedly. The reason for this was that industrial design had become increasingly specialized over the few intervening years, and so companies were now seeking professionally trained industrial designers, rather than relying on silversmiths who could also design products – such as

Robert Welch and his friend David Mellor. Nevertheless, Robert did work on a number of industrial-design commissions during the late 1960s and early 1970s, but they were beset with setbacks. His cast-iron cookware range for Lauffer of America proved to be a huge technical challenge, which took some three years to overcome. Another project, a range of stylish, modern stoneware to be made by Brixham Pottery in Devon also ran into difficulties, as the pottery could not produce the large quantities that had been initially envisioned. This latter project was essentially a craft-revival initiative and as such was very much of its time, with the 1970s seeing a huge resurgence of interest in the handicrafts and their preservation. This was evident in the staging of the 'Craftsman's Art' exhibition at the Victoria and Albert Museum in 1973, for which Robert designed and John Limbrey executed the shimmering Amethyst dish made from parcel-gilt silver decorated with delicate wirework inset with tiny purple gemstones. This unashamedly modern tour de force of silversmithing pushed both the technical and aesthetic boundaries of this age-old craft, thereby reinvigorating it for the late twentieth century.

Another similarly craft-orientated project was initiated in 1975 by the All India Handicraft Board, which invited Robert to visit India on a fact-finding mission and to create modern designs that would help to reinvigorate the country's traditional craft industries. The idea was that by producing modern designs using traditional craft skills, not only would these skills be preserved but also the resulting wares would be more suited to Western taste and could, therefore, be exported to bring in much-needed revenue to a country still in the earliest stages of industrial and economic development. This first trip to India lasted ten weeks and provided Robert with much food for design thought as he was taken around the country visiting various different metal workshops. He was especially taken with the lost-wax bronze casting he saw being undertaken in Kerala, and some nine years later he returned there for a more prolonged stay before creating a range of modern designs employing this ancient casting method.

India was, however, not the only foreign culture to which Robert was exposed in the 1970s: he visited Japan for the first time in 1979 at the invitation of Yamazaki Kinzoku Kogyo, a leading manufacturer of tableware that wanted to break into the US market. For this new client Robert designed the Regalia cutlery range, which had a then very fashionable Neo-Deco feel with its diagonally fluted handles that caught the light and shimmered. This was followed by similarly innovatively styled cutlery designs for Yamazaki, including the pistol-grip-handled Calibre (1979), the colourful plastic-handled Wave (1982) marketed as the 'Casual Collection' and Beach (1982), which came with its own 'cutlery tree' – a demountable hanging stand that in the early 1980s was seen as quite the latest thing in cutlery design, and reflected the increasing trend for less formal dining.

As well as his design work for Yamazaki, during the late 1970s and early 1980s Robert created the award-winning Kitchen Devils knife range (1979) and his classic plastic-handled scissors (1979) for Taylor's Eye Witness, while also working on bespoke silverware commissions, notably the Tower of London goblet (1978) and the altar cross and candlesticks for the Order of St John (1979). In addition, he designed a wide range of silver stock items for the shop during this period, including various pieces of jewellery set with semi-precious stones.[56] It was this remarkable creative versatility that established Robert's status as a talented multidisciplined designer, not only in Britain but also abroad, so much so that in 1979 he was awarded an M.B.E.

A New Sculptural Confidence

As an esteemed member of the international design community, Robert was chosen to be featured in the BBC's television series *Designers* in 1986. This 30-minute prime-time television programme on BBC2 revealed a modest and thoroughly charming man who cared passionately about what he did, and as such it helped to boost his reputation among the British public. Importantly, it showed him applying the same high standards of craftsmanship to everyday products, such as his mass-produced tableware for Old Hall, as to his unique silverware commissions. That

same year, Sue Roseveare interviewed Robert for the local *Focus* magazine and, writing about his mother's painting and his own design work as well as his children's youthful achievements, noted: 'There is no doubt Robert Welch and his family are exceptionally gifted people, which makes one reflect on the way in which the quality of precision, keenness of eye, feeling for shape and placing, insistence on perfection and pride in work seem to be transmitted unerringly from generation to generation.'[57] She had no idea quite how prescient her comment would turn out to be.

Yet while Robert's reputation grew, unfortunately his longest-standing and most loyal client, Old Hall, was facing increasing difficulties. The company had merged with the Prestige Group in 1970 and then was sold to the American tableware company Oneida in 1982. As Leslie Wiggin noted when Old Hall was finally forced to close its factory doors two years later, 'The problem was a change in fashion. The trade was ruined by the flood of cheaper Japanese stainless-steel ware … we just couldn't compete'.[58] Although Yamazaki produced high-quality wares, the vast majority of Japanese manufacturers produced markedly inferior stainless-steel goods, which because of their cheapness took stainless steel from the dining room back into the kitchen. And so an important chapter of Robert's design career ended, but as Old Hall closed, so other creative opportunities opened up.

That same year, as we have seen, Robert returned to India to create designs to be manufactured by bronze-casters in Kerala. Yet despite this intention, while he was out there he found the sights, sounds and colours of India so overwhelming to the senses that he could not gather his design thoughts in any meaningful way. In fact, he quickly realized that it would be better to leave the important business of designing until he had returned to the quiet calm of his studio in Chipping Campden. He did, however, spend a huge amount of time sketching the workers casting bronzes and other scenes of daily life, and in so doing he soaked up the heady atmosphere of India. The resulting collection of designs with their special verdigris patination was a sculptural triumph, skilfully marrying minimal geometric forms with age-old craft to create something that was utterly modern yet had an ancient emotional resonance.

Robert's ability to work on craft-based projects like the Kerala pieces, while developing more industrial projects, such as his Le Buffet kitchen tools for Samuel Groves & Co., was one of his great strengths as a designer, and ultimately put him in the rarified echelons of truly great shape designers – a genius of form – together with the likes of Tapio Wirkkala and Angelo Mangiarotti (1921–2012), both of whom were his contemporaries. But Robert's genius as a master form-giver was perhaps most emphatically revealed in two earlier silverware commissions received from the Victoria and Albert Museum and the British Museum, for candelabra in 1980 and 1983 respectively. For these designs Robert created numerous sketches, and was mindful not to lose the spirit of the early drawings during the design process. Both these designs revealed an increasingly sculptural tendency within his work, and were exceptionally beautiful examples of the silversmith's art.

Another 'silver' project undertaken by Robert during the mid-1980s was slightly less lofty in its aspirations, but nevertheless proved very commercially successful. In 1985, Robert was commissioned by his old colleague Donald McFall, now of Highland Craftpoint of Inverness, to develop a new product range for a small jewellery workshop, Shetland Silvercraft, based in the Shetland Islands – or, as McFall put it, to give 'a little twist to their production'.[59] The workshop's existing product line was not selling well and as a result the firm was struggling to keep its skilled workers in employment. In effect, this new range of designs was first and foremost intended as a job-preservation scheme. To that end Robert spent time at the Shetland Museum in Lerwick to try to find appropriate cultural inspiration for the project – which came in the form of a turned chess set made from cotton reels. With the chess pieces' different tops set on common bases, Robert had found a point of departure for his own design: a range of serving pieces with different figurative bronze finials (later silver-plated) depending on their uses. The butter knife had a cow-shaped finial, for example, while the honey spoon was adorned with a bee delving into a buttercup. Cleverly, these designs not only used the jewellery-making skills of the Scottish craftsmen, both in the execution of these distinctive castings and in the assembly of the complete products, but also combined them with the cutlery-making skills of the Sheffield-based company Harrison Fisher, which supplied the stainless-steel spoons, knives, scoops, and so on, with their bone-coloured plastic handles to which the finials were attached. This combination of handicraft and industrial production meant that the project encompassed both the hand and the machine. Launched in 1985, the range became a very popular gift item not only in the studio shop in Chipping Campden but also in Scotland. Indeed, it was so well-received that more designs were added to the collection two years later. This was followed in 1989 with Robert creating for the same workshop a collection of jewellery that, although quite modern in aspect, consciously reflected the use of spiral forms found in ancient Celtic metalwork.

The 1980s had brought great upheaval within the design community, as Post-Modernism swept in as the new and dominant language of design. Robert had, like most of his peers in the design world, been influenced by some of the more decorative aspects of

this major international style – as can be seen with his Yamazaki Serving Collection (1981–83) or his Neo-Deco uplighter for Lumitron (1984) – yet he never lost sight of the over-arching importance of function. And as the 1980s segued into the 1990s, Robert returned to his industrial-craft roots by exploring once again the creative possibilities of cast iron, with a range of highly original trivets. As he said in 1989 in an interview with Housewares magazine, 'Good design defies analysis. I work on pure instinct … There's nothing better than achieving a spot-on design for mass-production … I'm absolutely determined to get it right – the aesthetics, the production, the whole caboodle'.[60] Indeed, he found it helpful to work in almost total isolation with John Limbrey at his side in order to 'arrive at ideas totally uncontaminated … to come up with something totally fresh and different'.[61]

This is not to say that he was not subject to cultural influences: early in his career he had been inspired by the buildings of modernist architects, such as Ludwig Mies van der Rohe (1886–1969), Marcel Breuer (1902–1981) and Le Corbusier (1887–1965), which he had translated into crisp, precise lines. In the late 1980s and 1990s, however, he was inspired far more by the work of sculptors, such as Constantin Brancusi (1876–1957) and Alberto Giacometti (1901–1966), which was reflected in his use of sweeping forms and bold totem-like shapes. This was seen not only in his designs for silverware commissions such as the Silver Trust coffee sets (1992), with their distinctive spiralling forms, but also in his designs for mass production, such as his Dryad candlesticks

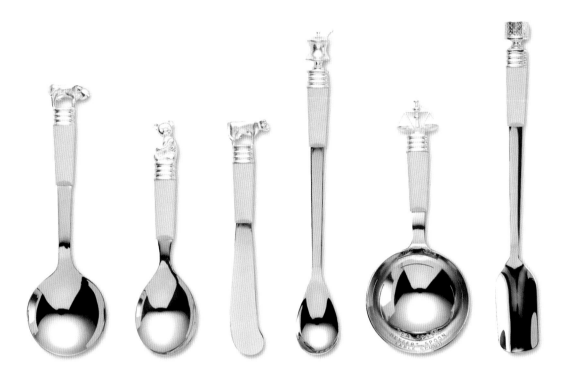

his Sparta lighting range (1991) and his Sea Drift Pebble vase (1998), all of which had a strong sculptural presence thanks to their bold massing and distinctly graphic profiles.

Now well into his sixties, Robert was still a design force to be reckoned with, and had no intention of slowing down or retiring. However, the prevailing taste during the late 1980s and 1990s for decorative and fussy designs was at stylistic odds with the type of work Robert was known for: clean, modern lines and functional forms. Also, thanks to the socio-economic turmoil of the 1970s and the early 1980s, many of his previous clients had either gone out of business or moved abroad, and instead of companies beating a path to his door, he was now having to find manufacturers to work with. Often, he sought out manufacturing partners just to ensure that he had new products to sell in the shops, such as the ever-expanding Dryad range, manufactured by B. Rourke & Co. and various lights produced by Chad Lighting – then both small one-man-band-type companies. Yet despite the various setbacks, which he listed in annual recollections at the back of his sketchbooks, Robert weathered the vagaries of fashion and continued to find success with the shops by selling good design directly to people who appreciated it. Having grown up surrounded by design, by the early 1990s it also seemed the right time for his children to take a more active role in the family business, yet with Robert still very much at the helm. Rupert joined the company in 1990, having previously studied at Sheffield Polytechnic before training as an accountant in the City of London. 'A natural mathematician' according to his mother, Rupert learnt the ins and outs of all aspects of the business over the next three years and then formulated a business plan, which proposed that the company switch to manufacturing its own designs under its own

Opposite: Patinated bronze bowl from the Kerala collection, designed by Robert Welch in 1984

Top: Six pieces from the Shetland Serving Collection designed by Robert Welch for Shetland Silvercraft, 1985

Above: RP220 Octopus and RP240 Tree pendants designed by Robert Welch for Shetland Silvercraft, 1989

name. Robert was, however, reluctant to adopt this seemingly risky strategy, probably because he had first-hand experience of how fraught with problems self-manufacturing could be from his earlier Campden Designs joint-venture. So, despite Rupert's conviction that this was the way forward, Robert stuck determinedly throughout the 1990s to what he had always done, working concurrently as an industrial-design consultant for various manufacturers and as a designer of bespoke commissions – his creative output balancing the mass-produced with the handmade. It was during this period that he also produced the majority of his large vibrant, colour-saturated oil paintings, mainly of landscapes and still-life subjects.

During the early 1990s, Alice Welch also started to play a vital role in the company, initially 'off her own bat' helping out with PR and creating the shop's window displays, until Robert suggested that she join the firm full-time.[62] She subsequently produced the company's first proper catalogue – previously Robert had issued simple broadsheets – in collaboration with Pentagram, the well-known design consultancy that had already undertaken various graphic projects for Robert Welch Designs, including the design of its logo in the 1980s. Lorenzo Apicella of Pentagram later redesigned the shop in Chipping Campden in the mid 1990s when it was expanded. Around the same time that their first catalogue was published, Alice and Rupert decided that they needed to promote the company's designs directly to the general public, and therefore took part in various consumer fairs, most notably the BBC Good Food Show at the NEC in Birmingham, as well as a host of other similar events. By using simple table displays to show their designs, they found that people immediately engaged with the products. Such fairs, along with various trade exhibitions, helped the company to gain real momentum during the 1990s. Alice recalls of their first Ambiente

show in Frankfurt that not one single person came to their stand, yet they persevered doggedly year after year, until people started to take notice of what they had on show, and then realize that it was really quite special in terms of its design and manufacture.

It was, however, the company's first outing at the Restaurant Show at Olympia in London in 1997 that would, with hindsight, prove to be a pivotal turning point. While exhibiting there a young designer called Gavin Pryke came on to their stand and Rupert began chatting with him. It transpired that Pryke had studied at the Royal College of Art, and had recently been appointed as an in-house designer for Virgin Atlantic Airways, which had big plans to regain the luxurious glamour that had been previously associated with first-class air travel in earlier decades. Quite simply, the airline wanted to offer the best service available and were on a design-fuelled mission to ensure their Upper Class cabins lived up to their name. Pryke and Rupert began an interesting discourse over the following months and eventually it was decided that Robert Welch Designs would create for Virgin Atlantic Airways a bespoke range of inflight cutlery, which would comprise eight rather than the standard four pieces. An adaptation of the Sea Drift pattern, this customized range was not only smaller and lighter, but arguably also better proportioned. After some deliberation about who would actually produce this prestigious cutlery commission, Rupert asked Virgin if they would give him the chance to self-manufacture and supply the cutlery, and Virgin agreed. Because of various agreements already in place, this cutlery order was eventually manufactured under the aegis of Gingko, Robert Welch Designs' distributor in the United States. Despite this, however, to all in intents and purposes 'the Virgin order' was the firm's earliest foray into proper self-production and certainly the cutlery was the first to bear Robert's name. And despite Robert's increasingly poor health due to a medical condition that had been first diagnosed in the mid 1980s, he found an immense amount of joy in witnessing his ideas being brought successfully to life by his own company for the very first time. He could see that the love and care he had lavished throughout his life on the initial pre-production development of designs was now being channelled by his children into the manufacturing and distribution side of things and the results were hugely encouraging.

Nevertheless, it was a phone call to the shop in 1999 that changed the course of the company perhaps more than anything else. On the line was someone from the restaurant chain Pizza Express, requesting a brochure to be sent to them, as they were looking for new cutlery to use in all their branches. Rupert instantly saw that this potentially significant order could be the financial springboard the company needed to start autonomously manufacturing under

the 'Robert Welch' name once and for all. Fortunately, Robert had been working on a new cutlery design for some time, so there was in effect an already existing design that could be put into production, albeit with a considerable amount of trialling and tweaking in order to hone it to balanced, Zen-like handling perfection. Undoubtedly, the earlier Virgin Atlantic commission gave Pizza Express the confidence to sign an agreement with Robert Welch Designs to provide a large quantity of this new cutlery. And so the process of taking the initial design concept to finished product commenced, overseen by Robert but with the assistance of Rupert. In early 2000, however, Robert's health began to falter, and so Rupert together with his brother William undertook the trip to the factory to inspect the first production run of this new cutlery range, which had by now been christened Stanton. While they were away, Robert's health deteriorated further, and on their return they rushed to see their father, who was now in hospital, so that he could inspect the gleaming samples of Stanton they had brought back with them. He was utterly delighted with the results and gave the design his unconditional blessing – as Rupert recalls, 'I felt that at that moment the baton had been passed'.[63] Two hours later Robert slipped peacefully away.

While the Robert Welch Design mantle had in effect been passed to the next generation, both Rupert and Alice knew that more than anything else their father's guiding ethos that 'everything can be better, everything can be improved'[64] must inform their future design decisions. It was indeed his greatest legacy to them. They subsequently hung a large photograph of Robert on the wall of the shop so that he could watch over them as they set out to create new products designed 'the Robert Welch way'.

Designing the Robert Welch Way

The year 2000 witnessed a momentous shift in the way Robert Welch Designs operated as a business, for at long last the control of production and distribution had been seized, and over the succeeding years both Rupert and Alice tirelessly worked to build upon their father's legacy and turn Robert Welch Designs into a world-class brand synonymous with design and manufacturing excellence. They did this not only from a design standpoint but also by trying to ensure that the perfection Robert had always pursued in the creation of form was translated into every aspect of how a product was manufactured and marketed. As Rupert observes:

'Although we aren't designers, we have Dad's creative genes and are just as obsessive as he was in getting all the ingredients right. The difference is that when one is in control of manufacture you can be a master of your own destiny, and consequently make sure that every product is imbued with a soul born out of love. People just don't realize how much work goes into every design or how full-time our commitment is to getting every element of it absolutely perfect. The collective energy of our close-knit team is wonderfully powerful and we actively embrace each other's ideas because that is how one develops great products.'[65]

Opposite: Sea Drift Pebble vases designed by Robert Welch, 1998

Above: Contemporary view of the Robert Welch Studio Shop in Chipping Campden

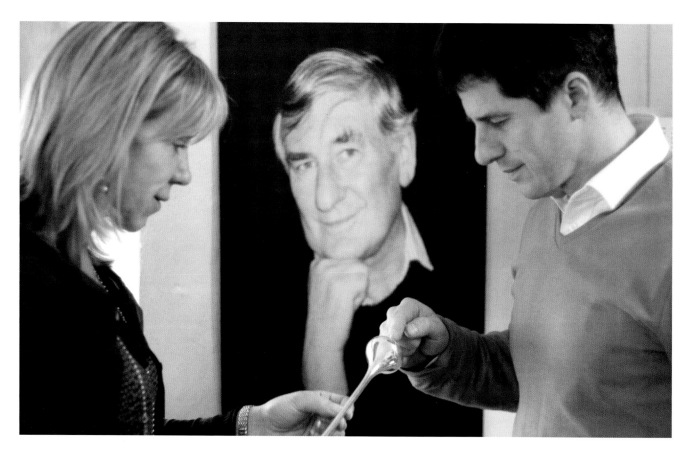

One of the first products to be created after Robert's passing, and with this striving-for-excellence mindset, was the Radford cutlery range; essentially a monobloc evolution of an earlier silver hollow-handled design known as Premier created by Robert in the 1980s. Far less expensive to produce than the earlier design, Radford went on to become the company's best-selling cutlery pattern, and was popular around the world thanks to its modern yet understated classical elegance and its impressive range of pieces. During the early 2000s, however, there was something of a hiatus as Rupert and Alice came to grips with running the company and steering its overall design direction. As a result, Robert's youngest son, William, joined the company after graduating from the Royal College of Art in 2001, and over the next four years he designed various products for the company, including four cutlery ranges – Pendulum, Comet, Vista and Deta – as well as some candlesticks. Around this time Alice instigated a design committee that included, apart from the three family members, the firm's trade-sales manager, its retail manager and its business consultant in order to promote a more strategic approach to design.

Realizing that the company needed a greater design capacity in order to grow, it was decided that another designer was required on the team to increase productivity and expand the range. As Alice observes, 'it was unrealistic to think we could keep the design side of the business entirely within the family' especially when their long-held goal had been to transform the company from 'a design house that sold things into a recognizable brand.'[66] By placing an advertisement in *Design Week*, they found Paul deBretton Gordon, who joined the design studio in 2005. Having studied product design at North Staffordshire Polytechnic (now Staffordshire University) before working as a freelance industrial designer for various Stoke-on-Trent companies as well as a shape designer for Wedgwood, deBretton Gordon was ideally suited to this new position, for he had an understanding of both craft and industry. Meanwhile, William, who had previously been an intern at Pentagram, decided to pursue his own independent design career and so Ruth Williams, on deBretton Gordon's recommendation, was brought in as an additional designer. A graduate of Loughborough University, Ruth had also worked at Wedgwood as a shape designer. The two were joined six months later by deBretton Gordon's wife, Kit, who had trained as a ceramic designer at Staffordshire before also working for Wedgwood.

This talented trio of form-givers set about creating a range of products that essentially channelled the design ethos of Robert Welch – they began 'designing the Robert Welch way'. Each possessed different design skills: Paul mainly concentrated on kitchenware, most notably the Signature range of knives, while Ruth focused on fluid designs for the company's 'living range', such as her extraordinary Windrush candlesticks, and Kit created various sculptural designs for both cutlery and homewares that would go on to become truly 'classic' Robert Welch designs, from her Molton cutlery to her Burford bathroom accessories. Although Ruth left in 2013 after creating a number of award-winning designs, Paul and Kit remain the company's main in-house designers. Every design, however, is developed in close collaboration with Alice and Rupert, who – although not having any formal design training themselves – are very much their father's children and as such have an extraordinary instinctive feel for the design process. Alice explains: 'My role is mainly at the front end … my eye is all about form, the perfection of form … and I am always responsible for writing the initial design briefs. Rupert handles more of the manufacturing side and always tries to push functionality as far as is humanly possible.'[67] Certainly Paul and Rupert have an especially close working relationship – echoing the creative synergy that Robert and John Limbrey enjoyed – and often there is, as Paul describes it, an almost 'spooky' intuitive understanding between them when they are developing a design. And while most of the current objects produced by Robert Welch Designs can be attributed officially to Paul and Kit, these products are also shaped to a very large extent by Rupert and Alice.

Recently the workspace in the Old Silk Mill was given a major refurbishment to bring it into the twenty-first century, and while today CAD software and 3-D printers have replaced traditional silversmithing tools and wooden models, the design philosophy remains the same. Similarly, the shop in Chipping Campden – alongside the recent one in Bath – continues to provide a tantalizing mix of innovative designs, both old and new, as it has done for more than 45 years. For at the heart of Robert Welch Designs is the belief that good design really does matter, and that every new product must push existing limits, whether aesthetically, functionally and/or technically. Put simply, there is no point in creating a design unless the aim is to produce the best product one can, and that is ultimately how to design the Robert Welch way. Under Alice and Rupert's careful direction, it is a proud legacy of design excellence that continues to be nurtured and evolved with a heartfelt passion. For as Robert Welch once observed, 'There has to be a flow of new designs all the time. And there are going to be failures, there's no doubt about that, but you have to have the faith and courage to keep on trying to do new things.'[68]

1972	Elected Honorary Fellow, Royal College of Art
1973	Younger son, William Leonard Welch, born
1973	*Design in a Cotswold Workshop* monograph published by Lund Humphries
1975	Visited India at the invitation of the All India Handicraft Board
1979	Visited Japan in order to design for Yamazaki Kinzoku Kogyo Created Member of the Most Excellent Order of the British Empire (MBE)
1984	Received Design Centre Award for Kitchen Devil Professional knife range Visited India to provide designs for bronze castings to be produced in Kerala
1985	Participated in a job-creation project for the Shetland Islands by creating designs for cutlery and jewellery
1986	Published *Hand and Machine* (biography) Featured in the BBC's *Designers* television series
1991	Opened second Robert Welch Studio Shop in Warwick
1993	Alice and Rupert Welch appointed directors of Robert Welch Designs Ltd, and over the coming years take increasing responsibility for the company's direction
1999	Following a substantial order from Pizza Express for Stanton cutlery, Robert Welch Designs Ltd, decides to manufacture designs under its own brand name, heralding a new chapter in the company's history
2000	Robert Welch died 15 March at the age of 70 in Warwick, after a prolonged illness (buried in Chipping Campden) Rupert and Alice Welch continue to direct the family-run business based on their father's belief in 'the poetry of moderation'
2001	Robert Welch's younger son, William, joins Robert Welch Designs as a designer, having studied product design at the Royal College of Art, London (graduating 2001)
2002	Received a FORM design prize at the Tendence Fair in Frankfurt for Comet cutlery
2005	Paul deBretton Gordon joins design team William Welch leaves Robert Welch Designs to pursue his own independent design career Paul deBretton Gordon appointed head designer at Robert Welch Designs Ltd Ruth Williams joins company as a designer (remains until 2013)
2006	Kit deBretton Gordon appointed designer at Robert Welch Designs
2009–11	Received a Red Dot Design Award, iF Product Design Award, three Excellence in Housewares Awards and a Good Design Award (Chicago Athenaeum) for Signature knife range
2010	Received a Red Dot Design Award for Bud cutlery
2011	Received two Good Design Awards from the Chicago Athenaeum, for Signature salt and pepper mills and Bud cutlery Received Excellence in Housewares Award for Signature salt and pepper mills
2012	Received Housewares Design Award for Signature knife range Kit deBretton Gordon appointed senior designer at Robert Welch Designs Opened third Robert Welch Studio Shop in Bath
2013	Received Red Dot Product Design Award for Molton cutlery Master silversmith John Limbrey died at the age of 80 (having worked with Robert Welch 1958–2000) Received two Housewares Design Awards (Cutting Edge and Top of the Table categories) for Signature knife range and Signature professional knife block, and Drift jugs
2014	Patricia Welch named Life President of Robert Welch Designs Paul deBretton Gordon appointed design director at Robert Welch Designs
2015	Robert Welch Designs celebrates the 60th anniversary of being based at the Old Silk Mill in Chipping Campden with the publication of *Robert Welch – Design: Craft & Industry*

Chronology

1929	Robert Radford Welch born on 21 May in Park Street, Hereford
1939	Welch family moved to West Malvern, Worcestershire
1939–46	Attended Lyttelton Grammar School in Malvern and Hanley Castle Grammar School
1946	Played with Second XI, Worcester County Cricket Club
1946–47	Attended Malvern School of Art, studying under Victor Hume Moody
1947–49	Served in the RAF as a wireless operator, based in Cambridge where he attended intermediate NDD (National Diploma in Design) classes at Cambridge School of Art
1949–50	Returned to Malvern School of Art Received the Charlotte Jacob Prize for Silversmithing
1950–52	Studied at the School of Silversmithing and Jewellery at Birmingham College of Art, under Cyril Shiner and Ralph Baxendale. Attained his NDD (National Diploma in Design)
1952–55	Studied at the School of Silversmithing at the Royal College of Art, London, under Professor Robert Goodden Attained his Des RCA Awarded the RCA Prize for Design in Three Dimensions and the RCA Silver Medal
1953–55	Visited Stockholm, Bergen and Copenhagen (using grants and a previously awarded scholarship)
1955	Set up his own studio and workshop at the Old Silk Mill, Chipping Campden, Gloucestershire Produced his first designs for production in stainless steel Appointed design consultant to Olde Hall Tableware, J. & J. Wiggin, Bloxwich (association continued until Old Hall's closure in 1984)
1956	Elected Member of Society of Industrial Artists (MSIA), later becoming a fellow (FSIA) in 1962
1956–62	Visiting lecturer for the Department of Industrial Design at Central School of Arts and Crafts, London
1957	Admitted to the Freedom of the Goldsmiths' Company by special grant (elected to Livery in 1982) Received first industrial-design commission for a product not made from metal, the Permutit water softener (launched 1959) Received a Design Centre Award for Campden toast rack
1958	John Limbrey joined the workshop as an assistant Awarded diploma for the Campden coffee set at Expo 58, the Brussels World Fair
1959	Married Patricia Marguerite Hinksman, whom he had met the previous year
1960	Awarded Silver Medal (with David Mellor) for Campden cutlery at the XII Milan Triennale Awarded Stainless Steel National Design Award by the National Industiral Design Council of Canada for SonA kettle
1960–71	Visiting lecturer for the Department of Silversmithing at the Royal College of Art, London
1961	Daughter, Alice Jane Welch, born Robert Welch Designs Ltd formally established on 7 April Created his first designs in cast iron
1962	Welch family moved to the White House in Alveston (remained family home until 2001) Received Design Centre Award for Oriana range of stainless-steel tableware
1963	Elder son, Alan Rupert Welch, born
1964	Received Design Centre Award for Merlin alarm clock
1965	Elected Royal Designer for Industry (RDI) – a faculty within the Royal Society of Arts Received Design Centre Award for Alveston (RW1) cutlery, later this design was modified in scale and rechristened RW2
1967	Elected Fellow of the Royal Society of Arts (FRSA)
1969	Opened the first Robert Welch Studio Shop in Chipping Campden Received the Observer Design Award

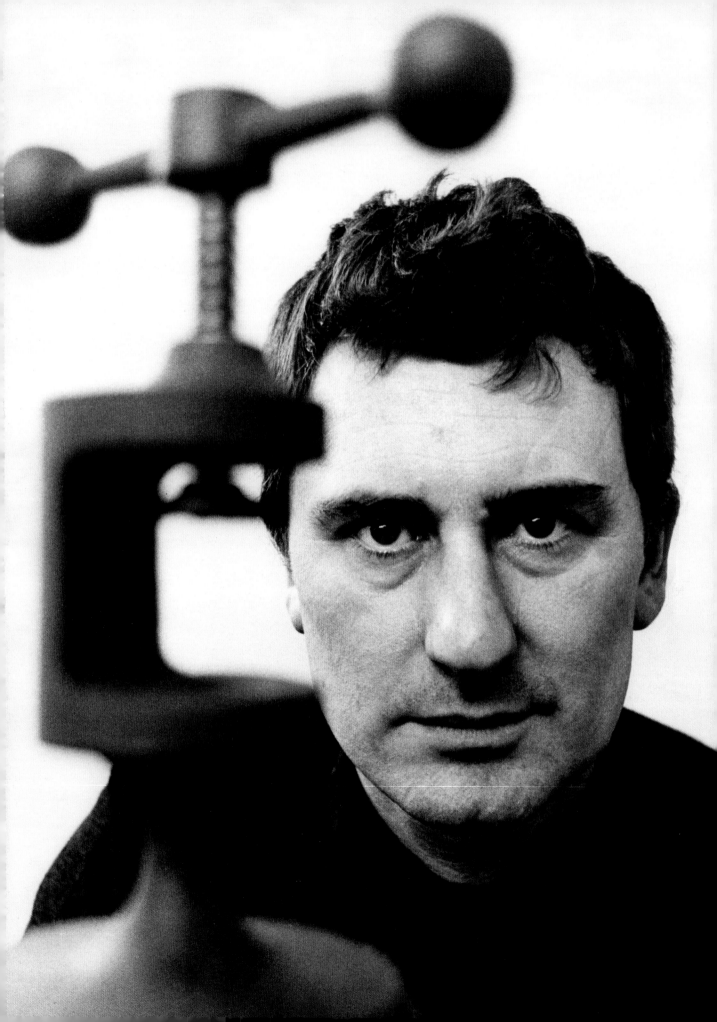

Chronology

Exhibitions

Group Exhibitions

1955	British Exhibition, Copenhagen
1956	An Exhibition of Modern Silver, Laing Art Gallery, Newcastle
1959	British Artist Craftsmen, US travelling exhibition organized by the Smithsonian Institution, Washington DC
1959	Watchmaker, Jeweller and Silversmith, Albert Hall, London
1959	Modern Silver, Goldsmiths' Hall, London
1963	Modern British Silver, Goldsmiths' Hall, London
1964	Inspiration Shakespeare Country, Stratford-upon-Avon
1965	Modern Church Plate, Manchester City Art Gallery
	Hand & Machine, The Design Centre, London
	The British Exhibition, Tokyo
1966	Hall-mark RCA (Silversmithing and Jewellery Students from 1955–1966), Royal College of Art, London
1966	The Sterling Craft: Five Centuries of Treasures from the Worshipful Company of Goldsmiths, London (toured USA as Ancient and Modern Masterpieces of British Gold, Silver and Jewelry, 1966–67)
1967	Public Treasure, Leeds City Art Gallery
1968	Vormgevers, Stedeljik Museum, Amsterdam
1969	British Design (10 British Designers), Rohsska Museum, Gothenburg, Sweden.
1973	The Craftsman's Art, Crafts Advisory Committee, Victoria and Albert Museum, London
1973	Birmingham Gold & Silver 1773–1973, Birmingham City Museum and Art Gallery
1975	Shopping in Britain, The Design Centre, London
1976	Treasures of London, Smithsonian Institution, Washington, DC
1976	Loot, Goldsmiths' Hall, London
1977	Explosion, Goldsmiths' Hall, London
1979	Homespun to Highspeed – A Century of British Design, Mappin Art Gallery, Sheffield
1980	Alternative Kitchens, Southampton Art Gallery
1980–81	Crafts South West (touring), Cornwall Crafts Centre, Trelowarren and the British Crafts Centre, London
1981	Drawing Technique & Purpose, Victoria and Albert Museum, London
1981	Designed in Britain – Made Abroad, Design Centre, London
1983	Design since 1945, Philadelphia Museum of Art, USA
1985	Serviezen in Metaal, Museum Boymans Van Beuningen, Rotterdam
1986–87	Eye for Industry: Royal Designers for Industry 1936–1986, Victoria and Albert Museum, London
1987	Design It Again, Design Council, London/Glasgow
1987	Building a Crafts Collection (Crafts Council), Holburne Museum of Art, Bath
1988–89	Craft Classics since the 1940s, Crafts Council Gallery, London
1990	The British Council, British Design Exhibition, Japan (touring)
1990–91	Finely Taught, Finely Wrought, Birmingham Museum & Art Gallery
1991	Fine Designs of 1960s Britain, University Gallery, University of Essex, Colchester
1991	Beyond the Dovetail, Crafts Council Gallery, London
1991	Industrial Metal Exhibition, Lincolnshire College of Art and Design
1991–92	The New Look: Design in the Fifties, Manchester City Art Gallery
1992	Decorative Arts Today, Bonhams, London
1992	British Goldsmiths of Today, Goldsmiths' Hall, London
1993	20th Century Silver, Crafts Council Gallery, London
1993	British Design: Catalyst for Commercial Success, Singapore
1997	Dish of the Day, British Council, Belgium
1997	British Master Goldsmiths, Goldsmiths' Hall, London
2012	British Design 1928–2012, Victoria and Albert Museum, London
2013	Designed to Shine, 100 Years of Stainless Steel, Millennium Gallery, Sheffield

Solo Exhibitions

1956	An Exhibition of Modern Silver and Stainless Steel by Robert Welch, Foyle's Art Gallery, London
1964	Silver by Robert Welch, Heal's (Tottenham Court Road), London
1967	Skjalm Petersen, Copenhagen, and Heal's (Tottenham Court Road), London
1974	Robert Welch: An Exhibition of Silver and Industrial Design, Crafts Advisory Commitee, Waterloo Place Gallery, London
1992	Skjalm Petersen, Copenhagen
1995	Robert Welch Designer-Silversmith, A Retrospective Exhibition 1955–1995 (travelling), Cheltenham Art Gallery and Museum, Holburne Museum and Crafts Study Centre (Bath), Manchester City Art Gallery, Birmingham City Museum and Art Gallery
2014	Robert Welch: Inspiration and Innovation, Court Barn Museum, Chipping Campden

1950s

Condiment set, 1953

This beautiful sterling silver and amethyst glass condiment set was one of Robert Welch's earliest designs, created while he was still a student at the Royal College of Art. The glass elements were actually made by Robert during a college visit to Stourbridge School of Art in 1953, as at the time the RCA did not have its own glassmaking facilities. With their softly rounded organic forms, the four pieces that make up the cruet set reflect the influence of postwar Scandinavian design, hardly surprising considering that the same year Robert had taken his first trip to Sweden where he met, among others, the well-known designer and gifted form-giver Stig Lindberg. Robert's design in turn signalled a fresh contemporary look for British silverware that was inspired by forms found in nature rather than being based on traditional antecedents. The set was subsequently awarded the Royal College of Art's 'Prize for Design in Three Dimensions', and was included in The British Exhibition held in Copenhagen in 1955 and later shown at the XII Milan Triennale in 1960. It was also displayed in 1956 at a solo exhibition of Robert's work held at Foyle's Art Gallery in London.

Designer:	Robert Welch
Materials:	Amethyst glass, silver mounts
Production:	Unique one-off piece executed by Robert Welch at the Royal College of Art, London

Above: Early photograph of the 'Amethyst glass' condiment set, 1950s (RW)

Stacking tea set, 1954–5

This compact two-piece stacking tea set – comprising a teapot and a hot-water pot – was one of several speculative designs Robert Welch created while studying at the Royal College of Art. Originally intended to be produced in satin-finish stainless steel, this prototype was never put into production. Made of satinized chrome-plated brass instead, this student piece not only revealed Robert's ability to work confidently in metals other than silver, but was also intended to approximate the look and feel of stainless steel. Then seen as a state-of-the-art material, this versatile alloy had already captured Robert's attention while he was travelling in Scandinavia as a student, for it had very different material properties to those of silver or EPNS (electroplated nickel silver), being not only tarnish-proof but also extremely hard and resilient. Rather than trying to mimic silverware, this design shows that Robert, even at this early stage in his career, was looking to create stainless-steel wares that had a crisp precision, well suited to the qualities of this thoroughly modern alloy. As a result of this approach, he would become an important pioneer in the stainless-steel revolution of the late 1950s and early 1960s.

Designer:	Robert Welch
Materials:	Satinized chrome-plated brass, plastic binding
Production:	One-off experimental design executed by Robert Welch at the Royal College of Art, London

Right: Early photograph showing the tea set unstacked, 1950s

Condiment set, 1955

This diminutive condiment set, comprising salt and pepper shakers, a mustard pot with spoon and a carrying tray, was Robert Welch's first design for J. & J. Wiggin and was essentially a modification of an earlier design that had been sold under the latter's Olde Hall brand. In April 1957 *Design* magazine noted that the main innovations of Robert's restyling were 'a triangular tray with curved sides and a refinement of the carrying handle'. The earlier condiment set had a rather curious handle with three raised bands that was reminiscent of an old-fashioned honey dabber and gave the whole design a distinctive Art Deco feel. In contrast, Robert's variation was altogether more organic in style. Interestingly, its distinctive O-topped handle was actually inspired by a similar element that had featured on a condiment set designed by the Danish silver and jewellery designer Harald Nielsen in 1941 – showing the direct influence of Scandinavian design on the young British designer. The same issue of *Design* magazine also featured another condiment set designed by Robert on its cover. This more radical design, which it noted was just about to be launched – although whether it actually was is a matter of conjecture – was intended to be easier to clean. The magazine also stated that it emphasized 'the value of unadorned shapes in stainless steel.'[69] Revealingly, Robert got his idea for this very modern design from watching the way metal tubing was being processed at the Olde Hall factory, with short lengths of tubular steel being cut diagonally in two 'in order to provide outlines for pressed spouts'.

Designer:	Robert Welch
Material:	Bright-finish stainless steel
Production:	From 1955, Olde Hall Tableware, Bloxwich, Staffordshire

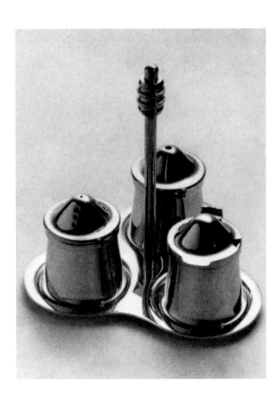

Below, left: Art Deco style condiment set manufactured by Olde Hall, 1950s, later redesigned by Robert Welch while still a student at the Royal College of Art

Below: Cover of Design magazine featuring another condiment set designed by Robert Welch, April 1957

Campden/Spring cutlery, 1956

The design of the Campden cutlery range was a collaboration between Robert Welch and his fellow RCA student and friend, David Mellor – who, like Robert, would become one of the most renowned British homeware designers of his generation. This alliance came about because Robert had been asked by Olde Hall to design a new stainless-steel cutlery range, while at the same time David had been asked by Walker & Hall in Sheffield to create a new range of cutlery. The two pooled their creative and technical resources, at the suggestion of the Council of Industrial Design, to create a design that could be produced by both companies. The original intention was that Walker & Hall would undertake the basic manufacture of the cutlery and the finishing and polishing would be done by Olde Hall. In the end, however, Walker & Hall undertook the complete manufacture of the range, while both companies retailed it. Walker & Hall sold it under the name Spring to the hotel and catering trade, while, rather confusingly, Olde Hall retailed it to domestic customers under the name Campden, in tribute to the location of Robert's new studio. The pattern was certainly very modern-looking, with its innovative short knife blades and slightly angular form, which recalled the edgy shapes of the famous Italian architect-designer Gio Ponti. It was subsequently awarded a silver medal at the XII Milan Triennale in 1960, and the range reputedly sold well. The confusion stemming from its double identity and the two designers' names attached to it, however, led the directors of Olde Hall to conclude that from then on the company would produce only exclusive patterns.

Above: Photograph of Campden cutlery used as the basis of a packaging design for Old Hall, 1960s. (RW)

Designer:	Robert Welch and David Mellor
Material:	Satin-finish stainless steel
Production:	From 1957 to 1972, Walker & Hall, Sheffield; re-tailed by both Walker & Hall, Sheffield, and Old Hall Tableware, Bloxwich, Staffordshire (known as Olde Hall until 1959) and later manufactured by Harrison Fisher, Sheffield, and Oneida, New York

Campden toast rack, 1956

Arguably one of Robert Welch's best-loved stainless-steel wares, the Campden four-slice toast rack was also one of his earliest designs to be put into mass production under the Olde Hall (later Old Hall) brand. Various scribbled preliminary sketches of this product reveal that Robert took quite a while to formulate the final design, the form of which was entirely inspired by a careful study of function – from its five rounded arch-like elements that allow the slices of toast to be inserted and extracted easily, to the integrated and ergonomically shaped handles at either end that facilitate carrying. While this classic toast rack was part of the larger Campden range of tableware (designed the same year), it also found commercial success as a standalone product, such was the strength of its design in terms of form, function and affordability. As a tribute to its innovative design, it received a Design of the Year award from the CoID (Council of Industrial Design) in 1957, which was presented to Robert by H.R.H. The Duke of Edinburgh. This was the first of many major awards that Robert would receive during his long and prolific career. The following year the toast rack was included in the council's annual 'Designs of the Year' exhibition of 1958. A larger, six-slice version (model no. 42913) of this 'New Look' design was also manufactured by Old Hall from 1962. As the leaflet that came in the box with these toast racks noted, 'Old Hall Tableware can last a lifetime. All it asks for is a little care' and it is remarkable how original examples of this iconic design often look as box-fresh as on the day of their first purchase, such was the high quality of both their design and manufacture.

Designer:	Robert Welch
Materials:	Satin-finish or bright-finish stainless steel
Production:	From 1957 to 1982, Old Hall Tableware, Bloxwich, Staffordshire (known as Olde Hall until 1959)

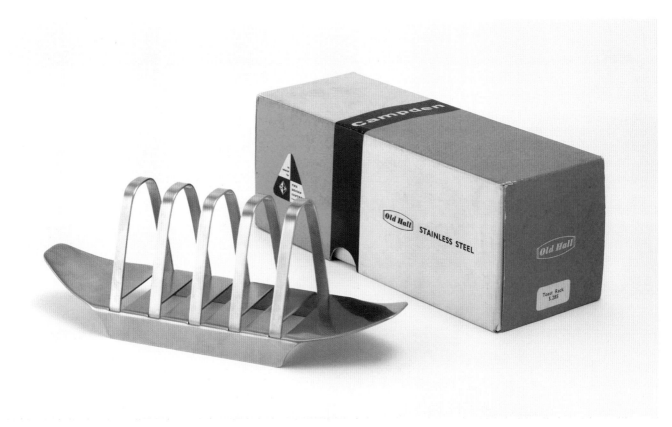

Opposite: Campden toast rack shown alongside its original packaging, which was also designed by Robert Welch and which additionally bears the Council of Industrial Design's distinctive kitemark

Right: Robert Welch explaining the design of the Campden toast rack to H.R.H. The Duke of Edinburgh, 1957

Campden coffee set, 1956

The Campden range was the first coordinated product line of stainless-steel wares to be designed by Robert Welch for Olde Hall Tableware, and as a group it was quite a departure for the Bloxwich company, being a design-led contemporary line that was pitched not only at the domestic retail market but also at the ever-growing catering sector. Of all the pieces in the range, it is perhaps the two pots and sugar bowl that make up the coffee service that are the most visually distinctive – with their satin-finish tapering bodies, rosewood knobs and side-jutting handles. These stridently contemporary designs epitomized the 'New Look' of the 1950s, which reflected an eagerness for more casual ways of living and a desire to look forward rather than backwards. Robert's designs based not on the traditional forms of coffee pots found in the West but rather on the shape of coffee pots used in the Middle East, must have seemed rather exotic when they were first launched.

Designer:	Robert Welch
Materials:	Satin-finish stainless steel, rosewood
Production:	From 1958 to 1974, Old Hall Tableware, Bloxwich, Staffordshire (known as Olde Hall until 1959)

Below: Ink and watercolour drawing by Robert Welch of the Campden coffee set, ca. 1956, showing an early variation of this design with rounded handles set on the same side

Campden three-part candleholder (model no. 44221), 1957

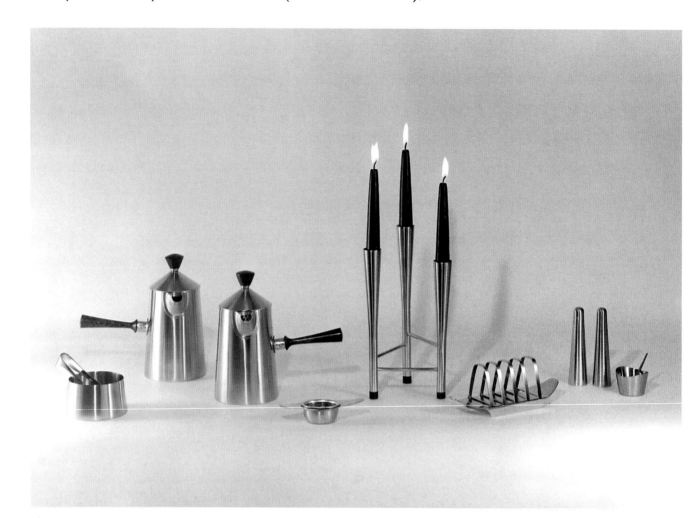

Having co-designed the Campden/Spring cutlery range with David Mellor in 1956, Robert Welch subsequently created various other products for Olde Hall to be added to the firm's new Campden range, including a triple-stemmed candleholder. This stainless-steel and teak design was unlike any that had been created before and, in common with the other pieces in the Campden range, had a stylish postwar modernity that exuded the casual sophistication so beloved by dinner-party-giving homemakers as well as by the burgeoning hospitality sector. Each fluted holder was a different height, while the crosspieces holding them together were also set at varying levels, thereby giving a sculptural dynamism to the ingeniously simple composition. Although designed for industrial mass-manufacture in stainless steel, the three-part candleholder's construction in many ways echoed that of the one-off, seven-branch silver candelabrum Robert was concurrently designing at the behest of Goldsmiths' Hall for inclusion in the Smithsonian Institution's 'British Artist Craftsmen: An Exhibition of Contemporary Work' (see page 68), albeit having a far simpler composition with fewer elements. In production for more than two decades with Old Hall, this classic design was also later manufactured by Robert Welch Designs in Chipping Campden in sterling silver, as a limited edition of 50 to celebrate the company's 50th anniversary.

Above: Publicity photograph showing the entire Campden range, 1950s (RW)

Designer:	Robert Welch
Materials:	Satin-finish stainless steel, varnished teak
Production:	From 1957 to 1976, Old Hall Tableware., Bloxwich, Staffordshire (known as Olde Hall until 1959)

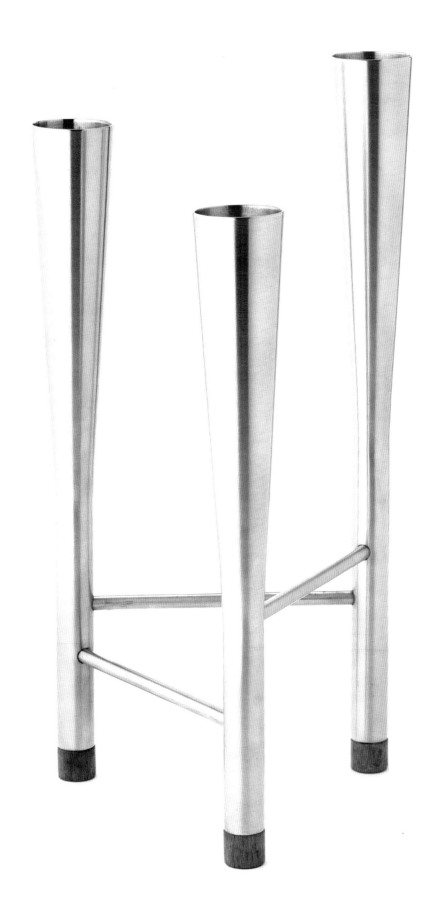

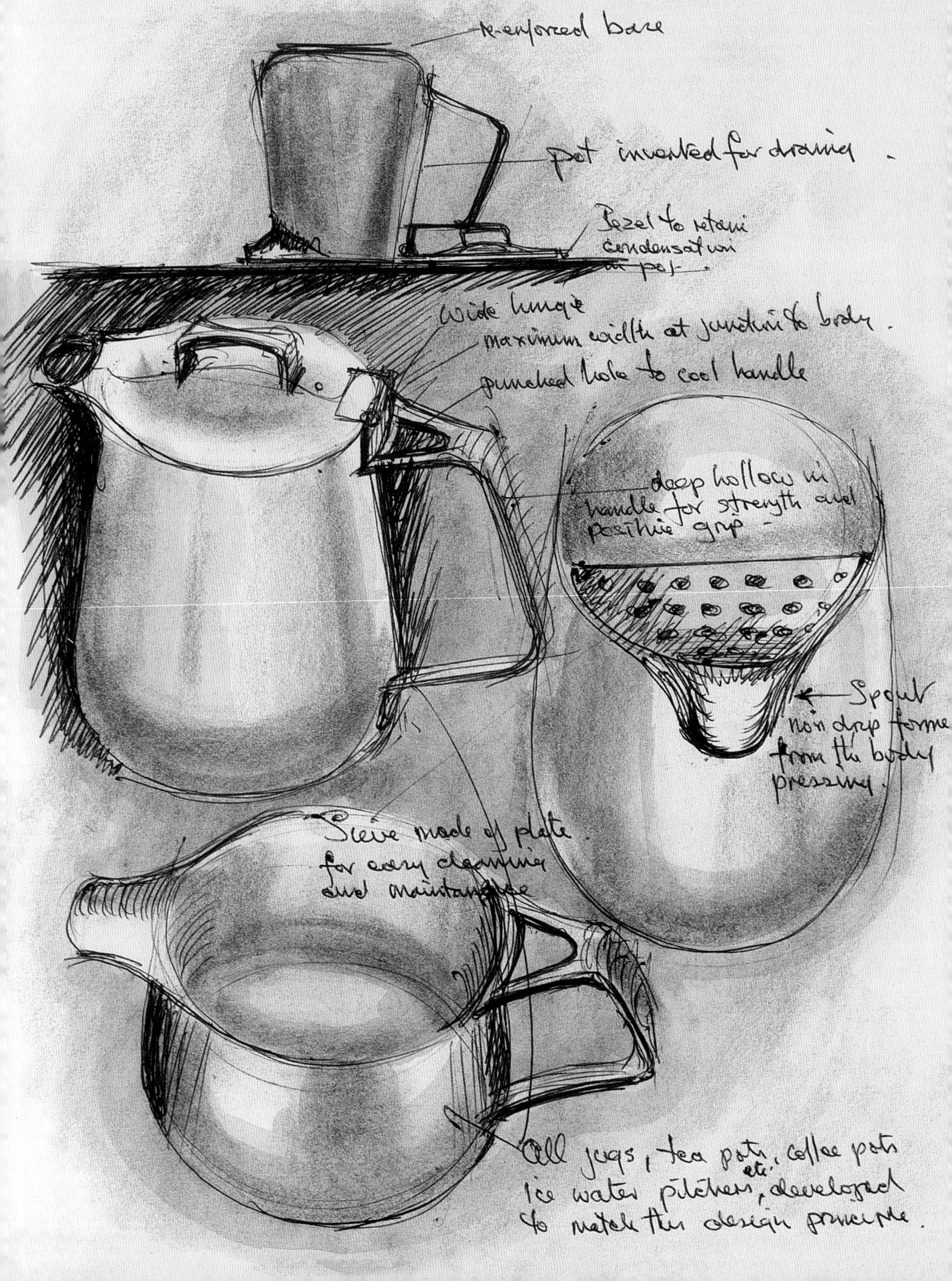

reinforced base

pot inverted for draining.

Bezel to retain
condensation
in pot.

Wide hinge
maximum width at junction to body.
punched hole to cool handle

deep hollow in
handle for strength and
positive grip.

Spout
non drip formed
from the body
pressing.

Sieve made of plate
for easy cleaning
and maintenance

All jugs, tea pots, coffee pots
ice water pitchers, developed
to match the design principle.

During the 1950s Olde Hall had its London office in Fenchurch Street, which just so happened to be around the corner from the headquarters of the Orient Line. Because of this proximity, Olde Hall's agent Harold Jacobsen from time to time received enquiries from Orient Line about the company's products. In 1956 Orient Line asked if there might be a suitable lavatory-brush holder for use on its ocean liners. The existing product made by Olde Hall, however, was just not durable enough for such a contract application. Because of this, the enquiry was forwarded to Robert Welch's studio, and Robert – in close collaboration with Olde Hall's works manager, Phil Robinson – created a prototype design that was, according to Robert, 'of true battleship strength and quality'.[70] The purchasing department of the Orient Line was so pleased with this robust new design that it placed a substantial order. Several months later, Robert received a letter from the company's director of supplies wondering whether he would be interested in creating a range of tableware for Orient's own ocean liner, the *SS Oriana*, which was due to

be launched in 1960. In fact, the Council of Industrial Design had recommended several designers including Robert, but during his interview he mentioned his earlier lavatory-brush holder design, which helped to inspire confidence in his abilities. Orient Line was even persuaded by Robert to consider using state-of-the-art stainless steel rather than old-fashioned silver-plated 'nickel silver' (a copper alloy). As Robert recalled, 'with my close association with Old Hall, the only company at that time capable of producing high-quality catering ware [from stainless steel], the equation fell into place and two years of intense work began.'[71] The resulting Oriana range was truly comprehensive in its scope, including not only cutlery, but also a host of serving articles, from vegetable dishes and ice buckets to a variety of pouring vessels. For this last category, Robert devised an elegant yet simple standardized jug shape with a low centre of gravity that was intended to provide a greater handling stability during rough sea crossings. This rational tapering form was not only used for different-sized pitchers, but also adapted with the addition of lids, sieves,

knobs or hinges to provide the main body elements of the range's teapots, coffee pots, hot-water jugs, and even its tall ice pitcher. This thoroughly durable and very modern holloware collection proved that with design skill and manufacturing excellence, stainless steel was more than a match for old-style electroplate, and perhaps even more importantly proved that it could be used to create wares that were stylishly modern rather than worthily utilitarian. The range was first used on the *SS Oriana*'s maiden voyage in December 1960; the following year Old Hall adapted the Oriana tea and coffee set for the retail trade, and from 1963 to 1975 it was also supplied to the catering trade.

Designer:	Robert Welch
Material:	Stainless steel
Production:	From 1960 to 1975, Old Hall Tableware, Bloxwich, Staffordshire

Above: Robert Welch in his studio contemplating pieces from the Oriana tableware range, ca. 1958

Opposite: Early publicity photograph of various designs from the Oriana tableware range, ca. 1960 (RW)

Right: Details from early publicity photograph of Oriana cutlery, 1957, taken using layers of glass to create a sense of visual depth (RW)

Apart from designing an extensive range of modern-looking stainless-steel serving and catering wares for the Orient Line to use on its brand-new passenger liner, the *SS Oriana*, Robert Welch was also commissioned to design a completely new cutlery range for this soon-to-be-launched vessel. Known as Oriana, the resulting set was remarkable for the shapely, ergonomic profiles of its pieces – which shared a sculptural quality with various cutlery designs being produced in Scandinavia, most notably the Focus range designed by Folke Arström in 1955. However, Oriana was even more sculptural with its undulating lines closely echoing the contours of the human hand and revealing the care Robert took to ensure that his designs were above all functionally perfect. Although the tableware for the *SS Oriana* was produced by Old Hall, this complementary cutlery range was instead manufactured by Mappin & Webb, the well-known jeweller and silversmith whose origins can be traced back to the Sheffield cutlery industry of the 1860s. The Oriana range, which was not only used on the cruise ship but also sold to the general public, was, however, something of a departure for Mappin & Webb

in that it was made from solid stainless steel rather than electroplated brass or sterling silver, for which the company was far better known. Sadly no longer in production, the wave-like Oriana pattern reflects the ascendency of organic design in the 1950s, and revealed that although Robert might have been based in the rolling Cotswold hills, seemingly far away from the centres of fashionable design, he was actually fully aware of the contemporary currents running through international design practice. Indeed, he absorbed them into his own formal vocabulary in order to create objects that epitomized the attributes of 'good design'.

Designer:	Robert Welch
Material:	Satin-finish stainless steel
Production:	From 1958, Mappin & Webb, Sheffield

Unlike Robert Welch's earlier silverware pieces, this extraordinary seven-branch candelabrum was designed without the use of any preparatory drawings or sketches. Instead, a model of the design was made using a trial-and-error process in the workshop, and this is undoubtedly why it has such a strong three-dimensional quality and a refreshing sense of formal innovation. It was commissioned by Graham Hughes, art director of the Goldsmiths' Hall, as one of a number of silverware designs to be included in the travelling 'British Artist Craftsmen: An Exhibition of Contemporary Work', which was sponsored by the Smithsonian Institution in Washington, DC and toured America from 1959 to 1960. Robert made his model of the candelabrum from lengths of wooden dowelling supplied by the local hardware shop, lathed into 'a random series of rounded and waisted forms',[72] which he described as 'unduloids'. These were then joined with randomly shaped wooden cross members that were glued in place. As soon as Hughes saw Robert's wooden model, he gave the go-ahead to execute the piece in silver. Interestingly, the design was directly inspired by a visit to a Jackson Pollock exhibition held at the Whitechapel Art Gallery in London in November and December 1958. As Robert

later recalled of the show, 'my first encounter with action painting was more than just stimulating';[73] it was in fact a deeply formative experience, which revealed to him how a strong sense of expressive immediacy could be achieved through creative spontaneity. That lesson was fully encapsulated in his design of this remarkably beautiful candelabrum. The piece's undeniable expressive qualities, as Charlotte Whitehead notes, are 'unusual to find in silver which is usually a very contained material'.[74] In 1991, while on loan to the exhibition 'New Look: Design in the Fifties' at Manchester City Art Gallery, the candelabrum was being stored in a warehouse that was unfortunately the subject of what is thought to have been an arson attack. Sadly, in the heat of the ensuing inferno this masterwork partially melted, but thankfully it was later painstakingly restored to its former glory.

Designer:	Robert Welch
Material:	Sterling silver
Production:	One-off exhibition piece commissioned by the Goldsmiths' Hall and executed by Robert Welch

Below: A photograph showing a wooden dowel being lathed to make up the model of the candelabrum, 1957

Nutcracker (model no. 44311), 1958

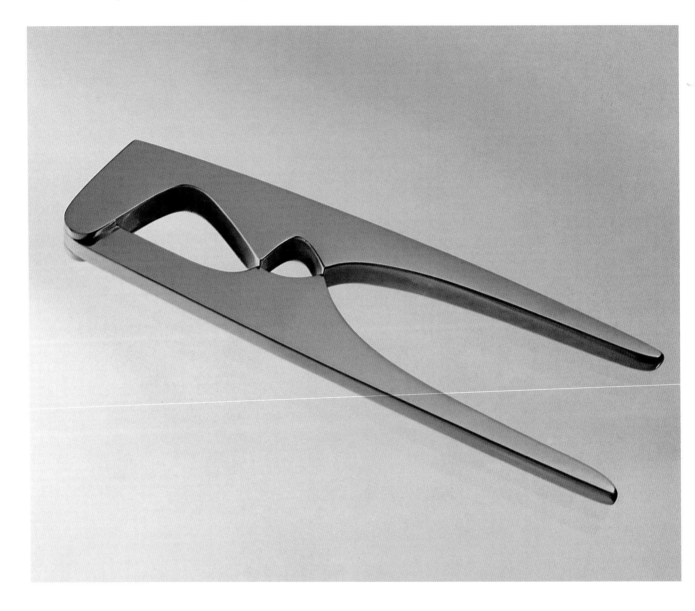

This early design by Robert Welch was first realized as a brass prototype, which he made in his workshop in Chipping Campden. Derrett End Lost Wax Casting of Droitwich subsequently developed a production model in 1958 using the lost-wax casting technique. This was the first design by Robert Welch to employ this ancient process, also known as *cire perdue*, which is notable for the precision it gives to castings. The manufacture was eventually transferred to Old Hall in 1961, but the design went out of production in the mid 1970s. It is, however, now prized by Old Hall collectors for its relative rarity and undeniable sculptural beauty. The longevity of its appeal has as much to do with its function as with its aesthetics: the attractive wave-like internal contours of the hinged cracker can hold varying sizes of nuts securely, while its two-pointed crests efficiently break their shells.

Above: Early photograph of the nutcracker, ca. 1958

Designer:	Robert Welch
Material:	Satin-finish stainless steel
Production:	From 1958 to 1960, Derrett End Lost Wax Casting, Droitwich for Robert Welch Designs; from 1961 to 1975, Old Hall Tableware, Bloxwich, Staffordshire

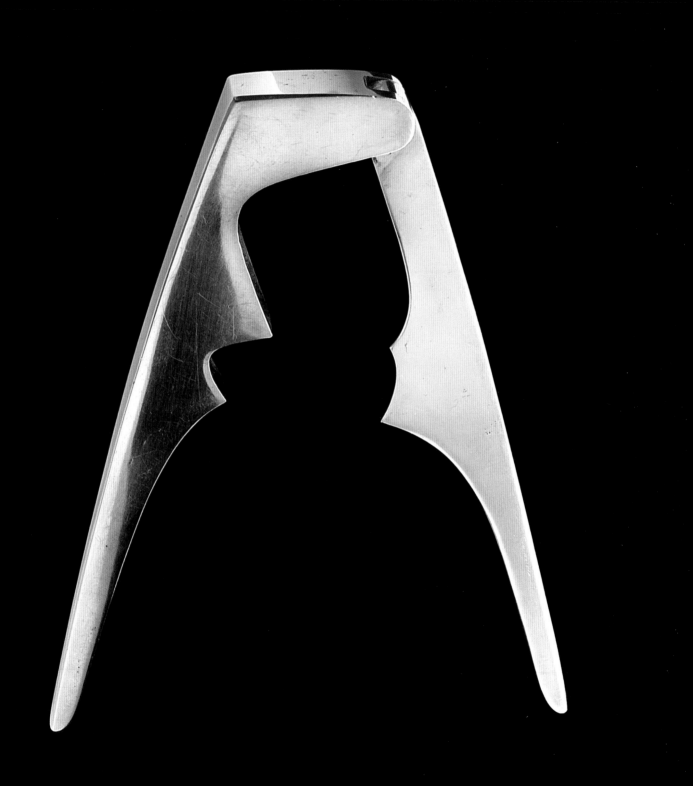

Cutlery prototypes for International Silver Corporation competition, 1959

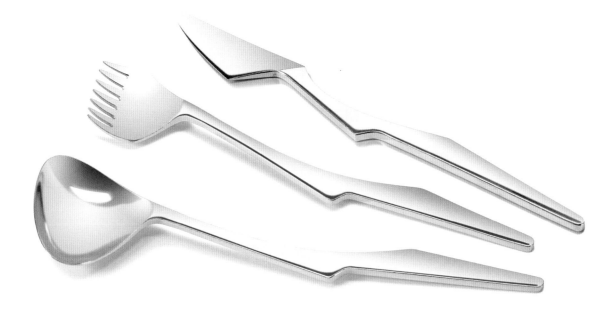

During the 1950s, a new sculptural confidence swept across the international design community, with the rigid geometry of the Modern Movement being rapidly replaced by a new organic sensibility that endeavoured to channel the abstract essence of nature into contemporary tools for living. As a talented form-giver, Robert Welch was, like other young designers, attracted to this fresh and more expressive approach to design, as these three experimental cutlery designs attest. These prototypes were created specifically for a cutlery competition held at the Museum of Contemporary Craft in New York that was sponsored by a well-known American silverware company, the International Silver Corporation of Meriden. Although based loosely on ergonomic studies, these highly sculptural designs were driven more by form than by function and had a stridently contemporary 'New Look' aesthetic. After Robert submitted two of the three designs to the competition, he began to feel that perhaps the designs had been guided too much by personal self-expression and not enough by functional considerations. This led to what can only be described as a damascene moment, with Robert deciding to go back to basics in his design of cutlery, which happily led to the development of the iconic Alveston range (see page 90). Yet despite this, these three designs reveal his complete mastery of form and are exquisitely beautiful objects in their own right.

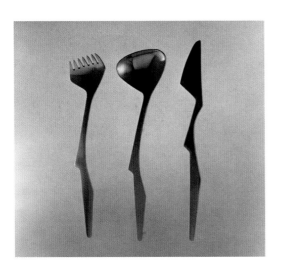

Left: Early photograph of cutlery prototypes, which was featured in Design *magazine, ca. 1959 (RW)*

Designer:	Robert Welch
Material:	Sterling silver
Production:	1959, prototypes executed by Robert Welch as competition entries

Broadway coffee and tea set, 1959

The village of Broadway is just down the hill from Chipping Campden and is often described as the 'Jewel of the Cotswolds'. During the early years of the twentieth century it was also a centre for both art and design, so it was fitting that when Robert Welch came to design this specially commissioned coffee service for the Worshipful Company of Goldsmiths, he named it after this ancient village of honey-coloured stone. The design of this silver and ebony service was based on the concept of cylindrical sections – as had been his earlier condiment set for Olde Hall that had been featured on the cover of *Design* magazine in 1957. The year before this coffee service was designed, the talented silversmith John Limbrey, who had studied at Birmingham College of Art, joined the Robert Welch workshop in Chipping Campden, and this remarkably beautiful design was the very first coffee (or tea) set that he made in silver.

Opposite, bottom: Pencil drawing by Robert Welch of the 'swan-necked' silver and ebony coffee set, ca.1959

Left: Broadway coffee set, shown with matching sugar bowl, ca. 1959 (RW) – in 1960 Old Hall made a stainless-steel version of this design

Designer:	Robert Welch
Materials:	Sterling silver, ebony
Production:	One-off commission from the Worshipful Company of Goldsmiths, executed by John Limbrey, Robert Welch Studio, Chipping Campden

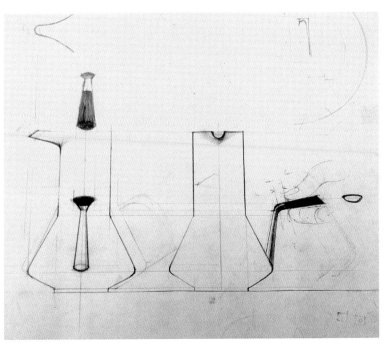

For his earlier stainless-steel and teak Campden coffee (see page 58) set for Old Hall, Robert had looked to Eastern precedents for inspiration – with the side-handles recalling those found on traditional Turkish coffee pots used throughout the Middle East. Similarly, for this exquisite coffee service commissioned by Goldsmiths' Hall, with its elegant swan-necked spout, he based his design on traditional Persian coffee-pot forms found in Iran. The design of this silver and ebony service, with its precise cylindrical and flared forms and its strongly attenuated spout and handle was however, stridently modern in aspect, albeit with a strong Eastern flavour.

Designer:	Robert Welch
Material:	Sterling silver, ebony
Production:	One-off commission from the Worshipful Company of Goldsmiths, executed by John Limbrey, Robert Welch Studio, Chipping Campden

Church plate for St Mary's Church, Swansea, 1959–65

Between 1959 and 1965, Robert Welch was commissioned to design 12 items of ecclesiastical silverware for St Mary's Church in Swansea. The initial patron was Cyril Davies, who was introduced to Robert by the Worshipful Company of Goldsmiths because he wanted to commission an altar cross and candlesticks as a memorial to his mother and father for presentation to St Mary's. This Gothic Revival-style Anglican house of prayer in the centre of Swansea had sustained extensive bomb damage during World War II, and it was rebuilt and rededicated only in 1958. As such, Robert's commission can be seen as part of the church's postwar regeneration – which is why the site-specifically designed pieces do not look back to earlier precedents but rather forward to a more optimistic space-age future. The original commission was added to by Canon Williams and other members of his congregation, and over the next few years various other pieces of church plate were commissioned including a chalice, a paten (communion tray), a ciborium (goblet used to hold consecrated wafers), a water ewer and lavabo (wash bowl), a pair of altar vases, a missal stand (lectern) and a processional cross. A specially designed aumbry (storage cabinet) was also built into the architectural fabric of the church to hold the pieces

when not in use. This suite of daringly and emphatically modern ecclesiastical silverware reflected the Church of England's desire to be seen to modernize during the late 1950s and throughout the 1960s. Through photographs alone, it is very difficult to gauge the scale of the pieces, especially the high altar cross, which is in fact impressively large, measuring just over one metre in height. More than anything, however, this commission demonstrated Robert's challenging of traditional design boundaries in order to create something strikingly contemporary, breathtakingly original and spiritually transcendent.

Designer:	Robert Welch
Material:	Sterling silver
Production:	From 1959 to 1965, executed by John Limbrey, Robert Welch Studio, Chipping Campden

LAMPS—in aluminium and acrylic
made in England

1960s

Above: Cotswold tea cup with gilded banding

Opposite: Early photograph showing all-white version of the Cotswold tea service, ca. 1960 (RW)

Right: Manufacturing mark designed by Robert Welch to be stamped on the underside of each piece

This elegant tea service was the first ceramic product designed by Robert Welch, and reveals his skill as both designer and craftsman for it marked the crossover from metals to other materials with very different physical properties. With its beautifully proportioned flaring shapes it demonstrates a mastery of form and function, while its restrained use of decoration – a simple band of gilding – imbues the design with a stylish yet understated sophistication that recalls similar fine china produced by the renowned German manufacturer, Rosenthal around the same time. Interestingly, Robert made prototypes of this design out of painted metal before it was manufactured in fine bone china. The design was produced in two variations, either all-white or white with a gilded banding. It was also conceived to be manufactured in yellow or black, but these colour options were never produced.

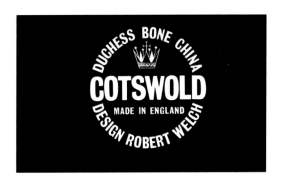

Designer:	Robert Welch
Material:	Glazed bone china with gilding
Production:	From 1962 Duchess China Works / A. T. Finney & Sons, Longton, Stoke-on-Trent, Staffordshire

Coffee suite for Churchill College, Cambridge, 1960–5

Receiving its Royal Charter in 1960, Churchill College in Cambridge was founded as the national and Commonwealth memorial to that great wartime statesman and leader, Sir Winston Churchill. It was intended to be a physical embodiment of his vision of how excellence in higher education could promote far-reaching benefits within a modern society.

Initially the college was housed in temporary buildings while its modernist brick and concrete campus, designed by the architect Richard Sheppard (1910–1982) was being constructed. On its completion, the campus won a Royal Institute of British Architects Architecture Award in 1968, with the jury noting, 'its merit is such that one has to search hard for criticism'.[75] The esteemed nuclear physicist Sir John Cockcroft, the college's first master, was responsible for commissioning Robert Welch in 1959 to create a modernist coffee suite for this new and shining beacon of higher education. The silverware pieces comprised a solid silver one-gallon coffee urn mounted on a stand, together with a matching sugar bowl and cream jug – and, like the building for which it was intended, the design was unequivocally modern with its clean, uncluttered lines. As Robert explained, 'The body of the urn was made as a cone and hammered into the required shape. The stand was made from heavy-gauge wires; the top rebated to take the stepped base on the urn, to avoid a pronounced demarcation between urn and stand.'[76] The subtle detailing of the set included an engraved inscription and the college crest, as well as rosewood inlays on the handles and urn tap. Rosewood was also employed for the closing cap and as a veneer for the base, which was made of laminated wood in order to negate any warping effect when the urn was heated by its spirit heater. As with his other bespoke commissions, Robert went to huge trouble to ensure not only that this suite was exquisitely executed, in this case by his right-hand man, John Limbrey, but also that it was functional – for instance, the urn's swing handle had a special locking device so that it would not go beyond a horizontal position and damage its silver body. It was such care for small details that raised Robert's work from the ordinary to the extraordinary. As well as this set, Robert carried out a further six silverware commissions for Churchill College between 1961 and 1968.

Designer:	Robert Welch
Material:	Sterling silver, solid rosewood, rosewood-veneered laminate wood
Production:	1960, one-off commission executed by John Limbrey, Robert Welch Studio, Chipping Campden

Below: Design drawing by Robert Welch of the Churchill College coffee set, ca. 1960

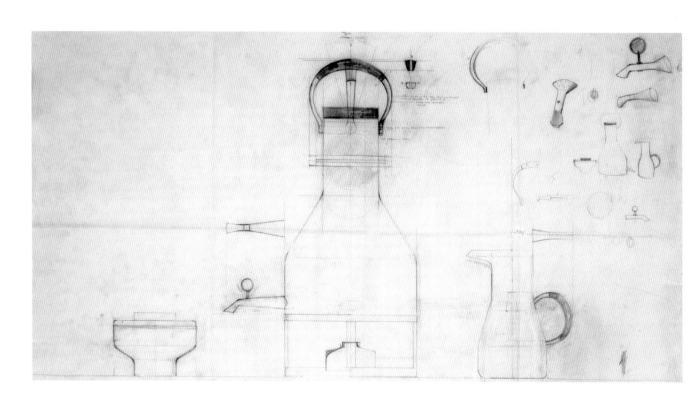

Inkstand for the City of Leicester, 1960

The Leicester-based jeweller and goldsmith George Tarratt commissioned this inkstand on behalf of the city's main department store, Lewis's. The City of Leicester was the recipient of this beautiful gift, which was intended as a new addition to its civic plate collection. Unlike most civic commissions of this kind, the design was unashamedly modern-looking, its distinctive cantilevered form inspired by one of the greatest buildings of the Modern Movement – Le Corbusier's famous Villa Savoye of 1928–31. The inkstand's sleek rectangular form comprised two square-cut glass and silver-lidded inkwells set either side of a rosewood-lined silver box engraved with the city's crest. These three elements were set on a rosewood base. The inkwells, made of highly polished cast blocks of glass, were specially fabricated by a lens manufacturer, while the silver box with its strip of rosewood revealing where its lid opens shows extraordinary attention to detail. The inside of the box is fitted out to hold a rosewood blotter, its paper-holding mechanism adjusted with a flush-set silver screw,

and a pair of rosewood fountain pens with gilt nibs. The strength of this design lies in its harmonious use of materials, which create a visual counterbalance between the optical reflection and transparency of glass, the warm solidity of the wood and the reflective quality of the burnished silver. A number of these inkstands were subsequently made as special commissions for other clients, most notably for the Worshipful Company of Goldsmiths as a presentation piece for Lord Holford, and for Ercol Furniture as a gift for the company's founder, Lucien Ercolani.

Designer:	Robert Welch
Materials:	Rosewood, optical glass, sterling silver
Production:	1960, bespoke commission executed by John Limbrey, Robert Welch Studio, Chipping Campden

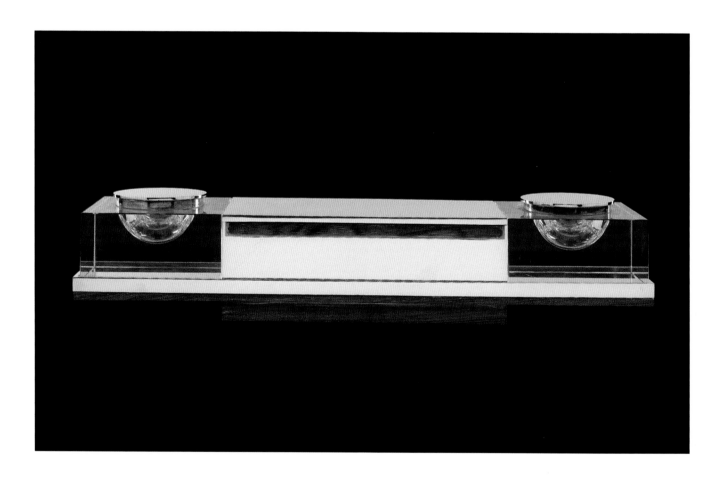

In the early 1960s Robert Welch designed a new wooden-handled kitchen knife specifically for British Home Stores (BHS). While the design did not make it into production, it did form the basis of a new cutlery range, known as Bistro, which was launched in 1963. With its rosewood handles and chunky form referencing traditional everyday French cutlery, as its name suggests, Bistro reflected the desire for less formal cutlery patterns that were suitable for increasingly casual styles of dining. Today, the Bistro range is no longer produced because its original handles were not suitable for dishwasher use. The current Trattoria range manufactured by Robert Welch Designs, however, is a modern variant of this much-loved 1960s classic, and instead of rosewood uses moulded dishwasher-proof handles made from high-grade acetal (polyoxymethylene or POM) plastic for a warm and engaging tactility.

Designer:	Robert Welch
Materials:	Bright-finish stainless steel, rosewood
Production:	From 1963 to 1982, Harrison Fisher of Sheffield for Old Hall Tableware, Bloxwich, Staffordshire (later Bistro Noir produced with thermoplastic handles by Old Hall from 1980 to 1982, and then later re-issued by Robert Welch Designs as Trattoria with polyoxymethylene plastic handles)

Merlin alarm clock, 1961

In 1956 the marketing and managing directors of Westclox – a successful Scottish clock-manufacturing company – decided that their product line needed reinvigorating, and that to do this a consultant designer should be brought in to create a brand-new range of modern clocks. The Merlin alarm clock was a direct result of this decision, with Robert Welch being chosen as the design consultant charged with updating Westclox's range of timepieces – from wall clocks to alarm clocks. While his first clock designs for the company were relatively traditional looking, the Merlin was, in contrast, strikingly modern. Prior to undertaking the design of the Merlin, Robert was briefed by the company's chief engineer, Cyril Ashwell, who with the electrical engineer Fred King was responsible for the development of the clock's internal mechanism. The electrically powered mechanism incorporated a 24-hour alarm with automatic resetting and a locking switch for when the alarm was not in use. Robert's job was essentially to skin this mechanism in a sculptural, modern-looking casing, and to that end he produced a series of prototypes made of wood or fibreglass, which he refined in discussion with Ashwell. The final product had a clam-like housing made of carmine red, 'Spanish gold' or white insulating plastic, a white metal dial on to which was printed simple black numerals and dots denoting one-minute increments, and luminescent spots marking the hours. The hour, minute and second hands were similarly easy to read – the first two having luminescent strips for nocturnal timekeeping, and the last being a simple line of red metal. Robert had hoped to use a different dial face devised by the graphic designers Colin Forbes and Alan Fletcher – who had recently designed his own letterhead, much to his satisfaction – but, as Robert noted, they were 'Alas, too far ahead of their time' for Westclox's management, and the presentation models that Fletcher Forbes Gill (the forerunner of Pentagram) had mocked up were rejected and subsequently 'packed up in a box, returned to Campden, and forgotten'.[77] Yet despite this, the Merlin clock was the most technically and aesthetically innovative design that Robert created for Westclox, and as *Design* magazine noted in 1964, it marked 'a new approach to popular British clock design, with the face well related to the body, controls well thought out, dial easily legible; but alas for the printing of the trademark'.[78] That same year, the design won a Design Centre Award, but as Westclox's chairman noted in 1968, 'CoID [Council of Industrial Design] styles just don't sell'. Despite the prestige this prize brought, it was not until five years after its launch that the Merlin alarm clock began 'showing signs of commercial appeal'[79] – presumably as the general public's taste finally caught up with its flagrantly contemporary Pop aesthetic.

Designer:	Robert Welch
Materials:	Plastic, painted metal, clock mechanism
Production:	From 1963, Westclox, Dumbarton, Scotland

Below, left: Exhibition drawing by Robert Welch of the Merlin alarm clock, ca. 1961

Below: Painted wooden model of the Merlin alarm clock with an alternative dial face designed by Fletcher Forbes Gill, ca. 1961

Judge Elegance cookware and kettle, 1961

In times gone by, itinerant gypsy tinsmiths known as 'tinkers' would travel from town to town mending people's worn-out pots and pans. Although the practice had largely died out by the early 1960s, *Design* magazine ran an article about a new range of cookware designed by Robert Welch under the banner 'No need for tinkers', presumably suggesting that it had been designed to withstand the rigorous tests of time. Known as the Elegance range, it had been conceived for large-scale mass production, and because of this Robert had been particularly mindful to design it in a way that reduced, as much as possible, the number of 'seconds' or rejects – which, of course, can have a detrimental effect on a manufacturer's bottom line. Another way that Robert was able to design economies into the range's manufacture was to employ common elements; for instance, a standardized knob was used across the whole range, while the pans all shared the same handle and ferrule, and the teapot and kettle both used the same spout. While the main bodies of the pieces were made of steel that was enamelled pale blue, yellow or black, the pan and kettle lids were made of anodized aluminium, which was not only lighter in weight, meaning it was easier for these parts to be lifted on and off while in use, but also importantly, less prone to chipping. In addition, Robert made sure that the pans stacked efficiently to save space. In this way, not only did the range have a distinctive contemporary elegance with its coloured enamel finishes and sculpted forms, but it was also highly practical.

Designer:	Robert Welch
Materials:	Vitreous enamelled steel, stainless steel, moulded plastic, anodized aluminium
Production:	from 1964, Judge Holloware Ltd, Cradley Heath, Stourbridge, Staffordshire

Above, left: Exhibition drawing by Robert Welch of the various designs in the Judge Elegance range, ca. 1961

Above: Publicity photograph of a stack of saucepans in the Judge Elegance range, ca. 1961 (RW)

Opposite, top: Judge Elegance kettle in pale blue enamelled finish

Opposite, bottom:: Photograph of Judge Elegance kettle, saucepans and coffee pot displayed on their packaging boxes, also designed by Robert Welch, ca. 1961 (RW)

Alveston cutlery, 1961

During the early 1960s the idea of good design as applied to the creation of better-performing contemporary 'New Look' homewares was increasingly gaining ground, and as a result numerous competitions and exhibitions were held around this time to attract the attention of an international audience of youthful designers. A well-known American silverware company based in New England, the International Silver Corporation of Meriden, held one such competition for the design of new silver cutlery patterns with generous prize money on offer, attracting entries from a number of countries. Robert submitted a couple of experimental designs to this competition (see page 72), but felt a little uneasy that his entries had been over-designed.

As Robert recalled: 'I submitted two designs in an experimental manner, and as soon as I sent off my entry I began to feel that I had been too self-indulgent; I realized that experiments in other areas had worked well enough, but the same principles did not necessarily apply to cutlery design'.[80] Feeling as though he had 'perjured himself' creatively, Robert set out to make amends by creating a new cutlery range that essentially went back to design basics, inspired by the honed and serviceable form-follows-function shapes that had historically been associated with the Sheffield cutlery industry. The resulting Alveston range, named after the village in which he and his family were then living, most definitely reflected contem-porary aesthetics, yet was also rooted in tradition being inspired by classical Georgian cutlery.

Essentially a modern evolutionary design based on ideal forms, the Alveston range is the most distinctive of all Robert's cutlery designs. It was first presented at a lecture he gave on the historical evolution of cutlery design to cutlery retailers in Sheffield, which was organized by the Council of Industrial Design in 1963. Officially launched a few months later, the range was originally manufactured by the Sheffield maker Harrison Fisher and retailed by Old Hall, and two years later received a prestigious Design Centre Award. The judges commended the range of seven pieces for its visually pleasing rounded forms and remarkably comfortable handling. Alveston was rechristened RW1 in the early 1980s, and was then modified in scale in around 2001 so as to accommodate the desire for slightly larger eating implements suited to more casual forms of dining. This variant was named RW2 and is still in production.

Designer:	Robert Welch
Materials:	Satin-finish or bright-finish stainless steel
Production:	From 1963, Harrison Fisher, Sheffield for Old Hall Tableware, Bloxwich, Staffordshire (a modified version of RW2 was created for Eurostar in 2005)

Below: Scaled design drawing of the Alveston cutlery range, ca. 1961 (6-piece place setting)

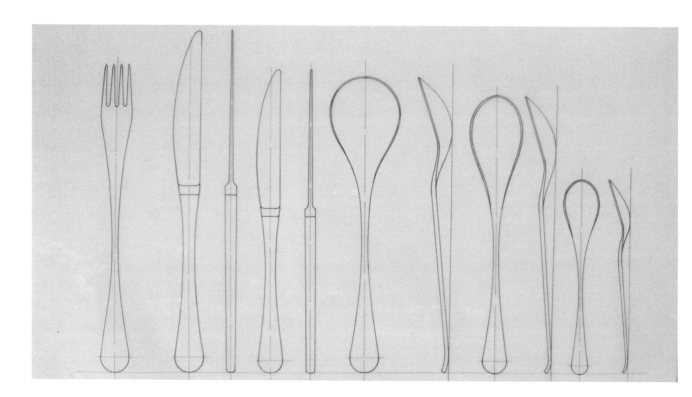

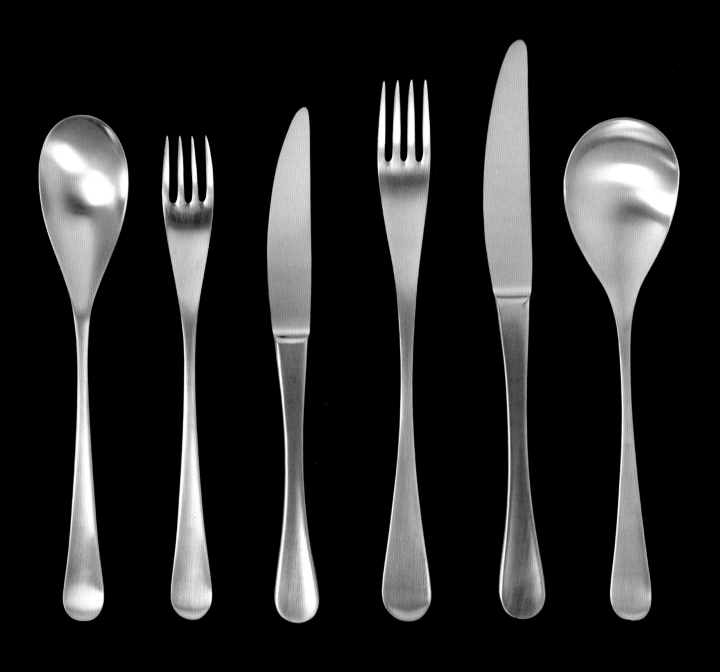

Alveston Tea Set, 1961–4

As we have already seen, from 1955 Robert Welch worked as a design consultant to Old Hall, creating numerous designs for supremely functional stainless-steel tableware. Although many of these holloware designs had a rather utilitarian and institutional aspect, they were beautifully designed and possessed a distinctive pristine quality that reflected Robert's skilful understanding of the delicate relationship between form and function. Among his many designs for Old Hall, the Alveston tea set stands out as an example of his remarkable ability to give expression to the inherent qualities of his materials, whether it was hard, shiny stainless steel or heavy cast iron.

Named after the Warwickshire village to which Robert and his family had just moved, the Alveston tableware range (which included his well-known set of award-winning cutlery) arguably comprised some of the finest stainless-steel designs ever produced. It is the Alveston tea set – unofficially known as the 'Aladdin's Lamp' service because of the teapot's distinctive shape – that is now the most sought-after item among collectors. Produced from 1964, this four-piece set was sold only to the retail trade, reflecting its more domestic appeal,

Above: Four-piece Alveston tea set shown with a stainless steel tray also manufactured by Old Hall

Left: The spout of the teapot being argon-welded on to its body at the Old Hall factory in Bloxwich, 1960s (RW)

and was initially offered solely in a satin finish, although a bright-finish option was made available from 1969 onwards.

A quintessential Mid-Century Modern design, the Alveston tea set, with its distinctive oil-lamp shape, reflected the era's more experimental approach to sculptural form, yet, unlike many later designs from the 1960s it did not abandon the Modernist credo of form following function – in fact, its rather squat form afforded it a low centre of gravity, which provided increased stability for pouring. One of its most appealing qualities is its sense of almost scientific precision, achieved using the ancient lost-wax process for the teapot's spout and flaring knob. This casting process provides excellent accuracy and was explained by Robert thus, 'a pattern is made in wax and invested in a plaster or clay mould; when it is dry, a cavity is made by melting out the wax and this cavity is then filled with molten metal'.[81] This technique had only recently begun to be used for commercially casting stainless steel – but as Robert's design demonstrated, it enabled the mass production of designs with relatively complex shapes that would have been unachievable through any other casting method then available. After casting, the spout

was argon-welded to the body of the teapot, which was itself made from two pressings that had been seamlessly welded together. The handle, which remained cool to the touch even when the teapot was in use, was also carefully considered, being angled in such a way as to provide the optimum degree of balance and control. The design's sense of precision was in many ways a projection of Robert's love of meticulous order, as his fellow RCA alumnus and close friend, the architect Ray Leigh remembers: 'It was always a contrast when visiting the Silk Mill, on one floor you had the Harts' workshop, which was like stepping back a hundred years, and then above it was Bob's workshop, which looked as though you could have practised open heart surgery in it.'[82]

Designer:	Robert Welch
Materials:	Satin-finish or bright-finish stainless steel
Production:	From 1964 to 1984, Old Hall Tableware, Bloxwich, Staffordshire

Campden Designs cast-iron range, 1961–ca. 1970

Robert Welch's interest in cast iron began in 1960 when he was commissioned by a foundry in the Black Country (the coal-mining area surrounding Birmingham) to create a design that it could manufacture and then market as its own. As Robert explained, 'They wanted to offset the uncertainty and fluctuation in the supply of castings to the motor manufacturing industry, so they were looking for a design for a cast-iron free-standing ashtray for contract use.'[83] Although this design did not prove commercially successful, probably due to its considerable weight, it did introduce Robert to the manufacturing potential of cast iron and as he noted, 'If the foundry was worried about the uncertainty of its market I was equally concerned about the haphazard inflow of commissioned silverwork and decided that if I could sell a candlestick in silver occasionally, then I could probably sell many more if they were made in cast iron and sold at a very reasonable price.'[84] This was a highly astute judgement that would eventually lead to a whole new area of design and manufacturing for Robert. Applying what he had learnt about working with cast iron from his earlier ashtray design, he created a sturdy candlestick in 1961 that he began producing – in fact, this was his first foray into batch production. With its rugged industrial-craft feel, the candlestick was perfectly in tune with the emerging

Opposite: Model nos. CD25, CD50 and CD20 (Hobart) candlesticks from the Campden Designs cast-iron range, designed 1961

Left: Graphic mock-up by Robert Welch for an in-store display, ca. 1962. Robert described this image as a 'forest' of candlesticks

CAST IRON BY ROBERT WELCH

Habitat generation, which was looking for less fussy and more youthful homeware designs. Originally known as the CD range (for Campden Designs), this became the blueprint for a whole new range of cast-iron homeware, which 'expanded rapidly to form a small family of related shapes, a prerequisite for being able to offer the concept as a viable collection'.[85]

Importantly, the candlesticks — which came in four sizes — together with the stylistically related fruit bowls (also designed 1961) photographed beautifully in black and white thanks to their distinctive undulating graphic profiles. These images appeared subsequently illustrated in *The Studio* magazine's popular *Decorative Art* yearbook in both 1964 and 1965. Inclusion in this famous and influential publication brought considerable interest from abroad, and Hagbarth Skjalm Petersen placed an order for 36 bowls (which until then existed only as sample pieces) to sell in his eponymous shop in Copenhagen. Bolstered by this interest, Robert made the trip to Denmark to meet this doyen of the Copenhagen design scene, who as a consequence increased his order considerably. Eventually, the manufacture of the

bowls and candlesticks, and other designs in the range, including the well-known nutcracker and pepper mill, was transferred from Campden Designs — a manufacturing joint venture between Robert and Wigmore Distributors — to Victor Cast Ware in the mid 1970s. After the temporary demise of Victor, the candlesticks and various other designs from the range were not produced for several years, but some were eventually put back into small-scale production by Robert Welch Designs around 1996 and at the same time the classic undulatingly profiled candlesticks were rechristened in tribute to Skjalm Petersen, whose first name was pronounced 'Hobart'.

Designer:	Robert Welch
Materials:	Red or blue vitreous enamelled or raw cast iron
Production:	from 1962, Campden Designs, Chipping Campden and later various selected designs produced from ca. 1975 by Victor Cast Ware, Telford, Shropshire (and from ca. 1996 by Robert Welch Designs, Chipping Campden)

In the early 1920s James Chantry, an engineer living in Sheffield – the centre of Britain's then thriving cutlery industry – perceived that there was a real need for a device that would enable a knife to maintain the correct blade angle while it was being sharpened. To this end, after conducting various experiments, he patented a sharpening mechanism in 1923. Around 1929 Chantry designed a knife-sharpening device that incorporated his patented mechanism, and marketed it as foolproof. Chantry's invention essentially replicated mechanically the movements used when sharpening knives with a handheld butcher's steel. In about 1940 the design was updated, and then in the early 1960s the well-known cutlery manufacturer Harrison Fisher, which had recently acquired the small company that produced the Chantry sharpener, decided the design of this device needed an overhaul. It commissioned Robert Welch, as it had previously worked with him.

While the earlier Art Deco-style product had two equal-sized grips (which looked rather like the ears of a cartoon rabbit), Robert's new design had instead one large gripping handle and a much wider base that extended under the handle to provide greater stability. Made of stove-enamelled cast Mazak – a zinc alloy – this new Chantry knife sharpener had a no-nonsense durability that has stood the test of time: many examples made in the 1960s are still in use today, as the two spring-loaded steels are totally and easily replaceable. Having been in production for more than 50 years, the Chantry knife sharpener is one of Robert's most enduring designs, and it is still on the market and is recognized for obtaining an impressively sharp knife blade, whether it has plain or serrated edges. In addition, it is incredibly easy to use, by simply inserting a knife into the central groove and pulling it towards you – showing how sometimes the simplest design solutions really are the best in practice.

Designer:	Robert Welch
Materials:	Stove-enamelled cast Mazak, sharpened revolving steel blades, metal tension springs
Production:	From 1964, Archant, Sheffield for Harrison Fisher, Sheffield (which changed its name to Taylor's Eye Witness in 2007)

Below, left: Early publicity photograph showing different-coloured finishes used for the Chantry knife sharpener, ca. 1963 (Enzo Ragazzini)

Below, right: Early publicity photograph demonstrating how to use the Chantry knife sharpener, ca. 1963 (RW)

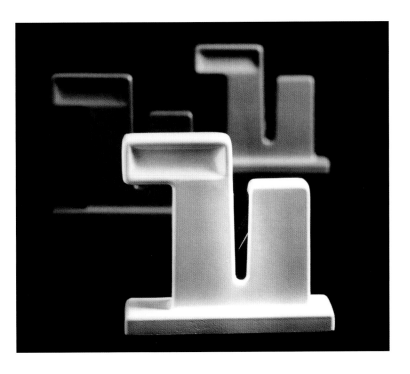

Heal's domestic silverware, 1963

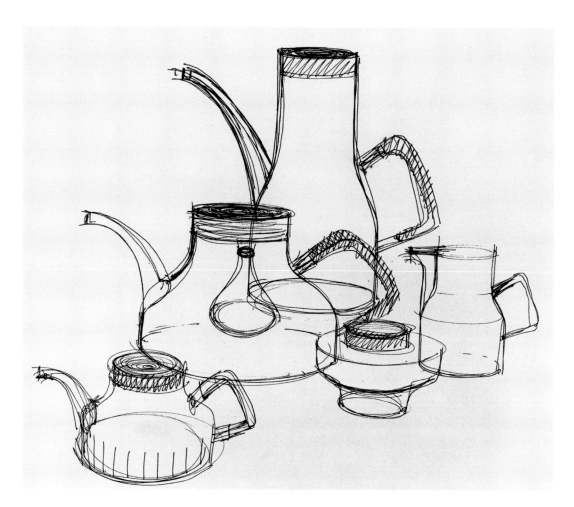

During the 1950s and 1960s, the well-known furniture store Heal and Sons on Tottenham Court Road in London was a leading promoter of youthful design talent, and as such was instrumental in introducing the fashionable contemporary 'New Look' into the British domestic landscape. The company had also been historically associated with the Arts and Crafts Movement, with its former chairman Ambrose Heal (1872–1959) a leading proponent of the style during the early decades of the twentieth century. It is, therefore, unsurprising that despite being a key promoter of British Modernism the firm was also a staunch supporter of craft-based design. Indeed, as the design historian Alan Crawford recalled, 'it was Heal's who were responsible for the major craft projects of the mid-1960s. In 1963 they decided to try to establish the habit at the upper end of the market of buying craftsman-made silver of modern design for wedding presents and so on.'[86] With this in mind,

Heal's asked Robert to design an entirely new range of modern silver tableware that could be displayed in a special showcase within the shop's 'Present Choice' department, with the idea that customers could specially order the entire range or a selection of pieces from Heal's and then the items would be produced in Robert's workshop in Chipping Campden. It was an entirely new concept for the commissioning of silverware and the response was, as Crawford put it 'steady but gradual'.[87] Importantly, it offered silversmiths such as Robert a new outlet to the domestic market, which meant they were less reliant on one-off bespoke workshop commissions or patronage from institutions such as the Goldsmiths' Company or church commissioners.

Mindful of the target market, Robert sought to keep the retail price affordable, and therefore used lathe spinning rather than time-consuming hand-hammering

to form the resulting range of silverware, which initially included an elegant tea and coffee service, a candlestick (available in two sizes), a condiment set, a sauce boat and matching tray, a vegetable dish, a sugar dredger and a wine goblet. This method of mechanized metal forming meant that the pieces had a slightly rippled surface, which needed further planishing by hand to obtain a completely smooth and lustrous finish, yet even so this method was far more labour-efficient than other traditional silversmithing techniques. Commissioned by Heal's in 1963, the range was exhibited the following year in a solo exhibition entitled 'Silver by Robert Welch' in Heal's flagship store. Because the range was seen as one of the finest examples of modern British craftsmanship, on several occasions pieces from the range were commissioned by Harold Wilson's government to use as state gifts, most notably by the Minister of State for Technology, John Stonehouse, in 1967 to take with him to Moscow as a present for the Russian government.

Above: Body of the coffee pot being seam-welded, ca. 1963 (RW)

Opposite: Various designs from the Heal's silverware range, designed from 1963

Designer:	Robert Welch
Materials:	Sterling silver, rosewood
Production:	From 1964, Robert Welch Studio, Chipping Campden, for Heal and Sons, London

Model no. CD60 (Hobart) nutcracker, 1964

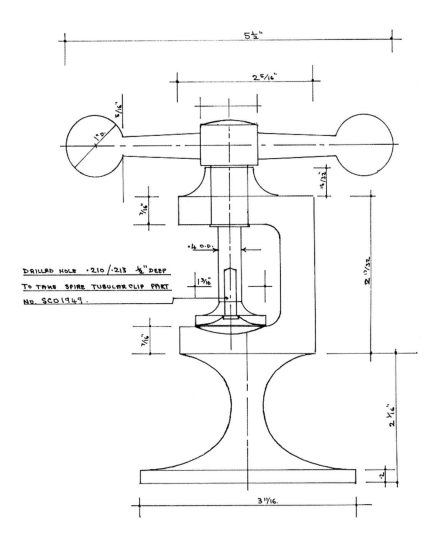

Left: *Scaled design drawing by Robert Welch of the model no. CD60 nutcracker, 1964*

Part of Robert Welch's extensive Campden Designs cast-iron range, the CD60 nutcracker was an unusual design in that it employed a screw mechanism rather than the more conventional hinged mechanism he had used in his earlier stainless-steel nutcracker design for Old Hall (see page 70). This sturdy tabletop design in solid cast iron blatantly reflected the growing awareness of industrial heritage and the need for its preservation during the early 1960s, and it is no coincidence that the old furnace at Coalbrookdale – the birthplace of the Industrial Revolution – only 65 miles northwest of Chipping Campden was rediscovered and excavated in 1959. The nutcracker's screwpress recalls those of early printing presses, while its robust, chunky form has a quasi-industrial quality – that

was perfectly attuned with the 1960s renewal of interest in Victoriana and the desire for more crafted, less polished 'authentic' homeware. The design was renamed 'Hobart' (like the related Campden Designs candlesticks) in tribute to Robert's friend Hagbarth Skjalm Petersen, the Danish design entrepreneur and gallery owner.

Designer:	Robert Welch
Material:	Vitreous enamelled cast iron
Production:	From ca. 1964, Campden Designs, Chipping Campden and later by Victor Cast Ware, Telford, Shropshire

Alveston carving set, 1964

One of Robert Welch's most distinctive designs, the three-piece Alveston carving set – comprising a two-pronged carving fork, a carving knife and a sharpening steel – can be seen as an evolution of the yew-handled carving set he created while he was still a student at the Royal College of Art, in that it shares a similar sculptural sensibility. The preliminary design sketches and pre-production versions of the Alveston carving set included a fork that had a relatively conservative form with a traditional nipped-in waisted section, an example of which is now in the permanent collection of the Philadelphia Museum of Art. Eventually, however, a more contemporary-looking solution was found with an undeniably free-flowing sculptural quality. Launched in 1964, a year after the Alveston cutlery collection, the carving set perfectly complemented this award-winning range. In 1968, following the landmark Vormgevers exhibition at the Stedelijk Museum in

Amsterdam, which included a number of designs by Robert, the museum purchased the Alveston carving set for its permanent collection, together with other classic Welch designs, including the rest of the Alveston cutlery range, the stainless-steel nutcracker and the Chantry knife sharpener. Although no longer in production, the Alveston carving set with its beautiful undulating contours, still reveals Robert's masterful form-giving skills, and as such it must be considered one of his most noteworthy designs.

Designer:	Robert Welch
Material:	Satin-finish stainless steel
Production:	From 1964, Harrison Fisher, Sheffield for Old Hall Tableware, Bloxwich, Staffordshire (later by Robert Welch Designs, Chipping Campden)

Below Left: Preliminary drawing by Robert Welch showing an early version of the Alveston carving fork and knife, ca. 1964, shown alongside matching Alveston 'fish carvers'

Below: Early publicity photograph of the three-piece Alveston carving set, ca. 1964 (RW)

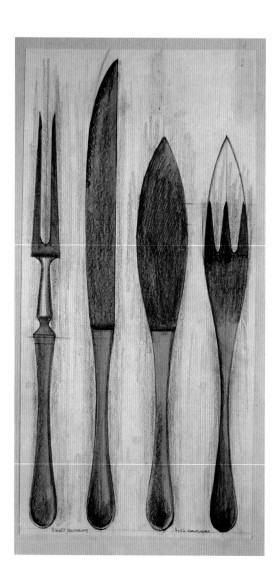

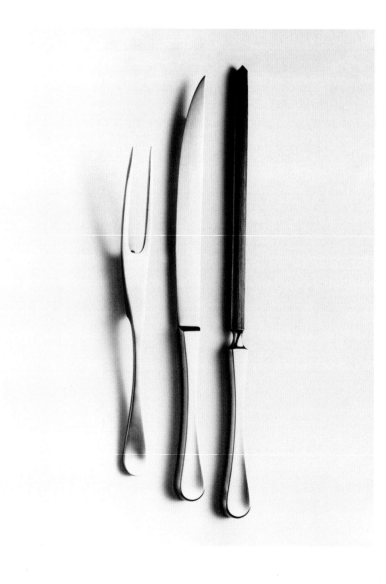

Comus canteen crockery, 1965

During the early 1960s, the Ministry of Public Building and Works was spending around £40,000 per annum on canteen crockery. However, its staff canteens across the country were largely stocked with thick, heavy and not particularly attractive patterns, which as the design commentator Gillian Naylor noted in *Design* magazine were 'neither presentable or practical'[88]. As part of a systematic policy to improve the standards of all the equipment in its remit, the ministry decided that it was essential to commission a new range of canteen crockery that could be used in its staff restaurants as well as in hospitals. Robert Welch was charged with this brief, since the ministry 'admired his practical approach to product design, and felt with his considerable experience of the stainless steel industry, he would appreciate the problem of designing for bulk purchase'[89]. They were entirely correct on this point, as many of the stainless-steel wares Robert had previously designed for Old Hall were intended first and foremost for institutional use – and as such were an already ubiquitous feature of canteens across Britain.

Working closely with the Stoke-on-Trent manufacturer J. & G. Meakin and the ministry's technical liaison officer for potteries, Arthur Bradbury, Robert and his office spent three months researching the project, including conducting detailed surveys in three ministry canteens in order to understand the typical handling, storing and usage of such institutional crockery. These surveys revealed that cleanliness and avoidance of chips and breakages depended largely on the handling of the crockery, but it was determined that human error was not responsible for every shortcoming and that often it was inherent flaws in the designs that made them susceptible to hygiene problems or vulnerable to damage in a busy canteen. For instance, the handles of cups were prone to chipping, while ridges on the undersides of plates allowed dirt to build up. Robert felt a more rational approach was needed

Below: Early publicity photograph of the Comus canteen crockery, 1965 (RW)

for the design of canteen crockery, and eventually, a brief was drafted that outlined the various requirements. These included the need for a complete meal to fit comfortably on a standard government tray measuring 18 by 12 inches, and that the two sizes of cup required should both fit the same-sized saucer. Another stipulation was that the new range should be able to be produced without the need for new machinery or special processes. The resulting Comus canteen range comprised three plates – instead of five as in the existing standardized patterns – that were lighter and smaller so as to fit better on a tray and be easier to carry. This crucial weight saving was achieved not only by reducing the plates' dimensions, but also by employing a concave rim rather than the thickened rolled rim traditionally used for utilitarian crockery. The two cups in the range were similarly thoughtful in their design, being safely and efficiently stackable and having robust yet ergonomically contoured handles that were easy to hold.

The range also included an egg cup, and each place setting cost around seven shillings to produce. Although this was not that much less expensive than other canteen ranges, the intelligence of Robert's design meant that fewer breakages saved money in the long run, and this in turn lessened administrative overheads for the commissioning ministry because of the reduced need for ongoing procurement. This range of elegant yet durable everyday crockery was also sold to the general public under the name Comus by its manufacturer, J. & G. Meakin.

Designer:	Robert Welch
Material:	Glazed ceramic
Production:	from 1966, J. & G. Meakin, Stoke-on-Trent, Staffordshire for the Ministry of Public Building and Works

Lumitron 3000 Series lighting range, 1966

The Lumitron lighting range designed by Robert Welch in the mid 1960s comprised eight models, including two table lamps, a floor lamp, two sizes of pendant light, and a wall light. As a product family, they shared an ingenious shade made up of an inner diffuser of white opalescent acrylic partially covered by an outer domed shade of either smoky grey or dusky purple acrylic. This shade assembly was held in place with two identical spun-aluminium fixtures pierced with ventilation holes for cooling. The lower fixture also contained the bulb holder and the on/off switch, which was operated by a hanging ball chain. Importantly, the range was based on the concept of interchangeability of standardized components in order to enable ease of manufacture, which meant the lamp parts needed virtually no modification between models. As Robert explained, even, 'the outer domes for the smaller lamps used the same tooling as the inner domes for the larger ones'.[90] When turned on, the lamps' two-tone shades produced not only a pleasing space-age optical effect, but also a warm and softly diffused luminescence.

Although the designs incorporated acrylic – then a state-of-the-art plastic that was especially favoured in Italy, with lighting designers working in an anything-goes sculptural aesthetic – Robert's lamps with their elegantly proportioned and mathematically precise forms had a strong visual refinement. Indeed, their Bauhaus-meets-Pop aesthetic could be said to have predicted the restrained yet fashionable Neo-Modern look of 1970s interiors.

Interestingly, unlike most of Robert's designs, which were the result of trial and error, the Lumitron range came about through a spark of creative thinking – a veritable design 'Eureka' moment. As he recalled, 'I was introduced to a small company, Lumitron, who specialized in contract lighting for architectural purposes. They asked me to submit designs; I had very little experience of work in this field, but somehow my Lumitron idea worked. I have never known a design concept appear, as this one did, in the proverbial flash of inspiration; it fell into place as if it were pre-ordained, and not just one lamp but a series of different types, each closely related to one another.'[91]

Certainly, as a design it has an undoubted 'rightness' as well as a characterful presence, which made it a firm favourite among British television-programme set designers in the late 1960s, and as a result it became a standard feature on sets such as the ever-popular Morecambe and Wise show.

Designer:	Robert Welch
Materials:	Polished aluminium, translucent smoke grey or purple acrylic and white opalescent acrylic
Production:	From 1966 to 1991, Lumitron, London

Opposite: Lumitron floor light and extendable pendant light

Below, left: Publicity photograph showing various lights from the Lumitron range, 1960s

Below, right: Publicity photograph showing the Lumitron light's double-dome shade

Manager 24-hour commercial wall clock, 1966

The Council of Industrial Design under the directorship of Gordon Russell was one of Robert Welch's greatest allies in the building and broadening of his design career. Indeed, it was the Council that first recommended him to the Scottish clock manufacturer Westclox in 1956, leading to one of his earliest industrial design commissions. This led to a very fruitful collaboration between designer and manufacturer that lasted well over a decade, during which time Robert designed dozens of timepieces for Westclox, from small alarm clocks to larger wall models – some quite traditional, while others were much more progressive. Among this latter category was the Manager range of wall clocks for office and institutional use, which utilized simple moulded plastic casings and printed aluminium faces. The clocks were available in two sizes (10 and 12 inches) and also with a choice of dial options, ranging from the relatively conservative with roman numerals to far more modern face displays. Produced by Westclox from 1967, the range had a no-nonsense practicality that made each clock easy to read even from quite a distance – showing once again that Robert was always mindful of the functional interface between a product and its user.

Left: A studio assistant making the model of the Manager wall clock, ca. 1966.

Designer:	Robert Welch
Materials:	Moulded plastic, printed aluminium, acrylic, various types of clock mechanism
Production:	From 1967, Westclox, Dumbarton, Scotland

Wall clock for the Ministry of Public Building and Works, 1966–7

Right: Scale design drawing by Robert Welch for the dial face of the 'Ministry' clock, ca. 1966

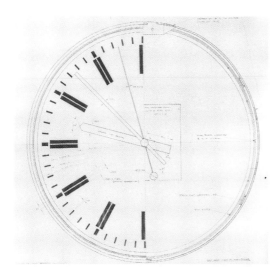

Having already designed a number of clocks for the well-known Dumbarton-based manufacturer Westclox, Robert Welch was an obvious choice when it came to the Ministry of Public Building and Works looking for someone to design a new standardized 'time-keeping' clock to adorn the walls of its numerous government offices. Designed the same year as his Manager range of wall clocks for Westclox this government-issue clock similarly employed a plastic casing and a simple metal face. This model, however, was also designed so that it could accommodate different types of mechanism and was produced in two sizes, either 12 or 16 inches in diameter. With its simple dial of spun aluminium, dark green plastic casing and bold graphic lines indicating hours and minutes, it was a veritable *tour de force* of modern purposeful design. Today, it is difficult to comprehend just how modern this minimalistic design must have seemed when it was first introduced; at that time most British clocks were still highly decorative in design, verging on the fussy, thanks to the fact that even then timepieces still had strong traditional associations with social position and status.

Designer:	Robert Welch
Materials:	Spun aluminium, enamelled metal, plastic, various types of clock mechanism
Production:	From 1968, Synchronome, Westbury, Wiltshire

Sauce boat (model no. 43784), ca. 1966

One of Robert Welch's best-known designs for Old Hall, the model no. 43784 translated the traditional form of ceramic sauce boats into glimmering stainless steel. During the 1960s, Old Hall stainless-steel tableware was so ubiquitous in British homes that it became known as the 'Wedding Present of the 60s' – in no small part thanks to Robert's seductively contemporary yet affordable creations, such as this sculptural masterpiece of modern stainless-steel design. A thoroughly utilitarian translation of his earlier silver sauce boat of 1956, this design had a capacity of half a pint, although a smaller quarter-pint model was

also manufactured by Old Hall. The firm also sold matching trays (as shown above), and later in the 1970s introduced a footed sauce boat also designed by Robert that was similarly sculptural and eminently functional.

Designer:	Robert Welch
Material:	Satin-finish stainless steel
Production:	From 1967 to 1984, Old Hall Tableware, Bloxwich, Staffordshire (a quarter-pint version was also produced, known as the model no. 43782)

Below, left: Scale design drawing by Robert Welch for the model no. 43784 sauce boat, ca. 1966

Below, right: Wooden model of the model no. 43782 sauce boat made in the Robert Welch studio workshop, ca. 1966

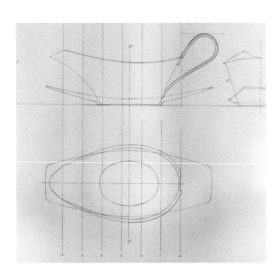

Dryad 70 architectural ironmongery range, 1966–7

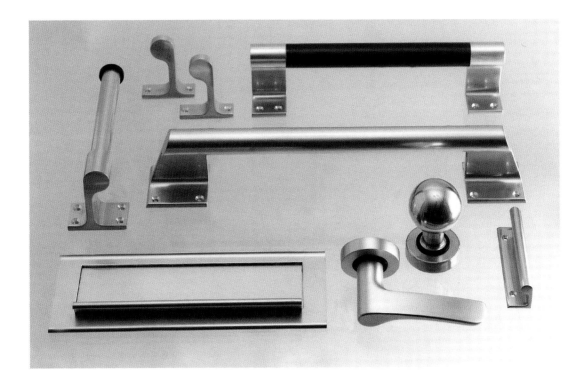

Believing that craft skills should be preserved in the face of rapid industrialization, Harry Peach (1874–1936) established Dryad Handicrafts in 1907 to produce a line of modern woven cane furniture that was successfully retailed both at home and abroad. Emboldened by his success, Peach went on to establish the Dryad Metal Works in 1926, putting the art metalworker William Pick in charge of operations. From the early 1930s until his death in 1964, Peach's youngest son Roger headed the company and was responsible for the design of its award-winning products. After Roger's death, his successor, Peter Ashberry, approached Robert Welch to design a new range of door furniture for Dryad. After much discussion, they decided that rather than using traditional casting methods, which produced slight blemishes when the cast items were anodized, they would base the design of the range on stock aluminium extrusions, which would negate the problem of unsightly imperfections. It was an ingenious solution, as from one stock extrusion it was possible to make a variety of designs, from towel rails to coat hooks. This use of standardized extrusions also meant the designs could be manufactured at relatively short notice and in relatively small batches if necessary. As Robert recalled,

'This was a great advantage in the 1960s when there were often difficulties in obtaining supplies of raw materials such as casting and forgings'.[92] The resulting Dryad 70 range, launched in the mid 1960s, was quite a design trendsetter for it predicted the pared-down industrial aesthetic that would become so popular with the emergence of the High-Tech style in the 1970s. In 1974 Robert added more designs to the range, including lever handles, pull handles, plate latches and locks, a safety ashtray, a tumbler, a toothbrush holder and a towel ring. Robert later created a similar range for Dryad, known as Simplan, which was launched in 1977 and based on a stock round bar element.

Designer:	Robert Welch
Material:	Satin-anodized extruded aluminium
Production:	From ca. 1967 to 1983, Dryad Metal Works, Leicester

Cake or fruit basket (model no. 41181), ca. 1968

One of Robert Welch's most visually striking designs, this cake basket had a strong pared-down quality that recalled the 'form follows function' ethos that guided the Bauhaus metalwork studio during the late 1920s and early 1930s – indeed, its strict geometry recalls the work of the pioneering Modernists Marianne Brandt (1893–1983)and Wilhelm Wagenfeld (1900–1990). Yet at the same time, this design – which was also described in Old Hall's catalogue as a fruit basket – predicted the strong movement in both art and design towards Minimalism during the early 1970s. A highly simplified design, the cake basket is made of just three elements – the gently concave plate, the ring-like base and the hinged, arching handle – all perfectly balanced thanks to a harmonious interrelationship between their mathematically precise proportions. Like many of Robert's other stainless-steel wares produced by Old Hall, the cake basket employed a satin finish, which gave it a more contemporary industrial aesthetic than that of a bright finish, which was more akin to the shiny lustre of EPNS (electroplated nickel silver).

Left: Early publicity photograph of the model no. 41181 cake/fruit basket, shown in use, ca. 1969 (RW)

Designer:	Robert Welch
Material:	Satin-finish stainless steel
Production:	From 1969 to 1984, Old Hall Tableware, Bloxwich, Staffordshire

Concord kitchen scissors, 1968

Featured in *Design* magazine in 1969, Robert Welch's Concord scissors were noted for their ergonomic shape, intended to assist in 'the cutting of awkward corners'. As with so many of Robert's designs for the home, the contoured form of these kitchen scissors was carefully considered from a functional standpoint with the handles featuring a useful bottle opener. The design also incorporated a toothed gripping section to provide assistance with the opening of difficult bottle and jar lids. While the overall design was made from high-quality and extremely durable chrome-plated carbon steel, the handle sections were stove-enamelled to provide better handling comfort as well as a bright modern aesthetic, and came in a choice of then highly fashionable colours: vibrant mandarin orange, olive green or duck-egg blue. Made by Harrison Fisher and sold under the firm's Taylor's Eye Witness brand, the scissors retailed for a democratically affordable 19s 6d – around £12.50 in today's money – which was, as *Design* magazine noted, a 'steel-plated snip', especially when one considers that they were designed and made to last a lifetime.

Below: Original packaging designed by Robert Welch for his Concord kitchen scissors, ca. 1968. This eye-catching lettering was used by Robert on various other graphic presentations for different products.

Designer:	Robert Welch
Materials:	Chrome-plated carbon steel, stove-enamelled paint
Production:	From 1968, Harrison Fisher, Sheffield

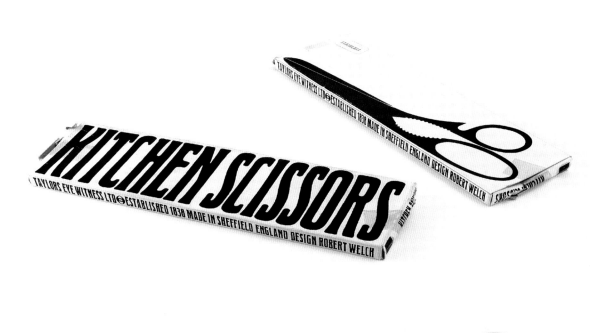

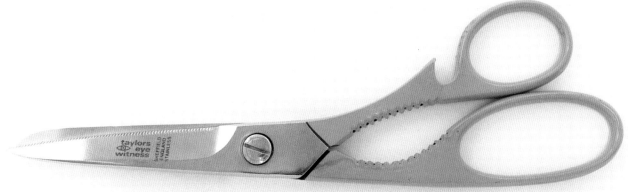

Serica glassware, 1968

When Old Hall acquired the Bridge Crystal Glass Company in 1969, it gave Robert Welch the opportunity to explore the creative potential of yet another material: glass. Named after a famous tea clipper, the resulting Serica glassware range was inspired by eighteenth-century tavern glasses. It was Robert's first glassware range and consisted of six differently sized drinking vessels: goblets, tumblers, a claret glass, a sherry glass and a liqueur glass. The range was offered in two versions, cut or uncut. As *Design* magazine noted when the range was launched, 'Because of the higher wastage through flaws in uncut crystal, the cut glasses cost no more than the uncut ones'.[93] Ranging in price from £1–16s to £2–16s and batch-produced, the fancier cut version was made available for retail purchase by Old Hall, while the uncut – and arguably more attractive – version was obtainable only as a special order. This latter version had the purer shape and perhaps better expressed the intrinsic form-giving and optical properties of lead crystal.

Designer:	Robert Welch
Material:	Uncut or cut full lead crystal
Production:	from 1969, Bridge Crystal Glass Company, Cradley, Worcestershire for Old Hall Tableware, Bloxwich (later by Robert Welch Designs)

Left: Sketch by Robert Welch of eighteenth-century goblets that inspired his own design for the Serica range, ca. 1968

Left: Early publicity photograph showing the 'cut' version of the Serica glassware collection, ca. 1968 (RW)

J.B. tea and coffee set, 1968

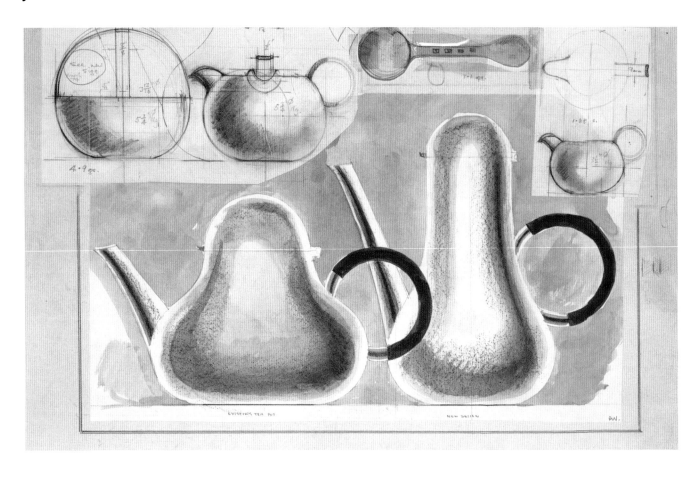

In 1962 Robert Welch and his family moved to Alveston, a small Warwickshire village just outside Stratford-upon-Avon. Living in the same village was the esteemed novelist and playwright J.B. Priestley with his wife, archaeologist Jacquetta Hawkes. After they had got to know each other, Priestley asked Robert if he could create a 'special pot' (a milk jug) that would match a fine Georgian coffee pot he already owned. As Robert would later remark, 'I use the word "match" loosely here – what he wanted was a pot that could be used from day to day and that would look like a piece made in the 1970s, but at the same time, it had to harmonize with his own rather ornate Georgian piece.'[94]

By channelling a classical Georgian sensibility into his own very contemporary design, Robert created not only this milk jug but also a matching rounded conical coffee pot with a domed lid, which – rather than having a traditional finial to open it – had a simple thumb lift unobtrusively positioned along the front edge of its lid. This ingenious feature meant that the pure curvilinear form of the pot was not spoilt by having a knob sticking out of its top. In fact, later versions of this seminal design had an even more pronounced bulbous form. Robert subsequently designed a matching teapot, cream jug, sugar basin, tea strainer and sugar spoon, and later in 1972 an oval rosewood tray designed and made by Tony McMullen at his workshop in Belbroughton in Worcestershire was added to this contemporary silverware range. Although the design originated as a bespoke commission, the J.B. set was serially produced over the succeeding years, albeit in relatively small numbers.

Above: Collaged design study by Robert Welch showing various pieces from the J.B. tea and coffee set, ca. 1968

Designer:	Robert Welch
Materials:	Sterling silver, laminated rosewood
Production:	From 1968, serially produced by Robert Welch Studio, Chipping Campden

Super Avon vacuum jug (model no. 43851) and coffee jug (model no. 43852), 1968

Throughout his career, Robert Welch – as William Morris had done before him – named the majority of his designs after the villages, towns and rivers that are to be found in the Cotswolds and surrounding vicinity. To this end, he designed the elegant Avon stainless-steel range for Old Hall in 1966, naming it after the well-known river that flows from Chipping Sodbury in South Gloucestershire to the wide-mouthed Severn Estuary. Two years later, inspired by various Japanese-made thermal coffee pots he had encountered on a trip to Scandinavia, and also presumably Arne Jacobsen's recently launched Cylinda-Line stainless-steel range, Robert created three new pieces: the Super Avon vacuum jug, coffee jug and iced-water jug. The first two were intended to be used in conjunction with the sugar bowl and cream jug of the existing Avon range. The new thermal jug had a one-and-half-pint capacity and utilized an easily replaceable vacuum lining made by the British manufacturer Aladdin, which allowed the liquids held in the jug to be kept either cool or warm for substantial lengths of time. The matching coffee pot, with its three-and-half-pint capacity, was similarly designed for practical function and as such incorporated a thick-gauge machined base so that it could be placed on a hotplate to keep its contents warm. All three designs had wide mouths intended for easy cleaning, while their contoured handles were made using the lost-wax casting process, giving the pieces a pleasing visual precision that elevated them from the utilitarian.

Left: Early publicity photograph showing the Super Avon model no. 43852 coffee jug, model no. 43851 thermal jug and the related model no. 43853 iced-water jug, ca. 1968 (RW)

Designer:	Robert Welch
Materials:	Satin-finish stainless steel (with "Aladdin" vacuum liner)
Production:	From 1969 to 1981 (coffee jug), from 1969 to 1974 (vacuum jug), Old Hall Tableware, Bloxwich, Staffordshire

Left: The Avon coffee set, previously designed by Robert Welch for Old Hall in 1966 (RW)

Flexi lighting range, 1968

Following the success of his earlier lighting range for Lumitron launched in 1966 (see page 110), Robert Welch designed another product family for this London-based firm two years later: the Flexi lighting range, which came in three sizes – two table versions and a floor-standing model. It was the direct result of Robert's research into possible design applications for industrial metal hose. Like the earlier Lumitron range, the Flexi lights incorporated a flaring 'tulip-style' pedestal base, but this element was made of stove-enamelled steel rather than polished aluminium. The Flexi range was also offered in a variety of colours

including bright red, yellow, white and mid-brown and featured extra stabilizing ballast in the form of a cast-iron inset hidden in its base. A section of off-the-peg chrome-plated heavy-duty tubing carried the necessary wiring and was held in place with a collar-like fitting. This bendy, tubular element then connected the weighted base to the spun-aluminium hemispherical shade, to which in turn a glare-reducing baffle and louvred light-filtering screen were fitted. Not only did this flexible tubing allow the shade to be rotated 180 degrees (with 'stops' incorporated into the design to prevent the internal wiring from twisting), thereby enabling a good degree of functional precision, but it also gave the design an appealing no-nonsense, industrial aesthetic. As such, it can be seen as a forerunner of the High-Tech look that dominated the early 1970s. Indeed, Flexi lights subsequently became a feature of many High-Tech interiors and were sold as exemplars of good design by the Design Council in its high-profile shop in London's Haymarket throughout the 1970s.

Left: Early publicity photograph of a Flexi table light intended to show the full flexibility of its stem, ca. 1968 (RW)

Designer:	Robert Welch
Materials:	Stove-enamelled steel, cast iron, chrome-plated metal hose, spun aluminium
Production:	From ca. 1968, Lumitron, London

Below: Mock-up of marketing booklet graphics by Robert Welch for the Flexi lighting range, ca. 1968

Goldsmiths' Hall Candelabra, 1968–70

Having received a commission for two large silver candelabra from the Worshipful Company of Goldsmiths, Robert Welch submitted a sketch for a proposed design that was 'covered with small hemispherical forms designed to have a shimmering effect by candlelight'.[95] The problem was how to produce this type of decorative finish; Robert puzzled over it for quite a while, but had been unable to come up with a workable solution. Then, as he recalled, 'quite by chance I got chatting to a man in a remote pub in mid-Wales during a family holiday. It turned out that I was talking to Mr. Butler, a Birmingham manufacturer who made the stainless-steel condiment set bodies that I had designed for Old Hall, by a process known as rotary swaging…I described my candelabra problems, and to my surprise, he said he thought he could help.'[96] As it happened, John Butler had acquired at a recent sale a nineteenth-century machine that had been used for making the ball-shaped winders found on antique hunter pocket-watches. He was sure that this chunk of industrial heritage could be adapted to produce the multi-ball surface finish that Robert was seeking to decorate the stems and branches of his candelabra. Sure enough, after undertaking various experiments, Butler was able to produce tubes of silver embellished with this distinctive three-dimensional ball-pattern. Robert's studio assistants, Paul Heneghan and John Limbrey then incorporated these into the overall design for the candelabra at the studio in Chipping Campden. The patron was utterly delighted with the resulting pieces, which were hugely innovative in terms of silversmithing. Unfortunately, after their presentation to the Court of the Company, one of the candelabra fell from a trolley on its way back to the vaults, on to a stone floor, and was badly damaged; it was returned to the Campden workshop where it was 'duly rebuilt'.[97]

Designer:	Robert Welch
Materials:	Parcel-gilt silver
Production:	One-off commission executed by Paul Heneghan and John Limbrey, Robert Welch Studio, Chipping Campden

Below: View of the Robert Welch studio/workshop in Chipping Campden with the Goldsmiths' Hall candelabrum shown in the foreground, 1970 (photo: Brecht-Einzig Ltd)

1970s

H.E. Lauffer cookware, 1970–4

Having shown his ability to design innovative cast-iron wares, Robert Welch was commissioned in 1970 by H.E. Lauffer of New Jersey to create a brand-new range of cookware comprising various cast-iron casseroles and frying pans. The company had already undertaken extensive market research and had prepared a detailed design brief, which emphasized the need for functionality. For example,

it called for the lids of all the casseroles in the range to double as serving dishes. Another requirement was that the product line be based on forms that would make it easy to expand the range at a later date – which led Robert to use either round or oval forms for the bases of the different wares. Another distinctive feature of Robert's design was the two ribs around the casseroles, from which the open handles were seamlessly developed. The lower rib was placed at the point where the pattern for the base divided into two parts for moulding, which meant that any excess metal left during the moulding process, known as flash, could be easily ground off the rib. Robert's design for the open handles was also process-driven, in that it enabled the lids and bases to be hung during the vitreous-enamelling process, making the whole procedure much easier.

Left: Publicity photograph showing two casseroles, a saucepan and a frying pan from the cast-iron cookware range designed for H.E. Lauffer, ca. 1974 (RW)

Designer:	Robert Welch
Material:	Vitreous-enamelled cast iron
Production:	From ca. 1972, Qualcast, Wolverhampton, for H.E. Lauffer, New Jersey

Above: Photograph of three stoneware coffee pots designed by Robert Welch showing the different types of coloured glazes used

Below: Publicity photograph of stoneware coffee set created by Robert Welch for Brixham Pottery, ca. 1970 (RW)

During the 1970s there was a huge revival of interest in craft, and Robert Welch, like other designers working at the time, was highly aware of the fact that craft skills were fast disappearing in the face of rampant industrial progress. With this in mind, during the 1970s and 1980s Robert undertook a number of creative collaborations with craft-based manufacturers, including the Brixham Pottery in Torbay, Devon. Initially, Robert designed for the pottery a coffee service with a very distinctive shape – with the handle and spout set on the narrowest part of the pot's body in order to make the overall footprint of the design as compact as possible. The coffee service, as well as later designs created by Robert for the pottery (including a condiment set and an oil bottle), featured a warm, mottled Tenmoku-style glaze, which produced random results in patterning and colour, thereby giving the wares a greater sense of handcrafted authenticity.

Designer:	Robert Welch
Material:	Tenmoku-style glazed stoneware
Production:	from ca. 1970, Brixham Pottery, Torbay, Devon

4000 Series kitchen tools, 1971

Opposite: Early plastic-handled versions of the kitchen tools designed by Robert Welch for Prestige

In 1970 Old Hall was absorbed into the Prestige Group – a much larger conglomerate of domestic metalware companies – and as Old Hall's chief design consultant Robert Welch began designing for the group around that time. During the early 1970s, Robert developed an idea for a range of kitchen tools that, unlike the existing tools being produced in Prestige's factory, were not riveted but rather made in one piece, which meant they would be far more hygienic and also aesthetically unified. Robert based his innovative concept on the traditional manufacture of spoons and forks using rolling, cutting and pressing techniques. However, these innovative designs remained on the drawing board until 1976, when the managing director of Prestige in West Germany, Paul Dreyer, visited the company's London office to discuss an upcoming visit to Japan and the idea of commissioning a new line of kitchen tools. Robert's designs, which had been lying in a drawer, were retrieved and taken by Dreyer to Japan, where the Kay Cutlery Company came up with 'a brilliant idea' for achieving the tools' one-piece construction. The firm suggested that the tools should be made in two parts, as in the English factory, but rather than riveted together they should instead be butt welded using a new

Below: Later all-metal versions of the kitchen tools designed by Robert Welch for Prestige

technique developed for use in the aircraft industry. Prestige took a leap of faith in Robert's revolutionary design and decided to invest in the necessary tooling and welding plant, which was financially not insignificant. Initially the kitchen tools, launched in 1977, were made with a moulded covering of heat-insulating plastic, which rather defeated the point of their one-piece construction and also had a tendency to melt. Eventually Prestige took a further leap of faith and began manufacturing Robert's design in all-metal. The range's subsequent commercial success was phenomenal, essentially redefining the design of kitchen tools and establishing a new manufacturing system for their production.

Designer:	Robert Welch
Materials:	Pressed stainless steel, moulded plastic
Production:	From ca. 1977, Prestige Group, West Germany

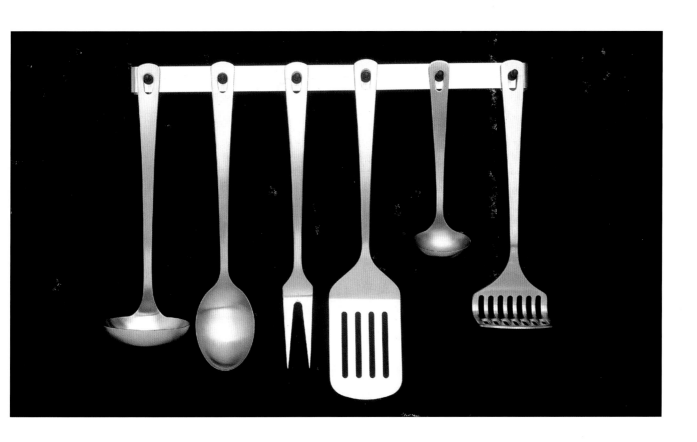

Ship's decanter and claret jug, 1972

One of the guiding characteristics of Scandinavian design has been the pursuit of 'ideal forms' that have evolved over decades and even centuries. Being fully aware of this approach to design from a very formative stage in his career, it is unsurprising that Robert Welch also frequently looked back to the design past in order to make sense of the design present, often basing his thoroughly contemporary designs on historic forms. The design of his Serica range of goblets (see page 118), for instance, was as we have seen based on late eighteenth-century tavern glasses. Similarly, the flattened and bulbous form of Robert's elegant silver-mounted ship's decanter of 1968 was inspired by the bell-shaped decanters used by sea captains in the early nineteenth century. Likewise, his beautifully proportioned

claret jug designed the same year was based on generic Victorian models. That is not to say that these two designs were copies of antiques, for they most certainly were not: rather, they were modern evolutions of perfectly honed forms, and as such they are timeless.

Below, right: Design drawing by Robert Welch for his claret jug, c.1972

Designer:	Robert Welch
Materials:	Sterling silver, free-blown lead crystal glass
Production:	From 1972, batch-produced by Robert Welch Studio, Chipping Campden

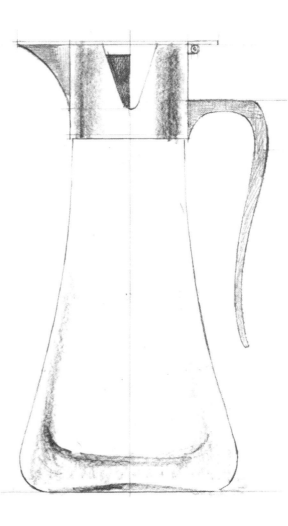

Amethyst dish, 1972

Throughout his career as a silversmith, Robert Welch pushed the aesthetic and technical boundaries of his chosen craft. The results were often as innovative as they were beautiful. Among all the silverware pieces produced by John Limbrey to Robert's design, there was one above all others that Robert felt was a 'tour de force of fine craftsmanship':[98] the Amethyst dish. Specially designed and made for the 'Craftsman's Art' exhibition held at the Victoria and Albert Museum in London in 1973, this extraordinary piece was made of parcel-gilt silver with its inside bowl covered in a rhythmically swirling pattern of delicate wirework into which were set small amethysts. This masterful composition evoked a sense of organic growth, with the pattern reminiscent of the germinated seeds from which both plant and human life evolve. It was a painstakingly difficult piece to execute; the silver wires had to be precisely soldered in small batches, making sure that the blowtorch being used did not accidentally melt either these wires or the wires and settings surrounding them. Every new year Robert would write a record of the successes and failures of the previous 12 months, and his observation of 1972 noted that the year marked 'the start of the great dish experiment with applied wires'.[99] Posing formidable technical challenges, this design is rightfully regarded as one of the defining successes of his silversmithing career.

Above: Design drawing by Robert Welch of the Amethyst dish, 1972 (RW)

Designer:	Robert Welch
Materials:	Sterling silver, silver wires, gilding, inset amethysts
Production:	ca. 1972–73 executed as a one-off piece by John Limbrey, Robert Welch Studio, Chipping Campden

Left: The silver wires of the Amethyst dish laid out in a complex pattern prior to being soldered on to the body of the dish

Far Left: Photograph of John Limbrey hammering a silver bowl into shape, in the same way as he would have made the Amethyst Bowl, ca. 1960s (RW)

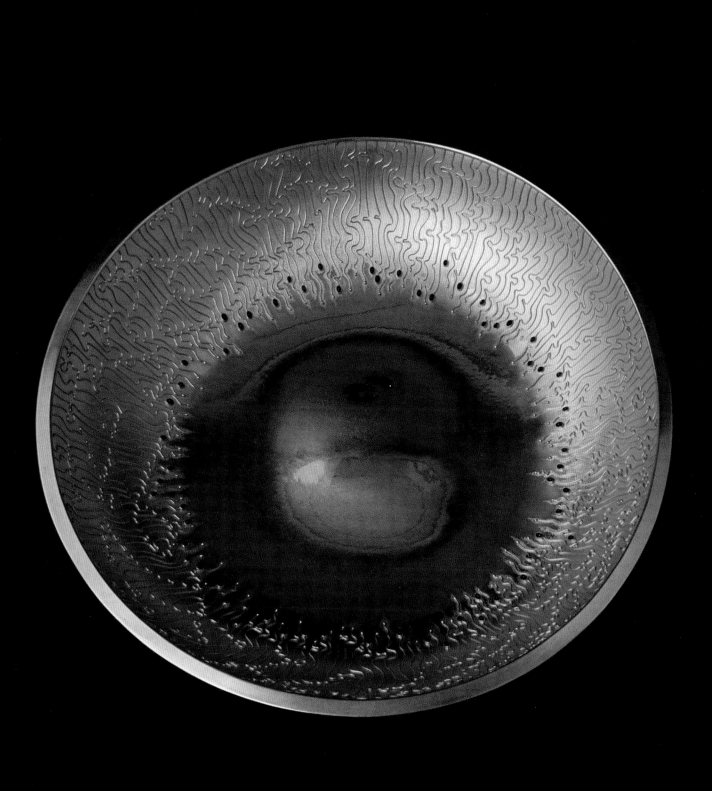

Tower of London goblet, 1978

One of the greatest icons of the British capital, the Tower of London not only protects the Crown Jewels, which are famously guarded by Yeomen Warders (known as 'Beefeaters'), but also has witnessed centuries of state pageantry, royal intrigues and bloody plots within its thick stone walls. Quite simply, more than any other building in the kingdom it resonates with British history. To celebrate the 900th anniversary of this historic building, the Department of the Environment approached Robert Welch to design a commemorative goblet that would be produced as a special limited edition. Despite being rather sceptical about the marketing of such commemorative objects, which had reached a tasteless peak during the Queen's Silver Jubilee in 1977, Robert was persuaded to accept the commission because it was to be entirely reliant on traditional handcraft techniques, and strictly limited to only 50 pieces. Robert's final design, which he sketched beautifully, incorporated a flaring lobed base reminiscent of a medieval chalice, and a band of engraved gothic script on a hatched background bearing the words 'Royal Palace & Fortress of the Tower of London', suitably inspired by the fifteenth-century Studley Bowl, one of the earliest and finest examples of English domestic silver in existence, and now part of the Victoria and Albert Museum's collection. Interestingly, some two and half decades earlier, Robert had sketched the Studley Bowl while training as a silversmith at Birmingham College of Art. Since the goblet was intended to mark the 900th anniversary of the founding of the White Tower (the central structure of the Tower of London precinct), Robert adorned the goblet's stem with a miniature representation of this medieval fortified keep, which he highlighted in parcel gilt. Yet despite all its historic connotations, Robert's Tower of London goblet was very much an object of its own time, and had a modern contemporary elegance thanks to its uncluttered simplicity. Unlike most commemorative limited-edition pieces, this design was expensive, selling for the princely sum of £790 in 1978 – making it, at the time, one of the most exclusive limited-edition products ever offered. Robert recalled, 'In all the celebrations and publicity for the event and souvenir articles that had been specially produced, there was not even a mention of the goblet, and to tell the truth I was relieved. I learnt later that all of them had been sold, presumably through very discreet advertising or by word of mouth.'[100] Each goblet

was made from thick-gauge silver that was painstakingly raised by hand by John Limbrey and then carefully finished to achieve a dramatic shimmering effect. As Robert noted, it was just as well that 1978 was not a particularly busy year for the workshop, since it allowed time for the prestigious commission to be completed. Years later, a press release issued by Court Barn Museum would observe, 'Through his career Welch took on a number of slightly off-beat commissions which resonated with his own beliefs about the importance of good design in everyday life and the role that design could play in supporting traditional craftsmanship and protecting jobs. This commemorative piece can be seen as part of the same inspiration. It represents his attempt to show that it was possible to produce a worthwhile and honest commemorative piece.'[101]

Above: John Limbrey shaping the cup sections of the Tower of London goblets, 1978 (RW)

Designer:	Robert Welch
Materials:	Parcel-gilt silver
Production:	From 1978, limited edition of 50 pieces executed by John Limbrey, Robert Welch Studio, Chipping Campden

Kitchen Devils professional knife range, 1979

The entrepreneurial businessman and consummate showman, Harold Bearston started selling a range of imported knives at agricultural fairs around the United Kingdom. His cutlery demonstration and sales pitch never failed to attract large gatherings, and as a result farmers and their wives were his first enthusiastic customers. So successful was his marketing technique that in the early 1960s he commissioned the Sheffield-based company Harrison Fisher to produce his own range of kitchen knives to be sold at low to mid-range prices. These knives were launched under the catchy 'Kitchen Devils' name – and so one of the most trusted brands in the kitchenware sector came into being. In 1979 Bearston asked Robert Welch to design a new premium range of knives that would be aimed at the top end of the market, which was then still dominated by foreign imports – in the region of 96 per cent. Bearston stipulated that these new knives must have full tangs, be comfortable to use and incorporate rivets to create an impression of high-quality manufacture to obtain consumer confidence. Robert's initial drawings were translated into models, and although he worked on a number of variants thereafter, the original design was adopted for full-scale mass production with virtually no changes being made. Aimed at professional chefs, this group

of 11 knives (together with a matching carving fork and blade-sharpening steel) set a new standard in the design of kitchen knives with its ergonomic contoured handles made of moulded-on plastic that allowed greater control. In acknowledgement of its innovative ergonomically informed design, the collection received a Design Centre Award in 1984 for being 'An Outstanding British Product' – a testament to its benchmark-setting design credentials. The judging panel, chaired by the industrial designer Kenneth Grange (b. 1929), would also note: 'The knives work well ergonomically – the shapes of both blades and handles are excellently thought out.'[102] Perhaps even more importantly, this range demonstrated that good design makes good business sense, for more than 600,000 units were sold within two years of the range's launch – capturing around 40 per cent of the UK market for professional chef knives.

Designer:	Robert Welch
Materials:	Stainless steel, plastic, brass
Production:	From 1979, Harrison Fisher, Sheffield (later Taylor's Eye Witness) for Kitchen Devils, Nottingham (currently manufactured by Taylor's Eye Witness)

Below: The entire range of Kitchen Devils professional knives, ca. 1979

Scissors, 1979

The same year as he designed his groundbreaking knife range for Kitchen Devils, the manufacture of which was subcontracted to Harrison Fisher, Robert Welch also created for the latter firm various new designs for plastic-handled scissors to be sold under its own Taylor's Eye Witness brand. Illustrated above are two models from the range: the shorter-bladed variant was intended to be used as a general-purpose/kitchen scissor, while the longer-bladed example was specially created for dressmakers – because even by the late 1970s home dressmaking was practised by a far greater number of women than it is today, and there was still a large and ready market for this type of specialized product. Although these two scissor designs were not the first to have contoured plastic handles – those famously designed by Olof Bäckström (b. 1922) and first produced by the Finnish company Fiskars in 1967 – they were, if anything, more ergonomically refined and arguably easier to handle. Still in production today, these 'classic' British scissors, which also come in left-handed versions, reflect the endurance of good design and the popularity of long-lasting products that are quite simply fit for purpose.

Above: Kitchen scissors (above) and dressmaking scissors (below)

Designer:	Robert Welch
Materials:	Stainless steel, moulded-on plastic
Production:	From 1979 to present, Harrison Fisher, Sheffield (later renamed Taylor's Eye Witness)

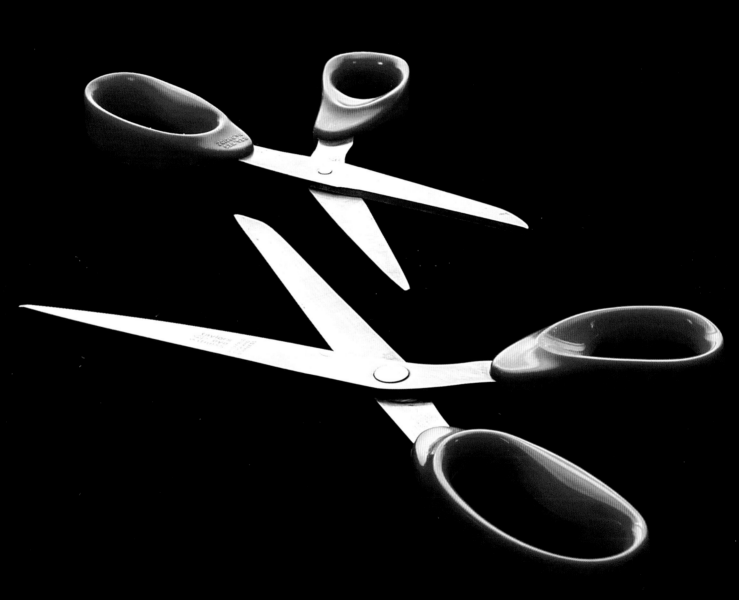

Above: John Limbrey tooling the hemispherical wires to create a knobbled pattern, ca. 1979 (RW)

Above left: Studio workbench with the wooden altar cross mount shown alongside the tooled silver rods, ca. 1979 (RW)

Left: Detail of the tooled silver wire inlay

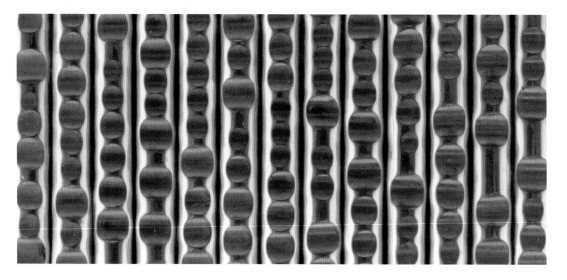

Altar cross and candlesticks for the Order of St John, 1979

The chairman and members of the Kent brigade of St John Ambulance – a well-known first-aid charity – commissioned Robert Welch to design and make this visually striking silver-and-rosewood altar cross and matching silver-plated candlesticks for St Gregory's Chapel in Canterbury Cathedral. The cross has an unusual construction in that the rosewood mount holds in place an inlay of tooled hemispherical silver wires, which were soldered together in order to give the impression of a seemingly random pattern but actually were carefully placed to ensure the most visually pleasing pattern possible. The resulting light-scattering knobbly surface, similar to that used by Robert for his earlier candelabra created for Goldsmiths' Hall (see page 126), gives the piece an attractive shimmering

quality even in low light. The pieces bear the insignia of the commissioning patron: on the candlesticks this takes the form of enamelled St John Ambulance badges set into blocks of clear acrylic, showing Robert's skill in mixing the old with the new.

Designer:	Robert Welch
Materials:	Altar cross: rosewood with tooled and soldered silver wire inlay, and inlaid badge / candlesticks: silver-plated with enamel badges set into acrylic blocks
Production:	1979, one-off commission executed by John Limbrey, Robert Welch Studio, Chipping Campden

Regalia cutlery, 1979

By the late 1970s, Japan had begun to Westernize rapidly and there was a growing demand for Western-style cutlery there, although chopsticks were, and would remain, the eating tool of choice. The Japanese manufacturer Yamazaki Kinzoku Kogyo not only wanted to respond to this new home-grown demand, but also wished to enter the lucrative American export market. With this aim, the company's product and marketing directors Hans Hallundbaek and Katherine Volkins (the former of whom had previously worked for Dansk), visited Europe with the aim of finding a suitable designer for this East-meets-West project. Because of Robert's impressive track record as an innovator in the field of stainless-steel design, they met him in 1979 and subsequently commissioned him to create a new, modern-looking range of cutlery specifically aimed at both the Japanese and American markets. As it happened, Robert had a year earlier been working on the design of a shimmering micro-faceted sidewall pattern for a new kind of car tyre, known as the Denovo, being developed by Dunlop for the Ford Metro. Although the project had eventually been shelved because of the high cost of the computerized milling machine needed to cut the facets on every tyre mould, Robert had spent considerable time and energy researching patterns that would scatter light effectively. Therefore, he knew exactly how to make a cutlery pattern shimmer on a table in a way no one had ever seen before. As Sue Roseveare wrote in *Focus* magazine in March 1982 of the pieces that made up the resulting Regalia range, 'They are small, light and delicate to hold – to suit the smaller hands of the Japanese'.[103] It was, however, the unusual fluting of the pieces' handles that set the design apart from other cutlery ranges. The mirror-polished opposing diagonal flutes bounced light off their shiny surfaces, giving the type of gleam usually associated with silver rather than steel. The success of Regalia led to the similarly fluted and light reflective Yamazaki Serving Collection (1981–2), which would likewise redefine the aesthetics associated with stainless steel as well as Robert's beliefs of how this metal alloy should be treated and finished. With its distinctive Post-Modern look, it was hoped that this 'New Wave' range would appeal to a younger demographic of consumers.

Designer:	Robert Welch
Material:	Bright-finish stainless steel
Production:	From 1980, Yamazaki Kinzoku Kogyo, Niigata, Japan

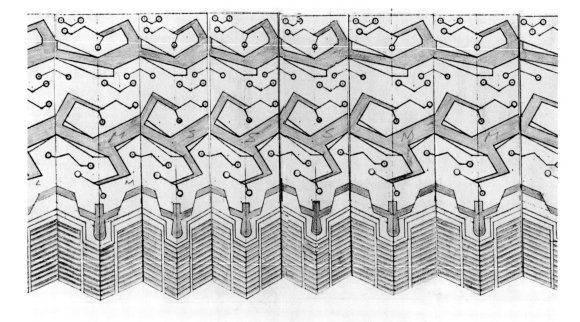

Left: Design drawing by John Limbrey of the tread and faceted sidewall patterning for Dunlop's Denovo tyre, 1978

Opposite, bottom: Yamazaki Serving Collection designed by Robert Welch, 1981–82

1980s

V&A candelabra, 1980

Although the Victoria and Albert Museum had not commissioned any silverware since the time of Sir Henry Cole in the late nineteenth century, Roy Strong, having been appointed its new director in 1974, decided that the museum's permanent silverware collection needed to have more contemporary pieces. To this end, he commissioned Robert Welch to design a pair of silver candelabra. As Robert would later recall, 'It proved to be a very sobering thing, once the first pleasure of the commission had subsided, to be asked to design a piece of silver for the collection of the Victoria and Albert Museum, for I knew that I was embarking on a piece that, all being well, would remain in the collection in perpetuity.'[104] Not really knowing where to start, Robert resorted to walking in the Malvern Hills, where often he found that he was able to think better than when he was surrounded by distractions in the studio. Gradually the design concept of candlebra made up of 'round juicy shapes', similar to those he had used for a presentational coffee service to commemorate St Lucia's independence in 1979, took form. He then made several tentative sketches based on blobular forms, which he subsequently showed to the keeper and deputy keeper of the V&A's metalwork department as well as to Strong. To his delight they all chose the design he himself preferred. A three-dimensional wooden model was then made to ensure that the piece would visually work from every angle, and once this had been given approval by the client, John Limbrey executed the two silver candelabra in the workshop. As an added special touch, around the bases of each candlebrum was engraved in Latin the words 'I put darkness in flight, rejoice the eyes, crowning the night, R.S. caused me to be made, V&A 1980'. Extraordinarily beautiful, these glistening candelabra fully expressed the magnificent properties of the material from which they were made, while at the same time revitalizing the silversmith's craft within a modern idiom.

Designer:	Robert Welch
Materials:	Sterling silver
Production:	1980, one-off commission for identical pair executed by John Limbrey, Robert Welch Studio, Chipping Campden

Far left: Preliminary sketch by Robert Welch of the V&A candelabra, 1980

Left: Painted wooden model of the V&A candelabra, 1980

Le Buffet serving utensils, 1983

Based in the West Midlands, Samuel Groves & Co. was founded in the 1820s and has for nearly 200 years been supplying the catering trade with superlative and hardwearing cookware. In 1953 the company launched the well-known Mermaid brand, which is still one of the most trusted names in bakeware. It was, however, during the early 1980s that the company conducted a market survey to prove that, thanks to the rapid growth of self-service buffets and carvery dining within the hotel, restaurant and pub sectors, there was a definite need for a new range of professional serving utensils. Although Robert Welch had already designed a highly successful range of kitchen utensils for Prestige (see page 132), they were nowhere near strong enough to cope with the pressures of a professional kitchen. Samuel Groves, therefore, commissioned Robert to design an entirely new range of professional tools that were 'at least double or treble the strength of the Prestige tools'[105] and that would have an unbendable one-piece stainless-steel construction with moulded-on plastic handles. Rising to the challenge of this exacting brief, Robert quickly realized that with catering supplies 'sturdy engineering is the keynote, and robust construction is of prime importance'[106] and so sketched a design for a modern-looking range of tools with an impressive sense of indestructibility. Very taken with this initial design drawing, the board of Samuel Groves immediately gave the project the go-ahead, and the range was subsequently launched under the Mermaid brand at the Hotelympia trade show in 1984. A durable and stylish answer to the catering trade's prayers, this range proved spectacularly popular and orders flowed in over the coming years. Still in production, it is one of the most commercially successful Robert Welch designs of all time.

Designer:	Robert Welch
Materials:	Pressed stainless steel, moulded-on plastic
Production:	From 1984 to present, Samuel Groves & Co., Birmingham

Surprise clock, 1983

In 1983 the Birmingham Assay Office decided it wanted to commission a gift for the Worshipful Company of Goldsmiths to commemorate the 700th anniversary of Henry III's introduction of quality standards for gold and silver articles. The problem was that because the Goldsmiths' Company was one of the oldest and wealthiest livery companies in the City of London it already had an impressive collection of plate containing every kind of object imaginable. After much deliberation, it was decided that the object should be a clock that 'did not look like a clock',[107] which could be used by the company's Prime Warden to keep a surreptitious eye on the timing of speakers and events when the company was holding its famous banquets. The resulting Surprise clock designed by Robert Welch and executed by John Limbrey was one of the more whimsical pieces that came out of the Chipping Campden workshop, yet even so it was meticulously detailed. For instance, when its hinged lid

set with amethysts and engraved with the company's arms and the assay office's emblems is opened to reveal the 'surprise' clock face, a beautifully engraved poem by Jonathan Swift also appears, ending with the following very appropriate lines: 'Thus we both shall have our ends, And continue to be special friends'. Made in parcel gilt, this design was a masterful example of silversmithing skill, revealing not only an imaginative response to an unusual brief, but also that the level of craftsmanship – at least in Chipping Campden – remained on a par with that of the august silversmithing masters of the past.

Designer:	Robert Welch
Materials:	Sterling silver, parcel gilt, glass, clock mechanism
Production:	1983, one-off commission executed by John Limbrey, Robert Welch Studio, Chipping Campden

British Museum candelabra, 1983

Although the British Museum is best known for its world-class collections of Egyptian, Roman and Greek artefacts, it also has a small but interesting permanent collection of twentieth-century designed objects – including a number of Old Hall pieces designed by Robert Welch. In 1982 Lady Pamela Hartwell, a noted society hostess and trustee of the British Museum, died and it was decided by a group of her friends that a fitting tribute to her memory would be to commission a set of six silver candelabra to be presented to the British Museum. The idea was that each would be engraved with a dedication and the donor's name, and that they could be used for formal dinner gatherings in the museum's Hartwell Room. In 1983 the museum's director, Sir David Wilson, met Robert Welch at the museum and provided him with a precise brief, stating that the design 'should be low and graceful, like a Viking Boat, and hold only two candles'.[108] On the train journey home, Robert visualized exactly what he thought the commissioner wanted, and the following day John Limbrey translated Robert's initial sketches into a model. At his next appointment with Wilson, Robert recalled saying that he really hoped he liked the design because he had absolutely nothing else to show him. Luckily, all went well and the dramatically sweeping design was approved; so Limbrey set to work to make the six identical pieces. Later Robert felt this design was especially successful because the final outcome had managed to retain the first spark of inspiration.

Designer:	Robert Welch
Material:	Sterling silver
Production:	1983, one-off commission for near-identical set of six executed by John Limbrey, Robert Welch Studio, Chipping Campden

Cast bronze wares, 1984

During the 1970s there was great interest in non-Western cultures, and especially their age-old handcraft traditions, which were seen to be under threat from increasing Western industrialization. The wares produced using traditional skills were also seen in the West as having an appealing authenticity, and there was a general consensus, especially among the international design community, that these craft traditions needed to be proactively preserved. During this period many leading European and American designers were approached by various foreign governments for help in revitalizing their craft industries in order to find new export markets, which would in turn help fund the development of their nations. To this end, in 1975 Robert Welch undertook a ten-week fact-finding survey of Indian art metalwork at the invitation of the All India Handicraft Board. During this first trip to India in a professional capacity, Robert highlighted the lost-wax casting of bronze in Kerala in Southern India for special consideration, and he was subsequently commissioned to write a report and set up a design programme to establish new markets for this ancient craft. He returned to India in 1984 for a more prolonged stay, with the aim of creating designs for such bronze castings, which could then be made by local craft workshops. Yet when he got there he found that he needed just to absorb the culture: 'India can be so overwhelming, the riot of colour and pattern, the smells, the heat, the number of human beings, the hundreds of thousands of clever craftsmen, the seemingly limitless possibilities for

Left: Patinated bronze chess pieces designed by Robert Welch, 1984

design, the sheer frustration of poor communications and travel, the difficulties of obtaining raw materials and the immense size of the country are just a few of the reasons why I have resisted as strongly as possible the temptation to commence design work there and then while in the country ... Instead I reserve my thoughts for the cool and temperate well-ordered calm of my studio in Chipping Campden.'[109] On his return to England, Robert created numerous drawings and precise models for a range of cast bronze wares, including a pestle and mortar, candlesticks, a candle-snuffer, a trivet and a set of chess pieces. Because the polished surface of bronze is difficult and time-consuming to maintain, it was determined that the designs should be patinated, and so Robert consulted an old friend from his RCA days, the sculptor Ralph Brown (1928–2013), who put

Left: Pen-and-wash sketch by Robert Welch of the bronze-casters of Kerala at work, 1984

Above (left to right): Pair of candlesticks, a candle-snuffer, and a pestle and mortar, all designed by Robert Welch and made of patinated bronze, 1984

him in touch with Kenneth Cook, who cast all his bronzes. Robert, with Cook's assistance, subsequently undertook numerous experiments to find just the right formula to create the required verdigris finish, using only substances such as elephant dung (obtained from Bristol Zoo) and turmeric, that would be readily available in the remote Indian workshops. After sending the models, drawings and templates, as well as careful instructions to India, Robert waited anxiously for several months until at last one day a huge parcel arrived with the finished products. On opening the package Robert and his colleagues were dumbfounded by the sheer beauty and manufacturing excellence of the work. Crucially, Robert had expertly managed, as he put it, to 'distil the flavour of the traditional form of this craft'[110],

and had then successfully translated this into a modern idiom so as to provide contemporary design-led products that were eminently suited to the Western market but based on age-old craft skills.

Designer:	Robert Welch
Material:	Patinated bronze
Production:	From ca. 1984, executed in the foundry of R. Venkitchalam Mannar, Kerala, India

Pestle and mortar (model no. RW320), 1984

Sometimes a design just has an inherent 'rightness', indeed, such products can often seem to have an effortless inevitability about them – they are 'ah yes, that makes perfect sense' solutions. Yet such a design usually has a quiet and understated demeanour, despite the sheer cleverness of the designer getting it so right. Robert Welch's cast-iron pestle and mortar is just such a design. Available in two sizes, this ingenious design has a handy pouring lip that also doubles as a holder for the pestle. Designed the same year as the Kerala bronzes, it shares a similar totemic quality with its elemental form having an engaging stripped-down functionalism. This reduction of form to functional basics recalls traditional Japanese kitchenwares – and gives the design an almost Zen-like quality that is timeless in its appeal.

Designer:	Robert Welch
Material:	Cast iron
Production:	From ca. 1984 to present, Victor Cast Ware, Telford, Shropshire

Above: Side view of the RW320 pestle and mortar showing its simple yet ingenious design

Left: Packaging designed by Victor Cast Ware, 1980s, which took over the manufacture and marketing of Robert Welch's cast-iron designs in the mid-1970s

Cookbook stand, 1986

Right: Early sketch of the cast-iron cookbook stand showing its adjustable tilt mechanism and its weighted cords, ca. 1986. Note the diagonal patterning on the book rest

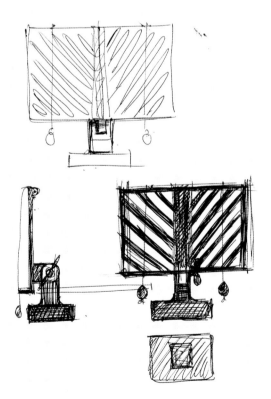

One of Robert Welch's best-loved cast-iron designs, this very heavy cookbook stand was designed to be sufficiently stable to cope with just about any size and weight of book. Its simple two-part construction was reminiscent of traditional lecterns found in churches, while its 'industrial craft' aesthetic complemented Robert's earlier Campden Designs cast-iron range (see page 94). Designed from a functional perspective, its simple screw mechanism enabled the book-rest section to be angled into the desired position for easier reading while cooking and preparing food, while two cords weighted with brass toggles were a simple way of keeping a recipe book turned to the right page. The distinctive pattern of the rest was suitably contextual, being inspired by the shape made by the pages of a book when placed in an open position.

Designer:	Robert Welch
Materials:	Enamelled cast iron, cord, brass
Production:	From ca. 1984 to present, Victor Cast Ware, Telford, Shropshire

161

Dryad candlesticks, 1988

Although the working of wrought iron has a long and illustrious history stretching back centuries, by the latter half of the twentieth century it was seen as just another age-old craft that was slowly dying out as blacksmith's forges closed their doors through lack of demand. Robert Welch saw the creative potential of this type of metalworking, however, and designed an extensive range of modern-looking candlesticks that utilized traditional blacksmithing skills. Each piece in the Dryad range – which also went on to include various lights, a table, a wine rack, fire irons, fire dogs and a plant stand – incorporated a spiral cage of finely wrought iron as its focal point. This distinctive motif may well have been an allusion to the logo of the Leicester-based Dryad Metal Works (a company Robert had previously worked with), which featured a dryad or nymph entwined in the trunk and branches of a tree. The Arts and Crafts illustrator and stained-glass artist, Paul Woodroffe (1875–1954), who had himself been a resident of Chipping Campden, probably designed this logo. The use of the name 'Dryad' was in all likelihood a nod to history on Robert's part, as throughout his career he was always acutely aware of the past and how it could inform the present in terms of design and making. This swirling and spiralling 'cage work' of iron strands required immense technical skill on the part of the maker, and Robert worked with the gifted blacksmith Brian Rourke to develop the range, since it was Rourke's Burnley-based company that was responsible for its later manufacture. Even today, the range is still hand-forged by one of Britain's foremost blacksmiths, thereby keeping a craft tradition well and truly alive into the twenty-first century.

Above: Early publicity photograph showing five different candlestick designs from the Dryad range, ca. 1988 (RW)

Designer:	Robert Welch
Materials:	Verdigris-, copper- or black-finish wrought iron (later epoxy-coated steel)
Production:	From 1988 to 2005, B. Rourke & Co., Burnley, Lancashire, and from 2005 to present, Robert Welch Designs, Chipping Campden

Cast-iron trivets, 1989–90

Having produced a number of iconic cast-iron designs during the 1960s, Robert Welch reignited his interest in this wonderful, though all-too-often overlooked, material during the late 1980s and early 1990s. The result was a comprehensive series of new wares, including a range of cast-iron trivets that featured abstracted pictorial representations – much like his earlier jewellery designs for Shetland Silvercraft (see page 36). The four large trivets had pierced patterns: a cat surrounded by mice; a squirrel surrounded by acorns; an octopus surrounded by fish; and a smiling sun surrounded by flowers. There were also at least seven more patterns for smaller 5-inch trivets. These handy and highly characterful designs were hugely popular during the late 1990s and early 2000s thanks to the resurgence of interest in home cooking, and were especially beloved by the so-called AGA crowd, as they were perfectly in keeping with the heavy-duty industrial-heritage aesthetic of these traditional-style stoves, which were themselves enjoying a huge revival. Still in production, these trivets, though heavily decorated and not overtly modern like many other pieces by Robert, must still be regarded 'Classic Welch' designs.

Clockwise, from above:
Trivets: Sun and Flowers,
1989; Octopus and Fish,
1989; Cat and Mice, 1990;
Squirrel and Acorns, 1990

Designer:	Robert Welch
Material:	Enamelled or powder-coated cast iron (originally only available in black but other colours were later added)
Production:	From ca. 1991 to present, Victor Cast Ware, Telford, Shropshire

1990s

Sparta was an ancient Greek city-state, its society famously dominated by the rigorous excellence of its military training. Consequently, the word 'spartan' now means simple and austere, as well as self-disciplined and restrained. During the 1980s and early 1990s, the emergence of Post-Modernism saw a revival of interest in Classicism, and the Sparta lighting range by Robert Welch reflects this trend. The stripped-down-to-basics attributes of the Spartan mindset must have appealed to Robert, who was always highly rigorous in his approach to design. Yet despite their overtly classical inspiration, this table lamp and pendant light were first and foremost functional yet elegant designs, rather than referencing Classicism in a tongue-in-cheek, ironic way, and as such they must be described as Late Modern rather than Post-Modern. Still in production some 25 years after they were launched, these elegant lamps with their shallow flaring shades were originally offered in either a chrome or antique copper finish. Not only do the shades perfectly conceal the bulbs, they also give the designs a distinctive graphic profile – a quality that is shared by many of Robert's designs, and which reveals his mastery of form-giving. Indeed, it is remarkable just how many acknowledged 'design classics' can be identified purely through their silhouettes, showing how important this characteristic is in the success of iconic designs.

Designer:	Robert Welch
Materials:	Antique-finish copper or chrome-plated steel
Production:	From 1992 to present, Chad Lighting, Birmingham

Galerie Cuisine (Campden) cookware, 1991

When Robert Welch received a commission from Cuisine Cookware of New York to design a new range of stainless-steel cookware, he was, in his words, 'determined that the design would represent the best in quality, performance and permanence'.[111] The resulting Galerie Cuisine collection had a number of notable features to improve performance: snug-fitting lids that were reversible for easy stacking, rounded inside corners, perfectly balanced handling and cool-to-the-touch hollow handles. The pans' three-ply base of stainless steel, copper and stainless steel also provided highly responsive heat-conductivity, giving chefs a great degree of control. The range when launched was described in its marketing brochure as 'a merger of function and finesse for the discerning cook', as well as 'a masterpiece of design and effortless utility'. Certainly the collection was ahead of the cultural curve, being a premium cookware range launched just as the interest in more elaborate kinds of cooking was taking off with the introduction of nouvelle cuisine in the early 1990s. Rather confusingly, the range is now sold under the Campden name; however, it still remains one of the best cookware ranges on the market, even though it was designed well over 20 years ago – proving just how enduring good design can be.

Designer:	Robert Welch
Materials:	Stainless steel, copper (sandwich base)
Production:	From ca. 1991, Cuisine Cookware, New York (later by Robert Welch Designs)

The Silver Trust coffee sets, 1992

The idea of establishing an organization to encourage and promote the work of contemporary British silversmiths was mooted by Lady Henderson at a meeting with the fashion designer Jean Muir and the silversmith Gerald Benney at the Goldsmiths' Hall in 1985. Officially founded two years later, the Silver Trust was ostensibly set up as a charitable trust to provide a collection of contemporary silverware for use in 10 Downing Street, as well as various British embassies around the world. The hope was that such commissions would help to publicize the work of contemporary British silver designers and makers both at home and abroad. Among the pieces that were commissioned were two identical hand-raised parcel-gilt coffee sets by Robert Welch, each comprising a coffee pot, cream jug, sugar bowl, spoon and tray. With their exquisitely hand tooled surfaces, spiralling flutes and furling handles inspired by ammonite fossils, the pieces revealed a greater sculptural bravado than any tea or coffee services Robert had previously designed. With their chased outer surfaces scattering a cool silver light, the pieces' internal surfaces were gilded to provide a contrasting glow of golden warmth. Personally presented by Robert to John Major, the Prime Minister at the time, these coffee sets are still used regularly by the current incumbents of 'Number Ten' and Chevening House, the official residence of the foreign secretary.

Designer:	Robert Welch
Materials:	Sterling silver, parcel gilt, antique ivory
Production:	1995, one-off commission executed by John Limbrey, Robert Welch Studio, Chipping Campden

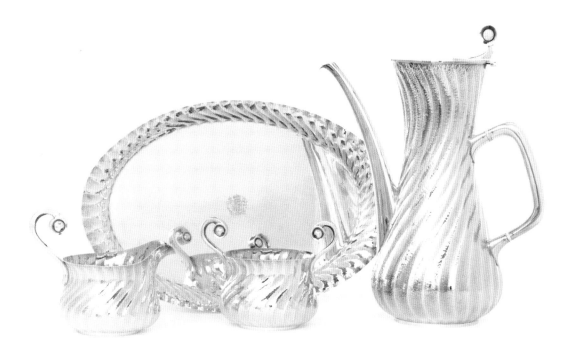

Ammonite Flat cutlery, 1993–4

Ammonite is one of Robert Welch's most distinctive designs, and was directly inspired by the spirals of fossils, which he bought from a specialist dealer in Lyme Regis and often incorporated into his jewellery designs. With its eye-catching motif formed on both sides of its handles, this cutlery range had a far stronger Post-Modern quality than others created by Robert during his long career – and as such was very much in tune with the international design trends of the early 1990s. Yet, it was just as carefully designed to function as well as his more classical cutlery designs. The pattern was originally designed for Ginkgo, an American cutlery company established by Wes and Janet Helmick in 1977. Initially, the pattern was available only as a rounded hollow design, but shortly afterwards a flatter solid stainless-steel variation (shown above) was introduced. A rather more expensive parcel-gilt option was also originally offered in the 1990s, with the shell spiral motif picked out in gold plate.

Left: Detail of Ammonite cutlery handle (flat version)

Designer:	Robert Welch
Materials:	Bright-finish stainless steel
Production:	From 1995, Ginkgo, Illinois, USA (later by Robert Welch Designs)

In 1995 the Cheltenham Art Gallery and Museum staged a major retrospective of Robert Welch's designs, and George Breeze, the museum's director, was in the habit of personally commissioning work from designers and artists whose work was shown there. He commissioned Robert to design a candelabrum to celebrate his and his wife's twenty-fifth wedding anniversary, stipulating that it should have five branches to symbolize the number of years they had been married – with twenty-five being a five times multiple of five. Another part of the brief was that the branches should start splayed out at the base, come together and then splay out again – to symbolize how the act of marriage brings a couple together and then allows the partners to expand their individual talents within the confines of their matrimony. The resulting five-stem candelabrum with its round base, arching branches and circular sconces met this exacting brief, and Robert specified that it should only be used with a certain type and height of church candle in order to balance its proportions perfectly. After undertaking this commission, Robert put the design, which he had by now christened the 'Breeze Candelabrum', into limited production, and it was subsequently sold in relatively small numbers through his studio shop in Chipping Campden.

Designer:	Robert Welch
Material:	Sterling silver
Production:	From 1997, limited production, executed by John Limbrey, Robert Welch Studio, Chipping Campden

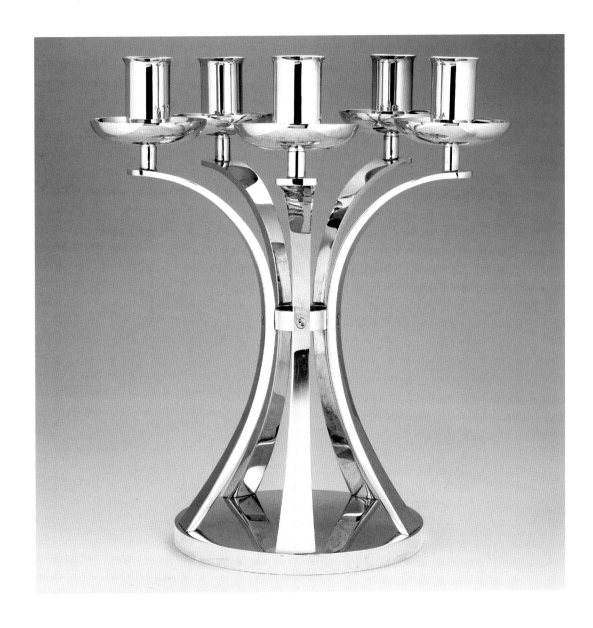

Sea Drift cutlery, 1995

During the 1990s Robert Welch's design work became increasingly fluid in line and organic in essence. This new quality was especially noticeable in a range of designs he produced under the title Sea Drift. This range included not only various cast-iron candlesticks and several ceramic pieces, but also a new and highly sculpted cutlery pattern that was quite different from any he had designed before, in that it had a strong gestural line with a contemporary feel; in fact, the pattern did not have the slightest vestige of Classicism about it at all. Launched in 1997 as both a solid flat and rounded hollow pattern, Sea Drift was inspired by the way bone handles on carving knives get gradually worn by the user's grip over time, so that their contours eventually conform comfortably to the shape of the hand. This organic pattern was seen as a breath of fresh air in the tableware world, so much so that in 1998 Robert was commissioned by Virgin Atlantic to create a smaller and lighter version for use in its Upper Class cabins – this specially designed thinner-gauge variation was so popular among the airline's clients that the butter knives were jokingly engraved with the words 'finest stainless steal'.

Below: Detail of Virgin Atlantic Sea Drift butter knife

Designer:	Robert Welch
Material:	Bright-finish stainless steel
Production:	From 1997, Ginkgo, Illinois, USA (later by Robert Welch Designs, Chipping Campden)

The Stanton cutlery range is a very important design for Robert Welch Designs, being not only Robert's last design before his death in 2000, but also the first design to be manufactured under his own brand. Having joined the family firm in 1990, Rupert Welch was convinced 'the future was to do it ourselves, to take an idea to manufacture',[112] but his father was quite resistant to this idea. However, in 1999 Pizza Express phoned to request a brochure, as it was looking for new cutlery for all its restaurants. Rupert immediately recognized that such an order might offer the company a springboard into the kind of self-manufacturing he had been envisioning. He managed to persuade the representatives of Pizza Express to drive up to Chipping Campden to see a new cutlery pattern that Robert had initially sketched some three years previously. They subsequently placed a substantial order, and so the design team in Campden began honing this elegant, modern-yet-classical design to pre-production perfection. While Rupert and his brother William were on a factory visit to inspect the first production run of the cutlery, Robert became ill, and on their return the brothers went to see their father in hospital to show him production samples. He was delighted with the results, and with his father's acceptance of these 'just launched pieces' Rupert felt 'the baton had passed',[113] for sadly his father passed away just a few hours later. This poignant ending was, therefore, the beginning of a new chapter for Robert Welch Designs.

Designer:	Robert Welch
Materials:	Bright-finish or satin-finish stainless steel
Production:	From 2000, Robert Welch Designs, Chipping Campden

Sea Drift candelabrum, 1996

Living and working in the Midlands, which is quite literally the heart of England and as far away from the coast as one can possibly get, Robert Welch relished the family's annual summer holidays caravanning in Porthmadog in North Wales and spending time at the nearby 'wild' campsite on Shell Island in Snowdonia National Park. Here, along this low-lying, windswept coastline with its grass-tufted sand dunes, big sky and bracing sea air, the Welchs would spend precious family time together. It was here that Robert relaxed and endlessly sketched, and with his well-honed eye found inspiration in nature – smooth sea-worn pebbles, swirling seaweed and gnarled driftwood. The Sea Drift candelabrum, with its four tentacle-like branches and asymmetrical form, was directly inspired by pieces of

driftwood found along the Welsh coastline, and was one of the most sculptural pieces he ever produced. The related single candlesticks (two versions), double candlesticks (two versions) and doorstop possessed similar shapes and were made from either cast iron or cast aluminium. The whole range was available in four different finishes: white, black, bronze or verdigris.

Designer:	Robert Welch
Materials:	Patinated or painted cast iron
Production:	From ca. 1996, Deeleys Castings, Walsall for Robert Welch Designs, Chipping Campden

Below: Photograph of prototype Sea Drift candelabrum and candlesticks, ca. 1996 (RW)

2000 to present

Radford cutlery, 2001–2

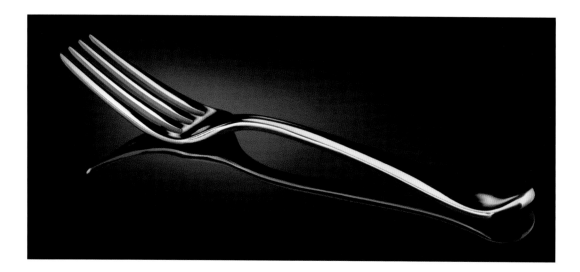

Radford is Robert Welch Designs' best-selling cutlery pattern thanks to its synthesis of the contemporary with the classical, which allows it to work well in various kinds of interior. Unlike many cutlery ranges it has been highly successful in both the retail and hospitality sectors, owing not only to its easy-on-the-eye modern classicism and perfectly balanced handling, but also to its impressive range. It comprises more than 50 different items, literally everything from grapefruit spoons and oyster forks to lobster picks and snail tongs. Its title is a tribute to Robert Welch's middle name, and the pattern was actually a monobloc evolution of an earlier and more expensive, silver or stainless-steel hollow-handled cutlery pattern known as Premier, which he had designed in 1984. This new and refined iteration with far more individual pieces was, as Rupert Welch recalls, conceived on the 'back of an envelope'. Yet despite this very humble beginning, the range was painstakingly developed by Rupert and John Limbrey over a couple of years until it achieved honed perfection. Since its launch in 2002, it has been appreciated across the world for its timeless 'not old, not new' aesthetic, as Kit deBretton Gordon so succinctly puts it, and reflects how Robert's rigorous design ethos has been carefully channelled into the development of the new products that now bear his distinctive signature.

Designer:	Rupert Welch and John Limbrey (based on earlier design by Robert Welch)
Materials:	Bright-finish stainless steel
Production:	From 2002 to present, Robert Welch Designs, Chipping Campden

Left and Right: Vector drawing of some items in the Radford cutlery range

Vista cutlery, 2003

Having taken an advanced mechanics course in Birmingham, William Welch – Robert's younger son – decided to follow in his father's footsteps and become a designer. To this end, he interned with Pentagram before applying to study at the Royal College of Art – where he was accepted, despite having no formal design training. At the RCA he won numerous accolades, including a Helen Hamlyn Award for a cutlery design for the physically impaired. After graduating, he joined the family firm as a designer and created a number of cutlery designs that had a distinctive gestural style. For instance, his Vista cutlery range was purposely designed to have a strong architectural feel, and was highly unusual in that the blades of the knives were designed to stand vertically on a table surface, thereby completely redefining the look of the traditional table setting. After spending four years working at Robert Welch Designs, William eventually decided to embark on his own independent design career. A number of his designs are still in production with the company, however, including this wonderfully poised yet sculptural cutlery design.

Designer:	William Welch
Material:	Bright-finish stainless steel
Production:	From 2004 to present, Robert Welch Designs, Chipping Campden

Opposite: Image of Signature deep bowl serving spoon showing its distinctive lipped handle that allows it to be efficiently hooked on to the Signature utensil stand

Signature utensils and stand, 2005–6

One of the defining features of designs adorned with the Robert Welch name is their clever left-field functionality. For instance, most kitchen tools have riveted handles or are stamped from metal, but the design team at Robert Welch decided instead to make a range of kitchen utensils that would use the same type of casting employed in the production of high-quality cutlery. The resulting designs possess similar qualities to well-made cutlery and, therefore, do not have the utilitarian look or feel generally associated with kitchen tools. Determined that the pieces should have kitchen-to-dining functionality, Paul deBretton Gordon, who was tasked with the utensils design and development, took great care to ensure that each piece had three points of contact, so it would not rock when placed on a table. Similarly, he also rethought how to store the tools. Normally kitchen tools are either hung from a rack or held in a utensil container. However, he came up with something radically different – a compact stand on to which the hooked utensils could be hung. In fact, this ingenious solution was almost stumbled on by Rupert Welch, who in one of the company's weekly design meetings grabbed an Arden candlestick and tried to hook the utensils on to it. The stand's design was subsequently evolved from this idea, and because of this it shares a similar 'signature' design DNA with the elegant candlestick that inspired it. With its lovely curves that define the negative space, it takes the idea of a rack and the idea of a container and fuses them into a hookable stand that is not only more functional but also unquestionably beautiful, with its elegant, sweeping lines.

Designer:	Paul deBretton Gordon
Material:	Stainless steel, POM (polyoxymethylene) or bamboo
Production:	From 2007 to present, Robert Welch Designs, Chipping Campden

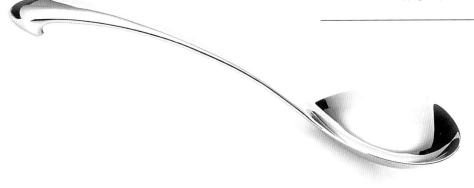

The development of the Signature knife range was initiated by Rupert Welch as a state-of-the-art evolution of Robert Welch's earlier Ergo knife range designed for Taylor's Eye Witness in the 1990s. In fact, during its development it was referred to in-house as Ergo 2. Initially, the design of the range was overseen by Rupert and the industrial designer Martin Drury, but when Paul deBretton Gordon joined the Robert Welch design team in 2005, he was charged with its overall development. Going back to the drawing board, Paul worked in close collaboration with Rupert, who was deeply involved with the engineering side of the design's development, and together they repeatedly consulted with various specialists and research institutions to create some of the best knives in the world. The resulting pieces incorporate ergonomic handles with oval backs that flatten out towards the blades to provide enhanced stability when cutting. Similarly, the handles, made from high-quality and extremely durable Delrin – an advanced polymer produced by DuPont – not only fit comfortably in the hand but also, importantly, angle the fully forged full-tang blades in such a way that they provide the optimum cutting action.

After spending two years perfecting the knives' design in consultation with professional chefs, deBretton Gordon decided that they should be offered with a specially designed easy-to-use knife sharpener that used a ceramic wheel device, so that the blades could be kept in tip-top cutting condition. He had observed that most people found traditional butcher's steels impossible to use, and that Chantry-type knife sharpeners, though fine to use on ordinary everyday knives, were too abrasive to use on high-end professional knives. Rupert then had the brilliant idea of incorporating the sharpener into the knife block so that each and every time a knife is used it can be easily sharpened before being slotted back into the block. Winning numerous prestigious awards for its innovative design, the Signature range set a new standard for kitchen knives, but, of course, the best proof of this is actually holding one of the knives in one's hands: it feels perfectly well-balanced and cuts with an impressive degree of precision.

Designers:	Rupert Welch and Paul deBretton Gordon
Materials:	Stainless steel, POM (polyoxymethylene)
Production:	From 2007 to present, Robert Welch Designs, Chipping Campden

Below: The various stages of manufacture, from steel bar to finished product

Arden candlesticks, 2006

Arden is the name of an area of countryside that stretches from the River Avon to the River Tame, mainly in the English county of Warwickshire. Like other places used by Robert Welch Designs in the naming of its designs, it is situated closed to the company's headquarters in Chipping Campden, and reflects how culturally rooted the company feels to this part of the world. The Arden range of candlesticks was created for the company by Ruth Williams, and the first design models were initially far chunkier in form. At Rupert Welch's insistence they were slimmed down again and again until their final slender and elegant form was achieved. Made from high-quality cast stainless steel and hand-finished, these candlesticks come in five different sizes and can be used individually or arranged as an attractive group.

Designer:	Ruth Williams
Material:	Bright-finish stainless steel
Production:	From 2007 to present, Robert Welch Designs, Chipping Campden

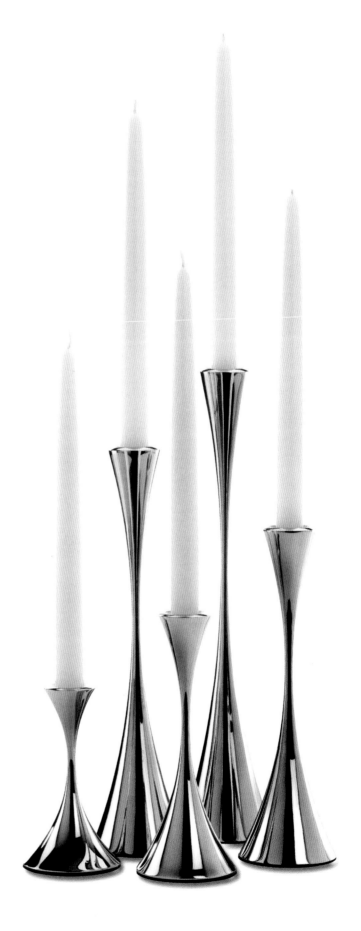

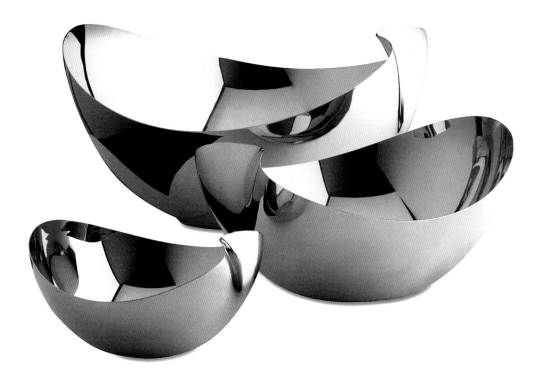

The title of this design was intended to allude to the fact that these three gleaming bowls were inspired by how traditional Russian dolls nest neatly into one another. They were created using then-state-of-the-art CAD software. Ruth Williams was responsible for the overall shape of this design, although all of the design team had some input into its final form. The reason for this was that the bowls' complex stacking form and the attractive, highly reflective mirror-polished finish proved to be a real challenge to produce, requiring the highest metalworking skills possible. While it might seem simple to make three stacking bowls from stainless steel, nothing could be further from the truth, for the designs' complex shape – curved on the top and with a knocked-in end – proved to be devilishly difficult to produce. Thanks to the manufacturing know-how of both the Robert Welch design team and the highly skilled craftsmen they work with, the technical challenges presented by this design were eventually overcome. The result is clearly more than worth all the painstaking trouble.

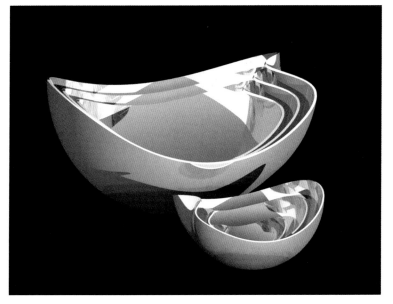

Designer:	Ruth Williams
Material:	Bright-finish stainless steel
Production:	From 2011 to present, Robert Welch Designs, Chipping Campden

Windrush candlesticks, 2007–8

This candlestick is named after the River Windrush, a tributary of the River Thames, which rises very close to Chipping Campden and winds through the Cotswolds. It is intended to recall the movement of running water with its dynamic flowing lines. Ingeniously, the candlestick can be used either as an individual piece, or interlocked to create a truly stunning candelabrum. The designer, Ruth Williams, recalls that the design came about relatively quickly, as once she had conceived the basic idea she enjoyed creating the flowing shapes that enabled them to interlock, thereby 'harking back to organic forms in nature'.[114] She also wanted to create a candlestick that allowed the user a degree of interaction, and the symbolism of two candlesticks intertwined has ensured that the design has become a popular wedding gift. In fact, up to three candlesticks can be interlocked, although arguably they look equally stunning when placed in a row on a windowsill or mantelpiece.

Designer:	Ruth Williams
Material:	Bright-finish stainless steel
Production:	From 2009 to present, Robert Welch Designs, Chipping Campden

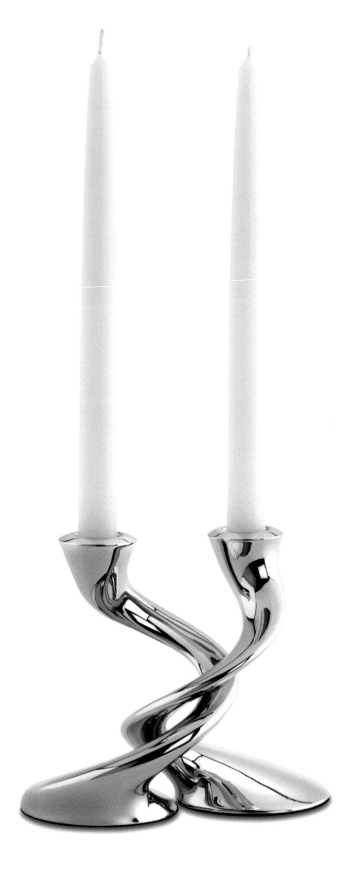

Molton candlesticks, 2007–9

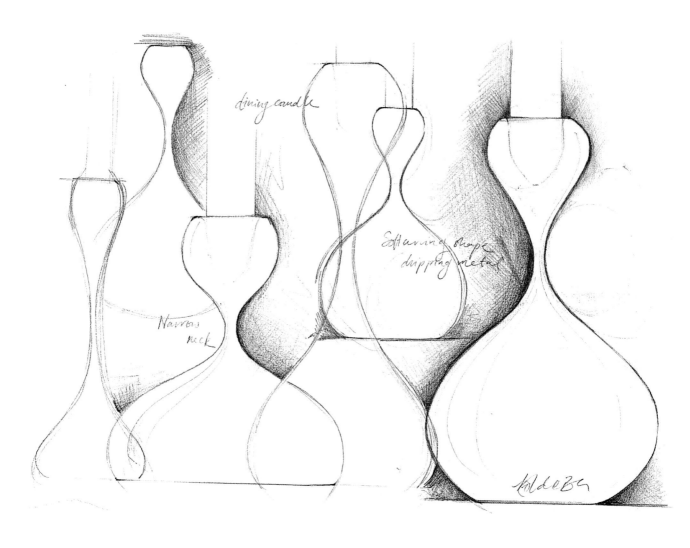

dining candle

Narrow neck

Softening shape dripping metal

Intended, as their designer Kit deBretton Gordon says, 'to emulate a piece of molten metal', the Molton candlesticks evoke pooling droplets. The idea for the range was to make a collection of interesting related but not matching shapes. The medium-sized candlestick was the first to be designed by deBretton Gordon and then she developed the larger model, while her colleague Ruth Williams came up with the related shape for the tealight holder. Like so many objects produced by the team at Robert Welch Designs, these beautiful and shapely mercury-like candlesticks technically pushed the factory that manufactures them, for each piece is made of a number of sections that are seam-welded together before being polished to a mirror-like finish. As deBretton Gordon notes, 'we only work with very skilled craftsmen and we are not trend-based. We want our designs to last forever and never to date, and the only way to do this is to develop shapes that are contemporary yet classical.'[115]

Above: Preliminary drawing by Kit deBretton Gordon of the Molton candlesticks, ca. 2007

Designers:	Kit deBretton Gordon (tall and medium candlestick); Ruth Williams (tealight holder)
Material:	Bright-finish stainless steel, glass
Production:	Medium candlestick from 2009 to present, tall candlestick and tealight holder from 2010 to present, Robert Welch Designs, Chipping Campden

Clove tealight holder, 2008

During the late 2000s and early 2010s, Ruth Williams was responsible for the design of many of the 'living products' launched by Robert Welch Designs, including these small but perfectly formed tealight holders. With their distinctive curved elliptical form they have a strong sculptural presence, despite their diminutive size. Like other designs by Williams, several tealight holders can be used together to create different groupings, but at the same time a single one works well too. When six are grouped together in a petal-like pattern, they look like the Chinese spice known as star anise, and this is what led the design to be christened with its suitably spicy name, Clove.

Designer:	Ruth Williams
Material:	Bright-finish stainless steel
Production:	From 2009 to present, Robert Welch Designs, Chipping Campden

Left: Two different groupings of Clove tealight holders

Designed by Ruth Williams, the Sesame tealight holders come in two different sizes and work either individually or as a visually striking pair. Although they are relatively simple in form, it took quite a while to settle on a suitable pattern for the pierced holes. After a lot of deliberation, the slotted pattern that had been previously developed by Paul deBretton Gordon for his Signature utensils collection (see page 183) was adapted to create the distinctive sesame-seed-like pattern used on the tealight holders. Allowing the light to scatter playfully, the Sesame tealight holders produce a warm glow that brightens even the coldest and darkest of nights – and as such they have a very Scandinavian flavour, which recalls Robert Welch's earlier products inspired by Nordic design.

Designer:	Ruth Williams
Material:	Bright-finish stainless steel
Production:	From 2009, Robert Welch Designs, Chipping Campden

Nest candelabrum, 2008

In 2008 Alice Welch wrote a design brief for a new candelabrum that would function as a statement piece but not take up too much space on a table. The resulting design by Kit deBretton Gordon took the form of a bowl-like 'nesting' structure with a unique central element made up of three curved arms, flanked by two similar, though shorter, outer arms. Viewed from different angles, the Nest candelabrum produces a host of interesting optical effects with its geometric curves and mirror-like reflections. The design pushed technical boundaries, and proved to be extremely complicated to manufacture, yet as with so many pieces produced by Robert Welch Designs, it gives the impression of effortless rightness. As this visually striking and highly sculptural centrepiece demonstrates, often simplicity in design is actually very complex to achieve.

Designer:	Kit deBretton Gordon
Material:	Bright-finish stainless steel
Production:	From 2009 to present, Robert Welch Designs, Chipping Campden

This range of elegant salt and pepper mills was originally intended to complement the Signature utensil stand and knife block (see pages 183–7) that were also designed by Paul deBretton Gordon. The refined simplicity of the products' form was informed first and foremost by function, with the domed top fitting comfortably into the hand and making the mills not only a pleasure to use but also easy to clean. Available in three sizes, they have an easy-to-remove pull-off top and a wide neck that enables effortless filling with either peppercorns or sea-salt crystals, or indeed dried herbs or spices, while the corrosion-proof CrushGrind™ ceramic mechanism can be adjusted using a concealed knob to regulate the precise size of granule. So durable that they have a lifetime guarantee, the mills have also received a Good Design Award from the Chicago Athenaeum, a Red Dot Award and an Excellence in Housewares Award – accolades that attest to their ingeniously simplified form and excellent functionality.

Designer:	Paul deBretton Gordon
Materials:	Bright-finish stainless steel, POM (polyoxymethylene), ceramic mechanism
Production:	From 2011 to present, Robert Welch Designs, Chipping Campden

Burford bathroom accessories, 2009

One of Robert Welch Designs' longest and most loyal clients has been the John Lewis Partnership: this creatively fruitful relationship has endured for many decades. In the late 2000s John Lewis's bathroom-ware buyer Leo Tye suggested that Robert Welch Designs should create a premium bathroom-ware range, which the partnership could sell in its department stores across the country. Kit deBretton Gordon was tasked with this undertaking, and she came up with a capsule collection of seven bathroom accessories, ranging from a toothbrush holder and soap dish to a vanity mirror and a soap dispenser. Rather than using chrome-plated brass, as most designs of this nature do, bright-finish stainless steel was adopted, which is far more durable. Likewise, the toilet brush was designed so that the brush element could be easily replaced, thereby increasing the product's life. Launched in 2010 as the Burford range, the collection proved to be so successful that John Lewis subsequently asked for a complementary range of bathroom fittings to be developed too.

Designer:	Kit deBretton Gordon
Materials:	Bright-finish stainless steel (mirrored glass and POM where applicable)
Production:	From 2010 to present, Robert Welch Designs, Chipping Campden

Below: Sketch by Kit deBretton Gordon of the different designs in the Burford range (including fittings), ca. 2009

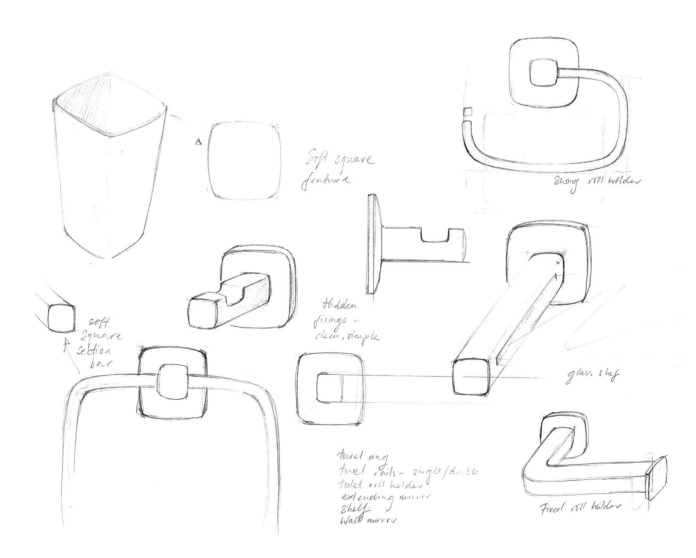

Bud cutlery, 2009

In the late 2000s Alice Welch decided that, with the emergence of more sophisticated types of dining, a new, elegantly refined cutlery range ought to be introduced into the Robert Welch product line. As Kit deBretton Gordon recalls, the brief was for 'an elongated cutlery that was bud-like and with a feminine aspect that would make it

suitable for fine dining ... I loved doing it, it was so unlike anything we had ever done before'.[116] Nevertheless, it took many painstaking months to develop the shape so that the subtle curve of the stem-like handles tapered comfortably into the hand. Bud's flowing organic lines, inspired by the buds of lotus flowers and water-lilies, set it apart from other slender-handled cutlery patterns, for it unequivocally captures the abstract essence of nature with its formal beauty. The range received a Red Dot design award in 2010.

Below Left: Early preliminary sketch by Kit deBretton Gordon related to the development of the Bud cutlery range, 2008

Designer:	Kit deBretton Gordon
Material:	Bright-finish stainless steel
Production:	From 2011 to present, Robert Welch Designs, Chipping Campden

Below: Preliminary design sketch by Kit deBretton Gordon of the Molton cutlery range, ca. 2011

The design of cutlery is one of the most specialized areas of design practice – for a fork or knife, if it is to be truly successful must work almost like a prosthetic aid. In order to design eating tools that are in harmony with the human hand, one must understand the subtle nuances of form and balance, and their complex interrelationship with ergonomics. Kit deBretton Gordon is such a designer, a veritable maestro of cutlery design. Her Molton set was inspired by the fluidity of molten metal and was designed to emphasize the unique material properties of stainless steel. With their curved lines and soft edges, the pieces were designed so that they not only feel comfortable in the hand, but also give the appearance of wrapping around a plate on a table setting.

Designer:	Kit deBretton Gordon
Material:	Bright-finish stainless steel
Production:	From 2013 to present, Robert Welch Designs, Chipping Campden

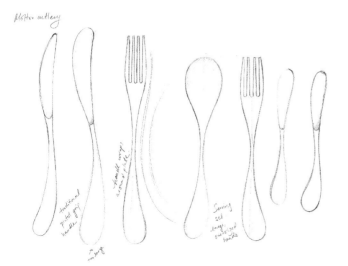

Drift jugs, 2012

As Kit and Paul deBretton Gordon recall, the Drift jugs 'were very much a team effort and the initial production was a nightmare because the design was so difficult to make'.[117] To start with, about 90 per cent of the production was rejected because it did not come up to scratch; since then the production problems have been more or less ironed out. The main reason for these teething problems was that these sculptural and size-graduated jugs, which are intended to function as 'serveware', have a relatively complex form that demands a high degree of skill to produce. Rupert Welch explains that when something is difficult to produce, there is often the fortuitous although unintended up-side in that it is much less likely to be copied, since when someone is trying to copy a design, if it is too much trouble they simply give up. Winning a 'Top of the Table' Excellence in Housewares Award in 2013,

and an iF product design award the following year, the Drift jugs were designed to function perfectly with their well-balanced handles, non-drip spouts, stable bases and ability to hold both hot and cold liquids. What draws the eye, however, is their soft, tactile curves and subtle yet contrasting finishes, with a mirror-like bright finish on the outside and a dull matt satin finish inside. It is this kind of meticulous attention to detail that sets such designs apart.

Designer:	Ruth Williams
Material:	Bright-finish and satin-finish stainless steel
Production:	From 2013 to present, Robert Welch Designs, Chipping Campden

Many of the products manufactured by Robert Welch Designs are conceived in collections, embracing a variety of stylistically related designs that share the same 'family' name. This practice harks back to Robert's naming of products he created for Old Hall all those years ago. Today, the company's impressive portfolio contains several designs that bear the name Arden, including this beautiful bowl. The idea for the design was prompted by the American retailer Crate & Barrel, which having successfully sold the elegant Arden candlesticks, asked whether a fruit bowl could be created to complement these striking designs. Ruth Williams worked on the initial sketches of the bowl, and then the rest of the design team developed it to production stage. Essentially very plain, it is turned into a stunningly beautiful piece by the addition of a chamfered edge and a striking concentric motif at its centre that induces happy memories of water rippling outwards in a pond. It is this type of evocative design language that provokes an almost subliminal emotional engagement between object and user.

Designer:	Robert Welch design team
Material:	Bright-finish stainless steel
Production:	From 2012 to present, Robert Welch Designs, Chipping Campden

Signature cookbook and tablet stand, 2012

Over the years Robert Welch's cast-iron cookbook stand has been a popular and useful item in many British homes. Yet times have changed, and people are increasingly using their electronic tablets to search for recipes online, so it was felt by the design team that a new kind of stand was needed for today's home cooks. Such a design would need to hold various sizes of book, any size tablet or even a single sheet of paper securely; also, it would need to be easily assembled and dismantled for compact storage when not in use, as well as being angle-adjustable for easy reading. The space-saving design created by Kit and Paul deBretton Gordon as an ingenious solution to this demanding brief is not only highly functional but also sleek and stylish when assembled. With a clear polycarbonate arm as a page holder and incorporating two strong magnets to hold single pages securely, the award-winning design, though originally intended for cooks, has become a firm favourite among musicians too.

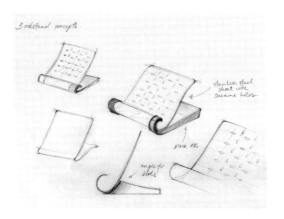

Left: Preliminary drawing by Kit deBretton Gordon showing various design ideas for the Signature stand, 2012

Designer:	Kit deBretton Gordon and Paul deBretton Gordon
Materials:	Bright-finish stainless steel, ABS, acrylic, magnets
Production:	From 2014 to present, Robert Welch Designs, Chipping Campden

Signature household scissors and stand, 2013

Right: Signature household scissors being stored in their matching stand

The design of the Signature scissors was the result of intensive research undertaken by Paul deBretton Gordon and Rupert Welch into what design elements are really needed to make a good pair of scissors. Using the state-of-the-art blade-testing facilities at the Cutlery Allied Trades Research Association (CATRA) in Sheffield, they analysed the characteristics of the finest professional task-specific scissors available and found that if blades were ground in a certain way they produced a far more effective cut. Using this data, they incorporated into the design of the Signature scissors similarly precision-engineered blades that cut effortlessly through a wide selection of household materials. Likewise, the ergonomic handles were designed to fit as comfortably in the hand as possible, while the matching black tapering stand is an attractive yet useful storage solution for when the scissors are not in use.

Designer:	Paul deBretton Gordon
Materials:	Stainless steel, POM (polyoxymethylene)
Production:	From 2014 to present, Robert Welch Designs, Chipping Campden

Contour steak knives, 2013

In France there is a long tradition of using beautifully crafted wooden-handled steak knives, and the design of the Contour knife was a very British response to this type of premium cutlery. Featuring hand-finished oiled-walnut handles and traditional stainless-steel rivets, it also incorporates a sharp serrated full-tang blade angled to provide optimum cutting performance, yet when the knife is laid on a table the edge of the blade does not come into contact with the table-top surface, thereby negating any possibility of scratching. Like other Robert Welch Designs cutlery, the Contour steak knife has been carefully designed to be ergonomic, so that – in contrast to other traditional-style steak knives – it fits comfortably into the hand.

Designer:	Paul deBretton Gordon
Materials:	Stainless steel, oiled walnut
Production:	From 2014 to present, Robert Welch Designs, Chipping Campden

Below: Publicity photograph showing the undulating lines of the Contour steak knife

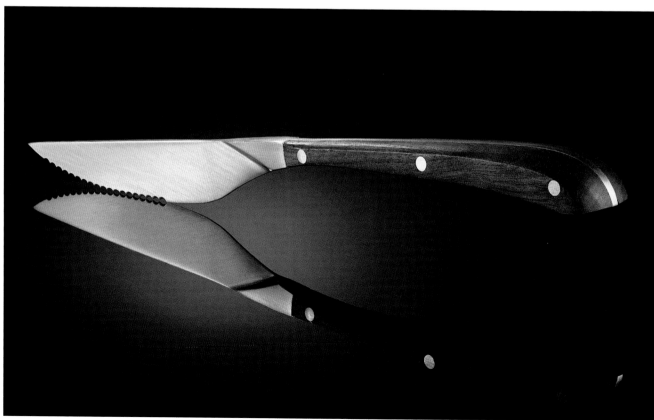

Signature storage jars, 2014

Now running the company that bears their father's name, Rupert and Alice Welch conscientiously maintain his commitment to innovative design, and are constantly encouraging their design team to push the boundaries aesthetically and functionally but also in terms of production. A case in point is the Signature storage jars. The idea at first was to produce a set of cylindrical jars that could stack, but through trial and error Kit deBretton Gordon determined that an elliptical base would in fact work far better as it could not be misaligned and therefore unstably stacked. Similarly, instead of polycarbonate, a different BPA-free co-polyester plastic was employed, which is far safer to use with foodstuffs while still being impact-proof and scratch-resistant. It was, however, the airtight silicone seal that proved the most difficult element to get right, and it took a huge amount of effort to ensure that it produced just the right noise and feel. While one usually registers such details only on a subconscious level, that type of haptic feedback is actually what elevates the experience of a product from the everyday to the deeply satisfying.

Below: Drawing by Kit deBretton Gordon detailing the stacking of the Signature storage jars, 2014

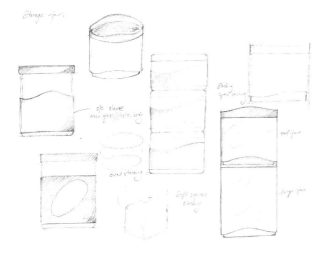

Designer:	Kit deBretton Gordon
Materials:	Tritan (co-polyester), polypropylene, silicone rubber, bright-finish stainless steel
Production:	From 2014 to present, Robert Welch Designs, Chipping Campden

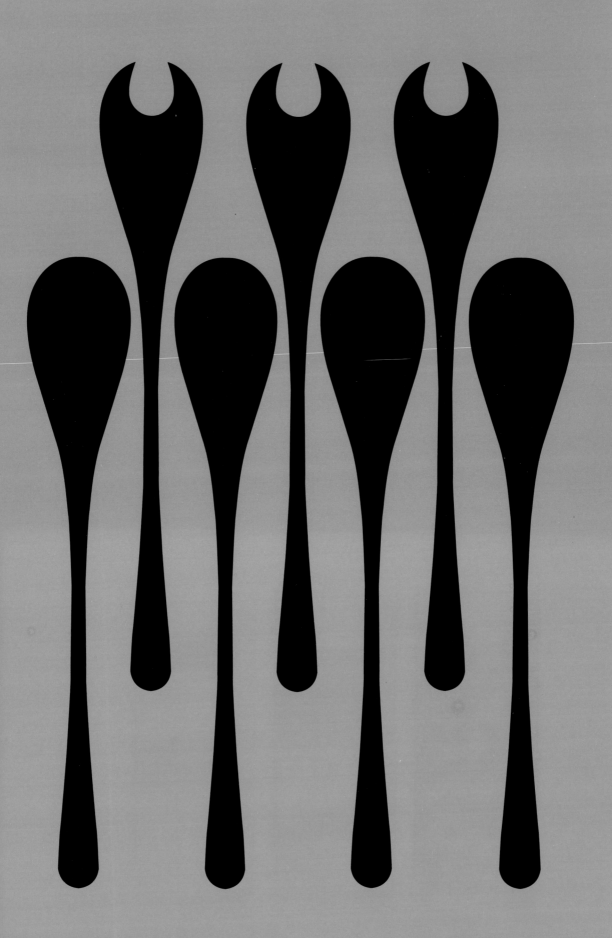

Selected additional designs

Selected additional designs:

Industrial Design – Products

Companion set, ca. 1958

Designer: Robert Welch

Materials: Cast iron, brass, wood

Production: Prototype

Manufacturer: Robert Welch, Chipping Campden

From 1960 onwards, most industrial designs were credited to Robert Welch Associates to recognize the contribution of others in his design team

Lynton washbasin, 1959–60

Designer: Robert Welch (in conjunction with Doulton's staff designer)

Materials: Glazed ceramic

Production: From ca. 1960

Manufacturer: Doulton Sanitary Potteries Ltd, Stoke-on-Trent, Staffordshire

One of several washbasins created for Doulton, Robert also designed other bathroom ceramics for Ideal Standard and Doulton Sanitaryware

Rocking horse, 1960

Designer: Robert Welch Associates

Materials: Plastic, metal

Production: Prototype

Manufacturer: Jury Holloware, Brierley Hill, Staffordshire

One of several experimental designs made from a new plastic known as Alkathene (low-density polyethylene)

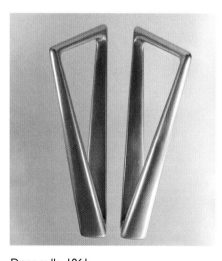

Door pulls, 1961

Designer: Robert Welch Associates

Materials: Anodized aluminium

Production: From ca. 1961

Manufacturer: Yannedis & Co., London

From a range of architectural fittings, including hospital door pulls, designed ca. 1961-2

Lawnmower grassbox attachment, 1961

Designer: Robert Welch Associates

Materials: Thermoplastic

Production: From ca. 1961

Manufacturer: Jury Holloware, Brierley Hill, Staffordshire for Qualcast, Wolverhampton

1001 carpet shampooer, 1962

Designer: Robert Welch Associates

Materials: Plastic, metal

Production: From 1962

Manufacturer: Hygiene Plastics, Parr Bridge Works, nr. Manchester

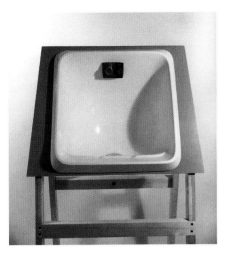

Washbasin for British Railways, 1960–1

Designer:	Robert Welch Associates
Materials:	Fibreglass, metal
Production:	Prototype
Manufacturer:	British Transport Commission, London

Lavatory for British Railways 1960–1

Designer:	Robert Welch Associates
Materials:	Fibreglass, metal
Production:	Prototype
Manufacturer:	British Transport Commission, London

Baby's bath, 1961

Designer:	Robert Welch Associates
Materials:	Plastic, metal, wood
Production:	Prototype
Manufacturer:	Jury Holloware, Brierley Hill, Staffordshire

One of several experimental designs made from a new plastic known as Alkathene (low-density polyethylene)

Beer pump, 1963

Designer:	Robert Welch Associates
Materials:	Stainless steel, plastic
Production:	Prototype
Manufacturer:	Guinness, Dublin

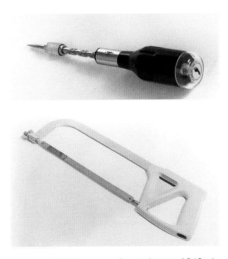

Footprint Tools screwdriver & saw, 1963–4

Designer:	Robert Welch Associates
Materials:	Steel, moulded plastic
Production:	From 1963–4
Manufacturer:	Thomas R. Ellin, Footprint Works, Hollis Croft, Sheffield

Garden spade, 1964

Designer:	Robert Welch Associates
Materials:	Tempered steel, plastic, elm
Production:	From 1964
Manufacturer:	Edward Elwell, Wednesbury, Staffordshire

Selected additional designs:

Industrial Design – Products

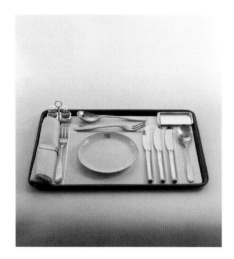

BOAC first-class inflight service, ca. 1965

Designer:	Robert Welch Associates
Materials:	Various
Production:	Prototype
Manufacturer:	Various for British Overseas Airways Corporation, (BOAC) London

Prinz kettle, 1966–7

Designer:	Robert Welch Associates
Materials:	Vitreous enamelled steel, stainless steel, plastic
Production:	From ca. 1968
Manufacturer:	Carl Prinz, Solingen, Germany

Prinz fondue set, ca. 1968

Designer:	Robert Welch Associates
Materials:	Stove-enamelled steel, wood
Production:	From ca. 1968
Manufacturer:	Carl Prinz, Solingen, Germany

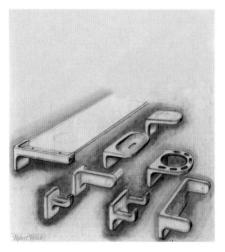

Albany bathroom fittings, 1976

Designer:	Robert Welch Associates
Materials:	Chromed or enamelled die-cast metal
Production:	From ca. 1977
Manufacturer:	Adie & Nephew, Birmingham (later by Celmac, Denton, Manchester)

Simplan architectural fittings, 1977

Designer:	Robert Welch Associates
Materials:	Extruded aluminium, cast aluminium
Production:	From 1977
Manufacturer:	Dryad Metal Works, Leicester

Denovo car tyre tread, 1978

Designer:	Robert Welch Associates
Materials:	Rubber
Production:	Prototype
Manufacturer:	Dunlop Tyres, Birmingham

Drawing compass, 1971

Designer: Robert Welch Associates

Materials: Enamelled metal, steel

Production: From ca. 1973

Manufacturer: W.J. Harris, Birmingham

Kitchen utensils, ca. 1971

Designer: Robert Welch Associates

Materials: Stainless steel, plastic

Production: Prototype

Manufacturer: H.E. Lauffer, New Jersey, USA

Tableware, ca. 1971

Designer: Robert Welch Associates

Materials: Ceramic, glass, enamelled cast iron

Production: Prototypes (cast-iron casserole produced)

Manufacturer: H.E. Lauffer, New Jersey, USA

Campden tableware, 1986–8

Designer: Robert Welch

Materials: Glazed earthenware

Production: From ca. 1988

Manufacturer: Poole Pottery, Poole, Dorset

Brunel coffee table, ca. 1998

Designer: Robert Welch

Materials: Enamelled steel, chrome tubular steel, wood

Production: From 1999

Manufacturer: Robert Welch Designs, Chipping Campden

The entire Brunel range, which included not only this table but various architectural fixture and fittings, was ingeniously made up using existing 'off-the-shelf' components

Virgin Atlantic inflight service, 2010–11

Designer: Paul deBretton Gordon

Materials: Stainless steel, glazed ceramic

Production: Production from 2011

Manufacturer: Robert Welch Designs, Chipping Campden

Selected additional designs:

Industrial Design – Clocks

Benita table clock, 1956–7

Designer:	Robert Welch
Materials:	Enamelled metal, glass
Production:	Prototype
Manufacturer:	Westclox, Dumbarton, Scotland

Believed to be Robert Welch's first design for Westclox

Mantelpiece clock, ca. 1959

Designer:	Robert Welch Associates
Materials:	Enamelled metal, glass
Production:	Prototype
Manufacturer:	Westclox, Dumbarton, Scotland

Wall clock, 1960

Designer:	Robert Welch Associates
Materials:	Ceramic
Production:	Prototype (1 of 2 face designs)
Manufacturer:	Westclox, Dumbarton, Scotland

Ritz wall clock, 1965

Designer:	Robert Welch Associates
Materials:	Brass, glass
Production:	From 1965
Manufacturer:	Westclox, Dumbarton, Scotland

Table clock, ca. 1965

Designer:	Robert Welch Associates
Materials:	Plastic, acrylic
Production:	Prototype
Manufacturer:	N/A

This model was inspired by Angelo Mangiarotti's Secticon range of clocks, an example of which was displayed on the mantelpiece of The White House, the Welches' family home.

Computim digital wall/desk clocks, 1969

Designer:	Robert Welch Associates
Materials:	Plastic
Production:	From 1969
Manufacturer:	Anglo Continental Clock Co, Newport Pagnell, Buckinghamshire

Astoria wall clock, ca. 1962

Designer: Robert Welch Associates

Materials: Enamelled metal, brass, glass

Production: From ca. 1962

Manufacturer: Westclox, Dumbarton, Scotland

Part of Westclox's Décor range, this electric or battery operated model was available in white, red and blue

Clearcall alarm clock, 1964

Designer: Robert Welch Associates

Materials: Plastic, acrylic

Production: From 1961–72 (modified in 1972)

Manufacturer: Columbia Division of General Time Corporation, USA,

A 'repeater' model, the Clearcall had an extra loud alarm for the hard of hearing

Melody alarm clock, 1964

Designer: Robert Welch Associates

Materials: Plastic, acrylic

Production: From 1964

Manufacturer: Westclox, Dumbarton, Scotland

Part of Westclox's Décor range, this electric or battery operated model was available in white, red and blue

Geneva table clock, 1972

Designer: Robert Welch

Materials: Cast iron

Production: From 1972

Manufacturer: Westclox Division of General Time Corporation, USA

The cog-like form of this clock face recalls the logo of Campden Designs. A wall version of this model was also produced.

Wall clock, ca. 1978

Designer: Robert Welch

Materials: Plastic (available in red or green)

Production: From ca.1978

Manufacturer: Westclox Division of General Time Corporation, USA

Wall clock, ca. 1989-90

Designer: Robert Welch

Materials: Cast iron

Production: From ca. 1990

Manufacturer: Victor Cast Ware, Telford, Shropshire

Selected additional designs:

Industrial Design – Lighting

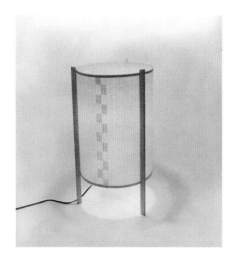

Table light, ca. 1955

Designer: Robert Welch (attributed)

Materials: Wood, textile/paper

Production: One-off (handmade)

Manufacturer: Robert Welch, Chipping Campden

Adjustable table light, 1958

Designer: Robert Welch

Materials: Enamelled metal, glass

Production: Prototype

Manufacturer: Francis Mackmin, London

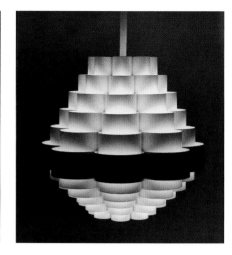

Pendant light, 1960s

Designer: Robert Welch

Materials: Unknown

Production: Prototype

Manufacturer: N/A

Consulate pendant light, 1973

Designer: Robert Welch

Materials: Stainless steel, enamelled steel, glass

Production: From 1973

Manufacturer: Lumitron, London

Desk light, ca. 1985

Designer: Robert Welch

Materials: Enamelled metal, tubular metal

Production: Prototype

Manufacturer: Robert Welch, Chipping Campden

November uplighter, 1990

Designer: Robert Welch

Materials: Chrome- and gold-plated wrought iron

Production: From 1990

Manufacturer: Chad Lighting, Birmingham

Pendant light, 1960s

Designer:	Robert Welch
Materials:	Unknown
Production:	Prototype
Manufacturer:	N/A

Chandelier, 1971

Designer:	Robert Welch
Materials:	Cast aluminium, glass
Production:	1971 (special one-off commission)
Manufacturer:	Robert Welch Studio for Browne's Hospital, Stamford, Lincolnshire

Consulate table light, 1973

Designer:	Robert Welch
Materials:	Stainless steel, glass
Production:	Prototype
Manufacturer:	Lumitron, London

Dryad table light, 1991

Designer:	Robert Welch
Materials:	Verdigris-, copper-, black-finish wrought iron
Production:	From 1992
Manufacturer:	Chad Lighting, Birmingham

Apollo table light, ca. 1998

Designer:	Robert Welch
Materials:	Stainless steel, enamelled steel
Production:	From 1999
Manufacturer:	Chad Lighting, Birmingham

Arden table light, 2007

Designer:	Kit deBretton Gordon
Materials:	Satin-finish stainless steel, textile
Production:	From 2007
Manufacturer:	Robert Welch Designs, Chipping Campden

Industrial Design – Cast Ware

Wynton Contracts ashtray, 1960

Designer: Robert Welch

Materials: Cast iron, aluminium

Production: From ca. 1961

Manufacturer: Loxwyn Ltd, West Bromwich for Peter Cuddon Furniture, Bristol

CD40 candlesticks, 1963

Designer: Robert Welch

Materials: Cast iron

Production: From 1963 (small batch production)

Manufacturer: Campden Designs, Chipping Campden, later by Victor Cast Wares, Telford, Shropshire

This oversized 'jumbo' candlestick was only produced in limited numbers, shown with smaller CD50 'Hobart' candlestick for scale.

CD55 candelabrum, 1964

Designer: Robert Welch

Materials: Cast iron

Production: From ca. 1964

Manufacturer: Campden Designs, Chipping Campden, later by Victor Cast Wares, Telford, Shropshire

Campden Design casseroles, 1967

Designer: Robert Welch

Materials: Enamelled cast iron

Production: From ca. 1965

Manufacturer: Campden Designs, Chipping Campden

Trinket box, match holder, ashtray, ca. 1967

Designer: Robert Welch

Materials: Cast iron

Production: Match holder: prototype / trinket box and RW75 ashtray: from ca.1967

Manufacturer: Campden Designs, Chipping Campden

RW55 candleholder and tablelighter, ca. 1969

Designer: Robert Welch

Materials: Cast iron

Production: From ca. 1970

Manufacturer: Campden Designs, Chipping Campden, later by Victor Cast Wares, Telford, Shropshire

Salt Cellar and CD90 pepper mill, 1964

Designer: Robert Welch

Materials: Cast iron, wood

Production: From ca. 1964

Manufacturer: Campden Designs, Chipping Campden, later by Victor Cast Wares, Telford, Shropshire

CD22 two-branch candleholder, ca. 1965

Designer: Robert Welch

Materials: Cast iron

Production: From ca. 1965

Manufacturer: Campden Designs, Chipping Campden, later by Victor Cast Wares, Telford, Shropshire

CD125 and CD130 Sundishes, 1966

Designer: Robert Welch

Materials: Cast iron

Production: From ca. 1966

Manufacturer: Campden Designs, Chipping Campden, later by Victor Cast Wares, Telford, Shropshire

New Generation cookware, 1969

Designer: Robert Welch

Materials: Cast iron, wood

Production: Prototype

Manufacturer: N/A

RW205 weathervane, ca. 1970

Designer: Robert Welch

Materials: Cast aluminium

Production: From ca. 1970

Manufacturer: Victor Cast Ware, Telford, Shropshire for Robert Welch Designs, Chipping Campden

Candleholder, 1971

Designer: Robert Welch

Materials: Cast iron

Production: Prototype

Manufacturer: H.E. Lauffer, New Jersey, USA

One of several decorative cast iron designs for Lauffer, it is unknown if these were ever put into production.

Selected additional designs:

Industrial Design – Cast Ware

RW130 coffee mill, 1975

Designer:	Robert Welch
Materials:	Cast iron, aluminium, wood (later ceramic)
Production:	From 1976
Manufacturer:	Victor Cast Ware, Telford, Shropshire

RW120 trivet, 1975

Designer:	Robert Welch
Materials:	Cast iron
Production:	From 1976
Manufacturer:	Victor Cast Ware, Telford, Shropshire

RW200 barbeque grill plate, 1975

Designer:	Robert Welch
Materials:	Cast iron (shown using two bricks)
Production:	From 1976
Manufacturer:	Victor Cast Ware, Telford, Shropshire

RW185 pestle and mortar, 1976

Designer:	Robert Welch
Materials:	Cast iron
Production:	From 1976
Manufacturer:	Victor Cast Ware, Telford, Shropshire

Contemporary (RW350) scales, 1982

Designer:	Robert Welch
Materials:	Stove-enamelled cast iron, brass
Production:	From 1984
Manufacturer:	Victor Cast Ware, Telford, Shropshire

Meat mincer / coffee grinder, 1983

Designer:	Robert Welch
Materials:	Cast iron, steel, wood
Production:	From ca. 1984
Manufacturer:	Victor Cast Ware, Telford, Shropshire

RW140 tongue press, 1976

Designer: Robert Welch

Materials: Cast iron, aluminium (later ceramic)

Production: From 1976

Manufacturer: Victor Cast Ware, Telford, Shropshire

Later in the 1980s a ceramic bowl was introduced and the design was subsequently marketed as a meat or pudding press

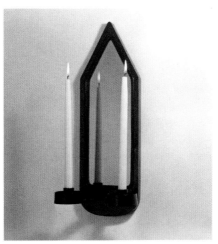

RW150 wall sconce, 1976

Designer: Robert Welch

Materials: Cast aluminium, mirror

Production: From 1976

Manufacturer: Victor Cast Ware, Telford, Shropshire

RW190 chandelier, 1976

Designer: Robert Welch

Materials: Cast aluminium

Production: From 1976

Manufacturer: Victor Cast Ware, Telford, Shropshire

RW380 tape dispenser, 1984

Designer: Robert Welch

Materials: Stove-enamelled cast iron

Production: From 1985

Manufacturer: Victor Cast Ware, Telford, Shropshire

Memo board, ca. 1984

Designer: Robert Welch

Materials: Cast iron

Production: From ca. 1985

Manufacturer: Victor Cast Ware, Telford, Shropshire

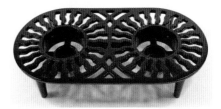

Table heaters, ca. 1984 & 1988

Designer: Robert Welch

Materials: Stove-enamelled cast iron

Production: From 1989

Manufacturer: Victor Cast Ware, Telford, Shropshire

Selected additional designs:

Industrial Design – Cast Ware

RW330 egg timer, 1984

Designer:	Robert Welch
Materials:	Cast iron, glass, sand
Production:	From ca. 1984
Manufacturer:	Victor Cast Ware, Telford, Shropshire

Two sizes of this design were produced, the larger for 3 minute 'runny egg' boiling, and the smaller for 5 minute 'soft egg' boiling

RW910 garlic press, 1988

Designer:	Robert Welch
Materials:	Cast iron, aluminium
Production:	From 1989
Manufacturer:	Victor Cast Ware, Telford, Shropshire

RW906 / RW905 salt/pepper mill, 1988

Designer:	Robert Welch
Materials:	Cast iron, brass
Production:	From 1989
Manufacturer:	Victor Cast Ware, Telford, Shropshire

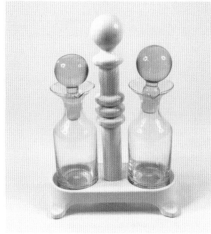

Liberty weighing scales, 1993

Designer:	Robert Welch
Materials:	Cast iron
Production:	From ca. 1993
Manufacturer:	Victor Cast Ware, Telford, Shropshire

Oil and vinegar stand, 1995

Designer:	Robert Welch
Materials:	Stove-enamelled cast iron, glass
Production:	From ca. 1995
Manufacturer:	Victor Cast Ware, Telford, Shropshire

Mug tree and kitchen roll holder, 1995

Designer:	Robert Welch
Materials:	Stove-enamelled cast iron
Production:	From ca. 1995
Manufacturer:	Victor Cast Ware, Telford, Shropshire

RW920 Owl string holder, 1990

Designer:	Robert Welch
Materials:	Cast iron, steel
Production:	From ca. 1990
Manufacturer:	Victor Cast Ware, Telford, Shropshire

RW930 Bull corkscrew and stand, 1990

Designer:	Robert Welch
Materials:	Cast iron, steel
Production:	From ca. 1990
Manufacturer:	Victor Cast Ware, Telford, Shropshire

RW970 nutmeg grater, 1992

Designer:	Robert Welch
Materials:	Cast iron, steel, brass
Production:	From 1993
Manufacturer:	Victor Cast Ware, Telford, Shropshire

Spice and herb carousel, 1995

Designer:	Robert Welch
Materials:	Cast iron, brass
Production:	From ca. 1995
Manufacturer:	Victor Cast Ware, Telford, Shropshire

Sea Drift doorstop, 1997

Designer:	Robert Welch
Materials:	Cast iron
Production:	From 1997
Manufacturer:	Deeleys Castings, Walsall for Robert Welch Designs, Chipping Campden

Sea Drift candelabrum, 1997

Designer:	Robert Welch
Materials:	Cast iron
Production:	From 1997
Manufacturer:	Deeleys Castings, Walsall for Robert Welch Designs, Chipping Campden

Selected additional designs:

Industrial Design – Stainless Steel

Darwin cake knife, 1953

Designer:	Robert Welch
Materials:	Stainless steel, gilding, acrylic
Production:	One-off
Manufacturer:	Student piece while at RCA

Condiment set, 1957

Designer:	Robert Welch
Materials:	Stainless steel, teak
Production:	Prototype
Manufacturer:	Old Hall Tableware, Bloxwich, Staffordshire

Campden condiment set, 1957

Designer:	Robert Welch
Materials:	Satin-finish stainless steel
Production:	From 1967 to 1968
Manufacturer:	Old Hall Tableware, Bloxwich, Staffordshire

Also known as model no. 41220

SonA kettle, 1960

Designer:	Robert Welch
Materials:	Stainless steel, plastic
Production:	Prototype
Manufacturer:	N.C. Joseph, Stafford-upon-Avon

The National Industrial Design Council of Canada awarded this kettle a Stainless Steel National Design Award in 1960

Dumpy (model no. 42831) sugar sifter, 1962

Designer:	Robert Welch (attributed)
Materials:	Satin-finish stainless steel
Production:	From 1962 to 1984
Manufacturer:	Old Hall Tableware, Bloxwich, Staffordshire

This sifter is believed to be a sleek redesign by Robert Welch of an earlier Old Hall model

Model no. 42913 toast rack, 1962

Designer:	Robert Welch
Materials:	Satin-finish or bright-finish stainless steel
Production:	From 1962 to 1984
Manufacturer:	Old Hall Tableware, Bloxwich, Staffordshire

This design was a 6-slice evolution of the earlier award-winning Camden toast rack of 1956

Campden tea strainer, 1958

Designer: Robert Welch

Materials: Satin-finish stainless steel

Production: From 1958 to 1984

Manufacturer: Old Hall Tableware, Bloxwich,
Staffordshire
Also known as model no. 44810

Model no. 44241 candleholder, 1958

Designer: Robert Welch (attributed)

Materials: Satin-finish stainless steel

Production: From 1958 to 1971

Manufacturer: Old Hall Tableware, Bloxwich,
Staffordshire

Oriana ice bucket, 1958

Designer: Robert Welch

Materials: Satin-finish stainless steel

Production: From 1961 to 1984

Manufacturer: Old Hall Tableware, Bloxwich,
Staffordshire
Also known as model no. 43210 and shown with model
no. 43213 tongs. This design was later modified for the
catering trades (from 1961)

Alveston candlesticks, 1962

Designer: Robert Welch

Materials: Satin-finish stainless steel

Production: From 1962 to 1971

Manufacturer: Old Hall Tableware, Bloxwich,
Staffordshire
Left to right: model nos. 44211, 44212, 44213

Model no. 44231 candleholder, 1963

Designer: Robert Welch

Materials: Satin-finish stainless steel

Production: From 1963 to 1966

Manufacturer: Old Hall Tableware, Bloxwich,
Staffordshire
This design was also produced as a vase with a closed base

Model no. 44111 ashtray, 1963

Designer: Robert Welch

Materials: Bright-finish stainless steel, plastic

Production: From 1963 to 1981

Manufacturer: Old Hall Tableware, Bloxwich,
Staffordshire

Industrial Design – Stainless Steel

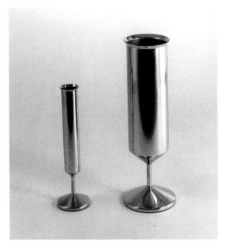

Alveston condiment set and dredger, 1963

Designer:	Robert Welch
Materials:	Satin-finish stainless steel, plastic
Production:	From 1963 to 1980
Manufacturer:	Old Hall Tableware, Bloxwich, Staffordshire

Also known as model nos. 41210 and 42821

Model no. 41370 hors d'oeuvres dish, 1964

Designer:	Robert Welch
Materials:	Stainless steel, teak
Production:	From 1964 to 1977
Manufacturer:	Old Hall Tableware, Bloxwich, Staffordshire

Alveston bud vase and flower vase, 1964

Designer:	Robert Welch
Materials:	Satin-finish stainless steel
Production:	From 1964 to 1972
Manufacturer:	Old Hall Tableware, Bloxwich, Staffordshire

Model nos. 45621 and 45611

Model no. 45811 preserve jar, 1968

Designer:	Robert Welch
Materials:	Satin-finish stainless steel, glass (liner)
Production:	From 1968 to 1984
Manufacturer:	Old Hall Tableware, Bloxwich, Staffordshire

Danesco kettle, 1974

Designer:	Robert Welch
Materials:	Stainless steel, plastic
Production:	Prototype
Manufacturer:	Danesco, London

Kettle, 1974

Designer:	Robert Welch
Materials:	Stainless steel, plastic
Production:	From 1974 to ca. 1982
Manufacturer:	Wejra, Skalborg, Denmark

The Danish manufacturer of this kettle was mainly involved in the production of munitions, and this design was an attempt at product line diversification.

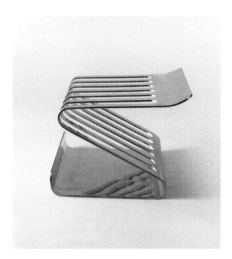

Toast rack, 1965

Designer: Robert Welch

Materials: Stainless steel

Production: Prototype (executed by John Limbrey)

Manufacturer: N/A

Butter dish and serving dish, 1967

Designer: Robert Welch

Materials: Satin-finish stainless steel

Production: From 1967 to 1978/1984

Manufacturer: Old Hall Tableware, Bloxwich, Staffordshire

Model nos. 42170 and 41976

Model no. 41200 condiment set, 1968

Designer: Robert Welch

Materials: Satin-finish stainless steel

Production: From 1968 to 1984

Manufacturer: Old Hall Tableware, Bloxwich, Staffordshire

Model no. 47400 candle lamp, ca. 1974

Designer: Robert Welch

Materials: Stainless steel, enamelled steel

Production: From 1975 to 1981

Manufacturer: Old Hall Tableware, Bloxwich, Staffordshire

Also offered with a smoked glass shade.

RWK 2250 candelabrum, 1992

Designer: Robert Welch

Materials: Bright-finish stainless steel, brass

Production: From ca. 1992

Manufacturer: B.D.K. Tableware, Walsall for Robert Welch Designs, Chipping Campden

Emirates napkin ring and sugar pot, 2012/14

Designer: Paul deBretton Gordon

Materials: Bright-finish stainless steel

Production: From 2012 and from 2014

Manufacturer: Robert Welch Designs, Chipping Campden

Industrial Design – Cutlery

Windrush cutlery, 1968

Designer:	Robert Welch
Materials:	Stainless steel or sterling silver
Production:	From 1970
Manufacturer:	Harrison Fisher, Sheffield

RW Child's Set, 1972

Designer:	Robert Welch
Materials:	Stainless steel
Production:	From ca. 1972
Manufacturer:	Harrison Fisher, Sheffield (later by Robert Welch Designs)

Twisted-handle cutlery, ca. 1975

Designer:	Robert Welch
Materials:	Sterling silver
Production:	From ca. 1975 (batch-production)
Manufacturer:	Robert Welch Studio, Chipping Campden

Fiddle cutlery, 1982

Designer:	Robert Welch
Materials:	Stainless steel
Production:	From ca. 1982
Manufacturer:	Yamazaki Kinzoku Kogyo, Niigata, Japan

Premier cutlery, 1984

Designer:	Robert Welch
Materials:	Sterling silver or stainless steel
Production:	From ca. 1984
Manufacturer:	Harrison Fisher, Sheffield for Villeroy and Boch's Courtier Collection

Merit cutlery, ca. 1987

Designer:	Robert Welch
Materials:	Stainless steel
Production:	From ca. 1987
Manufacturer:	Harrison Fisher, Sheffield for Villeroy and Boch's Courtier Collection

Calibre cutlery, 1979

Designer:	Robert Welch
Materials:	Stainless steel
Production:	From ca. 1979
Manufacturer:	Yamazaki Kinzoku Kogyo, Niigata, Japan

Wave cutlery, 1982

Designer:	Robert Welch
Materials:	Stainless steel, plastic
Production:	From ca. 1982
Manufacturer:	Yamazaki Kinzoku Kogyo, Niigata, Japan

Thames cutlery, ca. 1982

Designer:	Robert Welch
Materials:	Stainless steel
Production:	From ca. 1982
Manufacturer:	Ginkgo International, Woodridge, Illinois, USA

Dakota cutlery, 1987

Designer:	Robert Welch
Materials:	Stainless steel, gilding (or black-finish option)
Production:	From ca. 1987
Manufacturer:	Yamazaki Kinzoku Kogyo, Niigata,

Originally named Deco, this pattern reflects the strong influence of Post-Modernism with its playful reference of Art Deco-style ziggurat forms

Viceroy cutlery, 1987

Designer:	Robert Welch
Materials:	Stainless steel or sterling silver
Production:	From ca. 1987
Manufacturer:	Harrison Fisher, Sheffield for Villeroy and Boch's Courtier Collection

Ammonite Hollow cutlery, 1993–94

Designer:	Robert Welch
Materials:	Stainless steel
Production:	From 1995
Manufacturer:	Ginkgo International, Woodridge, Illinois, USA (later by Robert Welch Designs, Chipping Campden)

Industrial Design – Cutlery

Meridian cutlery, 1994

Designer:	Robert Welch
Materials:	Stainless steel
Production:	From ca. 1994
Manufacturer:	Ginkgo International, Woodridge, Illinois, USA

Sea Drift Hollow cutlery, 1996

Designer:	Robert Welch
Materials:	Stainless steel
Production:	From ca. 1996
Manufacturer:	Ginkgo International, Woodridge, Illinois, USA (later by Robert Welch Designs, Chipping Campden)

Trattoria Bright cutlery, 1996

Designer:	Robert Welch
Materials:	Stainless steel, POM (polyoyxmethylene)
Production:	From ca. 1996
Manufacturer:	Ginkgo International, Woodridge, Illinois, USA (later by Robert Welch Designs, Chipping Campden)

This dishwasher-proof range was based on the earlier wooden-handled Bistro pattern from ca. 1961

Torben Satin cutlery, 2006

Designer:	Ruth Williams
Materials:	Stainless steel
Production:	From 2007
Manufacturer:	Robert Welch Designs, Chipping Campden

This design was later adapted for inflight use in Virgin Atlantic's Upper Class cabins in 2011. A matching inflight ceramic tableware service was also created by Robert Welch Designs

Ashbury Bright cutlery, 2006

Designer:	Kit deBretton Gordon
Materials:	Stainless steel
Production:	From 2007
Manufacturer:	Robert Welch Designs, Chipping Campden

Vale cutlery, 2009

Designer:	Ruth Williams
Materials:	Stainless steel
Production:	From 2009
Manufacturer:	Robert Welch Designs, Chipping Campden

Pendulum cutlery, 1997

Designer:	William Welch
Materials:	Stainless steel
Production:	From ca. 1997
Manufacturer:	Ginkgo International, Woodridge, Illinois, USA

Comet Bright cutlery, 1999–2000

Designer:	William Welch
Materials:	Stainless steel
Production:	From 2007
Manufacturer:	Robert Welch Designs, Chipping Campden

Iona Bright cutlery, 2006

Designer:	Paul deBretton Gordon
Materials:	Stainless steel
Production:	From 2006
Manufacturer:	Robert Welch Designs, Chipping Campden

Palm Bright cutlery, 2009

Designer:	Ruth Willams
Materials:	Stainless steel
Production:	From 2010
Manufacturer:	Robert Welch Designs, Chipping Campden

This design was later adapted for inflight use in Emirates' First Class and Business Class cabins in 2011

Westbury Bright cutlery, 2011

Designer:	Kit deBretton Gordon
Materials:	Stainless steel
Production:	From 2011
Manufacturer:	Robert Welch Designs, Chipping Campden

Arden cutlery, 2013

Designer:	Kit deBretton Gordon and Ian Redfern
Materials:	Stainless steel
Production:	From 2014
Manufacturer:	Robert Welch Designs, Chipping Campden

Selected additional designs:

Silver Trophies

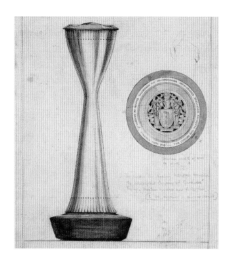

Flowers in Hospital trophy, 1953–5

Designer:	Robert Welch
Materials:	Silver, rosewood
Production:	1955, executed by Thomas James Boucher
Commission:	Worshipful Company of Gardeners

Thomas Boucher worked as a silversmithing technician at the Royal College of Art, London, and often helped students with the execution of their designs

The Silver Wink, 1960

Designer:	Robert Welch
Materials:	Silver, rosewood
Production:	1960, executed by Robert Welch Studio, Chipping Campden
Commission:	H.R.H. The Duke of Edinburgh

Made for an annual championship match held between Oxford and Cambridge universities' Tiddlywinks Societies, of which Prince Philip was president

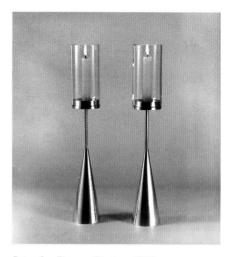

Prize for Elegant Design, 1960

Designer:	Robert Welch
Materials:	Silverplate, glass
Production:	1960, Robert Welch Studio, Chipping Campden
Commission:	Design Centre, London

These candlesticks were awarded to Neal French and David White for their Apollo tableware, which won the Duke of Edinburgh's Prize for Elegant Design in 1960

Starpacks trophy, 1961–2

Designer:	Robert Welch
Materials:	Parcel-gilt silver
Production:	From 1961, Robert Welch Studio, Chipping Campden
Commission:	The Institute of Packaging

Known as the 'Golden Egg', this design was presented as the Supreme Award by the Institute of Packaging three times during the 1960s

A.L. Wiggin trophy, 1964

Designer:	Robert Welch
Materials:	Silver, rosewood
Production:	1964, Robert Welch Studio, Chipping Campden
Commission:	J. & J. Wiggin

Executed for J. & J. Wiggin (manufacturers of Old Hall Tableware) for their five-a-side football tournament

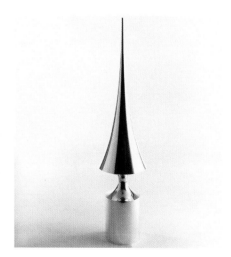

Honda trophy, 1965

Designer:	Robert Welch
Materials:	Silver
Production:	1965, Robert Welch Studio, Chipping Campden
Commission:	Honda Motor Trading Ltd

Two of these golfing trophies were commissioned by Honda Motor Trading Ltd for the Honda Parsomes Competition

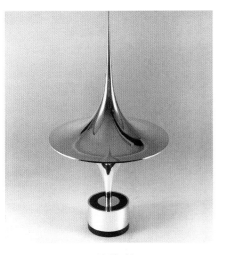

Elastoplast trophy, 1960–61

Designer:	Robert Welch
Materials:	Silver, rosewood
Production:	1961, Robert Welch Studio, Chipping Campden
Commission:	Clifford Bloxham & Partners

With its sharp pointed form, the award made a tongue-in-cheek reference to the fact that it was for a company that made bandages

Interplas trophy, 1961–63

Designer:	Robert Welch
Materials:	Silver, acrylic
Production:	1961, Robert Welch Studio, Chipping Campden
Commission:	Interplas (plastics industry exhibition)

This elegant trophy was awarded as the Supreme Award of the Interplas Exhibition to the German designer Dieter Rams on three consecutive occasions

(Unidentified) trophy, ca. 1961

Designer:	Robert Welch
Materials:	Silver
Production:	ca. 1961, Robert Welch Studio, Chipping Campden
Commission:	Unknown

Swimming trophy, 1965

Designer:	Robert Welch
Materials:	Silver, rosewood
Production:	ca. 1965, Robert Welch Studio, Chipping Campden
Commission:	Harrow and Wealdstone Boy Scouts Association

This elegant trophy was commissioned as a prize for a Boy Scouts' swimming competition

Football Manager of the Year trophy, 1965

Designer:	Robert Welch
Materials:	Silver, rosewood
Production:	ca. 1965, Robert Welch Studio, Chipping Campden
Commission:	Westclox

This ziggurat-shaped trophy was awarded several times to the legendary Matt Busby, and eventually given to him outright

International Ice Dancing trophy, 1973

Designer:	Robert Welch
Materials:	Silver, glass
Production:	1973, Robert Welch Studio, Chipping Campden
Commission:	Prestige Group

One of Robert Welch's major clients, the Prestige Group was a well-known sponsor of various skating competitions

Selected additional designs:

Ecclesiastical Design

Wafer box, 1956–7

Designer:	Robert Welch
Materials:	Sterling silver, parcel gilt
Production:	ca. 1957, Robert Welch Studio, Chipping Campden
Commission:	Cpt. Rev. Dunnett for Aldermarston Church, near Reading, Berkshire

Pectoral cross, 1957

Designer:	Robert Welch
Materials:	Sterling silver, gold plate
Production:	1957, Robert Welch Studio, Chipping Campden
Commission:	Bishop of Bangor

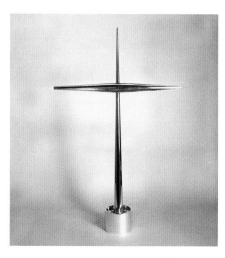

Altar cross (and candlesticks), 1961

Designer:	Robert Welch
Materials:	Sterling silver
Production:	1961, Robert Welch Studio, Chipping Campden
Commission:	W.R. Servaes, Director of the Orient Line for Northaw School, near Salisbury, Wiltshire

From 1958, John Limbrey was largely responsible for the execution of all handmade silver, including most, if not all, of the ecclesiastical commissions

Candlesticks and torchères, 1971

Designer:	Robert Welch
Materials:	Cast iron
Production:	1971, Ball Brothers (foundry), Stratford-upon-Avon, Warwickshire
Commission:	Dawber, Fox and Robinson (architects) for Mid Warwickshire Crematorium, Bishops Tachbrook

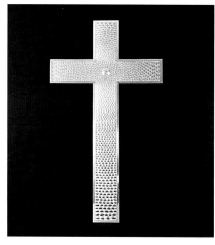

Wall-mounted cross, 1975

Designer:	Robert Welch
Materials:	Sterling silver, rosewood
Production:	1975, Robert Welch Studio, Chipping Campden
Commission:	St Mary's Church, Bridport, Devon

Design inspired by the graduated pebbles on nearby Chesil Beach in Dorset

Wafer box, 1977

Designer:	Robert Welch
Materials:	Rosewood, inlaid brass
Production:	1975, Robert Welch Studio, Chipping Campden
Commission:	In memory of Bob and Ella Arkell for Cutsdean Church, Gloucestershire

Chalice, 1962

Designer:	Robert Welch
Materials:	Sterling silver
Production:	1962, Robert Welch Studio, Chipping Campden
Commission:	The boys of Ratcliffe College, Leicestershire

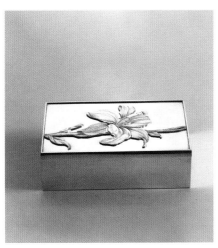

Wafer box, 1968

Designer:	Robert Welch
Materials:	Sterling silver, yew
Production:	1968, Robert Welch Studio, Chipping Campden
Commission:	Mrs Brooks in memory of her husband for the Church at Elmley Castle, Pershore, Worcestershire

Font, 1971

Designer:	Robert Welch
Materials:	Cast aluminium, acrylic
Production:	1971, Robert Welch Studio, Chipping Campden
Commission:	Canon Lambert for St Michael's Chapel, Rutgers University, New Jersey, USA

Chalice and wafer box, 1978

Designer:	Robert Welch
Materials:	Sterling silver, parcel gilt, rosewood
Production:	1971, John Limbrey, Robert Welch Studio, Chipping Campden
Commission:	Unknown

Portable communion set, 1991

Designer:	Robert Welch
Materials:	Sterling silver
Production:	1991, Robert Welch Studio, Chipping Campden
Commission:	Gift for St Andrew's Church, Shottery, Stratford-upon-Avon, Warwickshire

Wafer box, flagon and chalice, 1995–6

Designer:	Robert Welch
Materials:	Sterling silver, parcel gilt
Production:	ca. 1996, Robert Welch Studio, Chipping Campden
Commission:	All Saints Church, Wighill, Yorkshire

Selected additional designs:

Jewellery Design

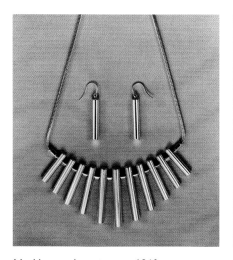

Necklace and earrings ca. 1960

Designer:	Robert Welch
Materials:	Gold-plated brass
Production:	ca. 1960
Manufacturer:	Dennison Watch Case Co., Handsworth, Birmingham

Necklace, ca. 1960

Designer:	Robert Welch
Materials:	Gold-plated brass
Production:	ca. 1960
Manufacturer:	Dennison Watch Case Co., Handsworth, Birmingham

Torque, early 1960s

Designer:	Robert Welch
Materials:	Gold-plated metal, semi-precious stones
Production:	Early 1960s
Manufacturer:	Dennison Watch Case Co., Handsworth, Birmingham

Bobble pendants and ring, ca. 1972

Designer:	Robert Welch
Materials:	Sterling silver or gold-plated silver
Production:	ca. 1972
Manufacturer:	Robert Welch Studio, Chipping Campden

Rutilated amethyst pendant, ca. 1972

Designer:	Robert Welch
Materials:	Sterling silver, rutilated amethyst
Production:	ca. 1972
Manufacturer:	Robert Welch Studio, Chipping Campden

Tourmaline pendant, 1972

Designer:	Robert Welch
Materials:	18ct gold, tourmaline
Production:	ca. 1972
Manufacturer:	Robert Welch Studio, Chipping Campden

Bracelet, 1960s

Designer:	Robert Welch
Materials:	Gold-plated brass
Production:	Early 1960s
Manufacturer:	Dennison Watch Case Co., Handsworth, Birmingham

Amethyst rings, 1960s

Designer:	Robert Welch
Materials:	Sterling silver, rough uncut amethysts
Production:	1960s
Manufacturer:	Robert Welch Studio, Chipping Campden

Quartz pendants, ca. 1972

Designer:	Robert Welch
Materials:	Sterling silver, quartz
Production:	ca. 1972
Manufacturer:	Robert Welch Studio, Chipping Campden

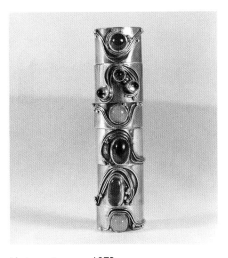

Various rings, ca. 1973

Designer:	Robert Welch
Materials:	Sterling silver, parcel gilt, semi-precious stones
Production:	ca. 1974
Manufacturer:	Robert Welch Studio, Chipping Campden

Known as 'Margaret's rings' these designs, like other jewellery pieces designed by Robert Welch, were executed by the silversmith, Margaret Fleming. She initially worked in the Robert Welch Studio in Chipping Campden before moving to Edinburgh, where she set up her own workshop and continued making pieces for Robert.

Ammonite pendants, ca. 1975

Designer:	Robert Welch
Materials:	Sterling silver, polished fossils
Production:	ca. 1975
Manufacturer:	Robert Welch Studio, Chipping Campden

From 1972 onwards, Robert Welch incorporated various ammonite fossils into his jewellery designs, and throughout the 1970s created jewellery pieces set with not only fossils, but also various semi-precious 'specimen' stones

Oyster shell fossil pendant, ca. 1975

Designer:	Robert Welch
Materials:	Electro-formed silver, polished fossil
Production:	ca. 1975
Manufacturer:	Robert Welch Studio, Chipping Campden

Selected additional designs:

Domestic Silverware

Sauce boat, 1956

Designer:	Robert Welch
Materials:	Sterling silver
Production:	1956 (one-off piece)
Manufacturer:	Robert Welch Studio, Chipping Campden

This early silverware design was essentially the blueprint for Robert Welch's later model no. 43782 sauceboat for Old Hall, made from stainless steel

Candleholder, 1960

Designer:	Robert Welch
Materials:	Sterling silver, with oxidized recesses
Production:	1960 (one-off piece)
Manufacturer:	Robert Welch Studio, Chipping Campden

Tea set, 1961

Designer:	Robert Welch
Materials:	Sterling silver, nylon
Production:	1962 (one-off piece)
Manufacturer:	Wakely and Wheeler, London

This sculptural tea set was commissioned by Graham Hughes and is in the permanent collection of Goldsmiths' Hall

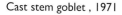

Cast stem goblet , 1971

Designer:	Robert Welch
Materials:	Sterling silver
Production:	1971
Manufacturer:	Robert Welch Studio, Chipping Campden

Oval tea pot and hot water pot, 1971

Designer:	Robert Welch
Materials:	Sterling silver, ivory
Production:	From 1971 (batch production)
Manufacturer:	Robert Welch Studio, Chipping Campden

Candelabrum, 1972

Designer:	Robert Welch
Materials:	Sterling silver
Production:	1972 (private commission)
Manufacturer:	Robert Welch Studio, Chipping Campden

At least three variations of this one-off commissioned design were made, including one with a looped carrying handle

238

Condiment set, ca. 1962

Designer:	Robert Welch
Materials:	Sterling silver
Production:	From ca. 1962 (batch production)
Manufacturer:	Robert Welch Studio, Chipping Campden for Asprey & Co., London

Candlesticks, 1963

Designer:	Robert Welch
Materials:	Sterling silver
Production:	From 1964 (batch production)
Manufacturer:	Robert Welch Studio for Heal's, London

These elegant candlesticks were part of the original silverware range Robert Welch designed for Heal's in 1963

Dumpy condiment set, 1963

Designer:	Robert Welch
Materials:	Sterling silver, rosewood, glass liner (mustard dish)
Production:	From 1964 (batch production)
Manufacturer:	Robert Welch Studio for Heal's, London

Rose bowl, ca. 1973

Designer:	Robert Welch
Materials:	Sterling silver
Production:	ca. 1973 (one-off piece)
Manufacturer:	Robert Welch Studio, Chipping Campden

Carafe with inset amethysts, 1973

Designer:	Robert Welch
Materials:	Sterling silver, amethysts
Production:	1973
Manufacturer:	Robert Welch Studio, Chipping Campden

This exquisite gem-studded carafe relates to the design of the Amethyst bowl in that it incorporates silver wires laid in an organic pattern and small amethyst cabochons

Hackworth coffee pot and teapot, 1973

Designer:	Robert Welch
Materials:	Sterling silver, ivory
Production:	From 1973 (batch production)
Manufacturer:	Robert Welch Studio, Chipping Campden

These pieces were originally commissioned by Lt. Col. Hackworth and then later were batch produced for sale in the Robert Welch Studio Shops

Selected additional designs:

Ceremonial Silver

 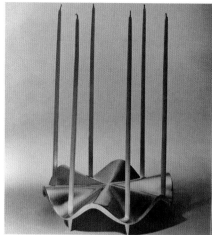

Double-panned fruit bowl, 1955–6

Designer:	Robert Welch
Materials:	Sterling silver, parcel gilt
Production:	1956, 1 of 2 pieces, Robert Welch, Chipping Campden (with assistance from Hart's Silversmiths)
Commission::	Worshipful Company of Goldsmiths for presentation to Imperial College of Science and Technology, London

Candleholder, 1958

Designer:	Robert Welch
Materials:	Sterling silver
Production:	1958, 1 of 3 pieces, Robert Welch Studio, Chipping Campden
Commission:	Greenlands Association, Henley Business Administration College, Henley-on-Thames, Oxfordshire

Candelabrum, 1958

Designer:	Robert Welch
Materials:	Sterling silver
Production:	1959, one-off, Robert Welch Studio, Chipping Campden
Commission:	Gordon Russell on behalf of the CoID for presentation to Sir Walter Warboys on the occassion of his knighthood. Warboys, an Australian-born businessman, was chairman of the CoID from 1953 to 1960, and was instrumental in the establishment of the Design Centre in London.

 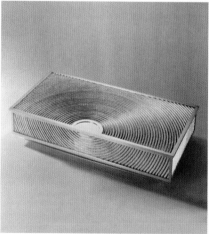

Repoussé dish, 1971

Designer:	Robert Welch
Materials:	Sterling silver, parcel gilt
Production:	1971, 1 of at least 2 pieces, Robert Welch Studio, Chipping Campden
Commission:	Churchill College, Cambridge, for presentation to Dr Denys Armstrong. Another example was made for Donald Anderson, chairman of the P&O Line.

Oval tea pot and hot water pot, 1971

Designer:	Robert Welch
Materials:	Sterling silver, parcel gilt, cedar wood
Production:	1974, one-off, Robert Welch Studio, Chipping Campden
Commission:	J.R. Phillips & Co. for presentation to Courvoisier of France

Furniture Makers loving cups, 1977

Designer:	Robert Welch
Materials:	Sterling silver
Production:	1977, 1 of 2 pieces, Robert Welch Studio, Chipping Campden
Commission:	Worshipful Company of Furniture Makers to commemorate the Queen's Silver Jubilee

Candelabrum for RSA, 1965

Designer:	Robert Welch
Materials:	Sterling silver
Production:	1965, 1 of 6 pieces executed by Raymond Marsh, Robert Welch Studio
Commission:	Royal Society of Arts, London

Clock, 1965

Designer:	Robert Welch
Materials:	Sterling silver, glass, clock mechanism
Production:	1965, one-off, Robert Welch Studio, Chipping Campden
Commission:	The King's Royal Rifle Corp, Winchester, Hampshire

Bobblesticks candleholders, 1971

Designer:	Robert Welch
Materials:	Sterling silver, parcel gilt
Production:	From 1971, batch-production, Robert Welch Studio, Chipping Campden
Commission:	Presented to H.R.H. Princess Margaret by the Cincinnati Engineering Company, and then later batch produced

Epergne, 1978

Designer:	Robert Welch
Materials:	Sterling silver
Production:	1978, one off, Robert Welch Studio, Chipping Campden
Commission:	Directors of Hoskins & Horton for presentation to William George Ainge Russell

Glaxo wine goblet, 1987

Designer:	Robert Welch
Materials:	Sterling silver
Production:	1987, one-off, Robert Welch Studio, Chipping Campden
Commission:	Glaxo Holdings, London (a number of variants of this design were also made for Glaxo)

Cheltenham coffee service, 1995

Designer:	Robert Welch
Materials:	Sterling silver, ivory
Production:	1995, one-off, Robert Welch Studio, Chipping Campden
Commission:	Cheltenham Art Gallery and Museum

Footnotes

1. William Whatley, *Robert Welch, Designer and Silversmith* (thesis), University College, Cardiff, 1973, p.2

2. Robert's father Leonard Radford Welch survived one of the worst maritime disasters in British history, the sinking of the HMS *Iolaire* just off Stornoway in the Outer Hebrides in 1919 – with only 75 of the 280 passengers onboard surviving. Later Robert went on a pilgrimage to Stornoway and sketched the landscape that had been the backdrop to this tragic disaster.

3. Quoted in *Victor Winstone, Personal Recollections of a Design Legend*, p.1 – see:http://www. oocities.org/hvf_win/Welch01.htm

4. William Whatley, *Robert Welch, Designer and Silversmith*, p.3

5. Ibid, p.6

6. Ibid, p.7

7. Fiona MacCarthy, 'Robert Welch Obituary', *The Guardian*, 23 March 2000

8. William Whatley, *Robert Welch, Designer and Silversmith*, p.8

9. Terry Grimley, 'Craftsman with a Silver Touch' article, *Birmingham Post*, 10 June 1995

10. William Whatley, *Robert Welch, Designer and Silversmith*, p.9

11. Patrick Guest first worked for Gollins Melvin Ward, before setting up his own architectural practice, Mayorcas & Guest

12. Svenska Slöjdföreningen (the Swedish Council of Industrial Design) later became known as Svenska Form

13. William Whatley, *Robert Welch, Designer and Silversmith*, p.9

14. Victor Winstone, *Personal Recollection of a Design Legend*, p.1

15. William Whatley, *Robert Welch, Designer and Silversmith*, p.10

16. Ibid, p.11

17. Victor Winstone, *Personal Recollection of a Design Legend*, p.1

18. See: http://www.oldhallclub.co.uk/html/steady_progress_1945-1960.html

19. The addition of 12% chromium to steel makes it stainless

20. Robert Welch, *The Design and Production of Stainless Steel Tableware* (thesis), Royal College of Art, London, 1955, p.3

21. Ibid, p.5

22. Ibid, p.13

23. Ibid, p.14

24. Ibid, p.14

25. William A. Whatley, *Robert Welch, Designer and Silversmith*, p.11

26. Ibid, p.12

27. Harold Pyment's father Jim had been the foreman of the Guild of Handicraft's cabinetmaking workshop

28. Gordon Russell lecture delivered to the Royal Society of Arts, London in 1978 – quoted in *Robert Welch: Designer-Silversmith, A retrospective exhibition 1955–1995* exhibition catalogue, Cheltenham Art Gallery & Museums, 1995, p.19

29. William A. Whatley, *Robert Welch, Designer and Silversmith*, p.14

30. Ibid p. 14

31. John Ruskin, *Lectures on Art, 1870 – Lecture 3: The Relation of Art to Morals*, sect. 95

32. William Morris, 'The Lesser Arts' (lecture), 1877 quoted in *The Collected Works of William Morris*, ed. May Morris, 24 vols., Longman, Green, London, 1910-15, 22: 26-27

33. *Designs of the Year 1958* (catalogue), Council of Industrial Design, London, p.28

34. *Design* (Issue 100), Council of Industrial Design, London, April 1957, p.31

35. *Design* (Issue 114), Council of Industrial Design, London, June 1958, p.44

36. Bill Stanton, 'Profile of a Designer – Robert Welch, Artist Craftsman', *Stainless* (Issue No.2), November 1974, pp.8–11

37. Robert Welch and Alan Crawford, *Robert Welch – Design in a Cotswold Workshop*, Lund Humphries, London 1973, p.10

38. 'Announcing The Design Centre for British Industries' (insert) – *Design* (Issue no.82), Council of Industrial Design, London, 1955

39. Patricia Welch, interview by Charlotte Fiell, Chipping Campden, Glos., October 2014

40. Ibid

41. *Designers: Robert Welch* (BBC2 documentary film), British Broadcasting Corporation, London 1986

42. *British Artist Craftsmen: An Exhibition of Contemporary Work*, Smithsonian Institution, Washington, DC/Ambassador Pub. Co., London, 1959, foreword

43. William Whatley, *Robert Welch, Designer and Silversmith*, p.36

44. Patricia Welch, interview by Charlotte Fiell

45. Ibid

46. *Homes & Gardens*, January 1965, p.31

47. Patricia Welch, interview by Charlotte Fiell, Chipping Campden, Glos., October 2014

48. Ibid

49. Ibid

50. Ray Leigh, interview by Charlotte Fiell, Chipping Campden, Glos., August 2014

51. Graham Hughes, 'Robert Welch, Goldsmith and Silversmith' (article) , *The Connoisseur*, July 1963, p. 193

52. William Whatley, *Robert Welch, Designer and Silversmith*, p.25

53. Patricia Welch, interview by Charlotte Fiell, Chipping Campden, Glos., October 2014

54. *Mobilia* (Issue 145), August 1967, p.23

55. Robert Welch, *Hand & Machine: Robert Welch, Designer – Silversmith*, Robert Welch, Chipping Campden, 1986, p.21

56. According to documents and letters held in the Robert Welch archive it would appear that the majority of the jewellery designed by Robert Welch was executed by Margaret Fleming, who initially worked in his studio in Chipping Campden and then later established her own workshop with another jeweller in Edinburgh, where she continued producing pieces for him. There are, however, various pieces of jewellery (as well as stone-set, twisted-handled, silver spoons) that bear another RW maker's mark – also assayed in Sheffield, but in a distinctive elongated script rather than in slanted lettering, and set in two vertical rectangles rather than a single horizontal rectangle. Pieces bearing this alternative RW maker's mark have previously been misattributed to Robert, but were actually designed by Ralph Weston of Nether Edge, Sheffield. Like Robert, Weston also worked in stainless steel, albeit within the realm of jewellery design, and similarly had designs that were manufactured by Oneida.

57. Sue Roseveare, 'Robert Welch: Designer and Silversmith of Chipping Campden', *Focus*, March 1982, p.35

58. Roland Smith, 'End of the Line for a Grand Old Family of Steel' article, unknown source, dated 18 April 1984, ref: Robet Welch Archives

59. *Designers: Robert Welch* (BBC2 documentary film), British Broadcasting Corporation, London 1986

60. *Housewares*, November 1989, p.18

61. Ibid, p.19

62. Alice had previously trained as a make-up artist and then worked for a leading spa in London before working as a beauty therapist with her mother in Warwick

63. Quoted by Rupert Welch, 'The Ashbee Lecture: The Design Legacy of Robert Welch', Court Barn Museum, Chipping Campden, 14 September, 2014

64. Ibid

65. Rupert Welch, interview by Charlotte Fiell, Chipping Campden, Glos., November 2014

66. Alice Welch, interview by Charlotte Fiell, Chipping Campden, Glos., October 2014

67. Ibid

68. *Designers: Robert Welch* (BBC2 documentary film), British Broadcasting Corporation, London 1986

69. *Design* (Issue 100), Council of Industrial Design, London, April 1957, p.31

70. Robert Welch, *Hand and Machine*, p.123

71. Ibid, p.123

72. Robert Welch, *Hand and Machine*, p.49

73. Ibid, p.49

74. Charlotte Whitehead, One-to-One Event talk, Court Barn Museum, Chipping Campden, 19 July 2014

75 *Design* (Issue 237), Council of Industrial Design, London, September 1968, p.24

76. Robert Welch and Alan Crawford, *Robert Welch – Design in a Cotswold Workshop*, p.18

77. Robert Welch, *Hand and Machine*, p.184

78. *Design* (Issue 186), Council of Industrial Design, June 1964, p.56

79. *Design* (Issue 229), Council of Industrial Design, January 1968, p.34

80. Robert Welch, *Hand and Machine*, p.126

81. Robert Welch and Alan Crawford, *Robert Welch – Design in a Cotswold Workshop*, p.30

82. Ray Leigh, interview by Charlotte Fiell, Chipping Campden, Glos., August 2014

83. Robert Welch, *Hand and Machine*, p.157

84. Ibid, p.157

85. Ibid, p.158

86. Robert Welch and Alan Crawford, *Robert Welch – Design in a Cotswold Workshop*, p.11

87. Ibid, p.12

88. *Design* (Issue 220), Council of Industrial Design, April 1967, p.35

89. Ibid, p.35

90. Robert Welch and Alan Crawford, *Robert Welch – Design in a Cotswold Workshop*, p.40

91. Robert Welch, *Hand and Machine*, p.192

92. Robert Welch and Alan Crawford, *Robert Welch – Design in a Cotswold Workshop*, p.181

93. *Design* (Issue 240), Council of Industrial Design, December 1968, p.72

94. Robert Welch, *Hand and Machine*, p.28

95. Robert Welch and Alan Crawford, *Robert Welch – Design in a Cotswold Workshop*, p.50

96. Robert Welch, *Hand and Machine*, p.52

97. Ibid, p.53

98. Ibid, p.53

99. Robert Welch, 'Annual Record of 1972', Robert Welch Papers, Robert Welch Archive

100. Robert Welch, *Hand and Machine*, p.57

101. 'Court Barn Museum acquires a Tower of London Commemorative Goblet', press release, Court Barn Museum, Chipping Campden, March 2013

102. '1984 Design Council Awards' Press Release, 1 May 1984, p.1

103. *Focus*, March 1982, p.35

104. Robert Welch, *Hand and Machine*, p.62

105. Ibid, p.153

106. Ibid, p.150

107. Ibid, p.67

108. Ibid, p.77

109. Ibid, p.101

110. Ibid, p.102

111. Galerie Cuisine brochure, ref: Robert Welch Archive

112. Rupert Welch, 'The Ashbee Lecture: The Design Legacy of Robert Welch', Court Barn Museum, Chipping Campden, 14 September, 2014

113. Ibid

114. *Designed in Chipping Campden* (website video), Robert Welch Designs, Chipping Campden, see: http://www.robertwelch.com/Content.aspx?id=1102516

115. Kit and Paul deBretton Gordon, interview by Charlotte Fiell, Chipping Campden, September 2014

116. Ibid

117. Ibid

Selected Bibliography

Books

Andrew, John and Derek Styles, *Designer British Silver: From Studios Established 1930–1983*, Antique Collectors' Club, Woodbridge, Suffolk, 2014

Bennett, Michael, *Robert Welch designs for Old Hall Tableware*, Appin Press, Birkenhead, 2009

Fiell, Charlotte and Peter Fiell, *Industrial Design A-Z*, Taschen, Cologne, 2001

Fiell, Charlotte and Peter Fiell, *Masterpieces of British Design*, Goodman Fiell, London, 2012

Fiell, Charlotte and Peter Fiell, *Tools for Living: A Sourcebook of Iconic Designs for the Home*, Fiell Publishing, London, 2010

Hughes, Graham, *Modern Silverware throughout the World 1880–1967*, Studio Vista, London, 1967

Jackson, Lesley, *The New Look: Design in the Fifties*, Thames & Hudson, London, 1981

Larkman, Brian and S.H. Glenister, *Contemporary Design in Metalwork*, John Murray, London, 1963

Larkman, Brian, *Metalwork Designs of Today*, John Murray, London, 1969

Welch, Robert and Alan Crawford (intro), *Robert Welch – Design in a Cotswold Workshop*, Lund Humphries, London, 1973

Welch, Robert, *Hand & Machine: Robert Welch, Designer – Silversmith*, Robert Welch, Chipping Campden, 1986

Exhibition catalogues

British Artist Craftsmen: An Exhibition of Contemporary Work, Smithsonian Institution, Washington D.C./Ambassador Pub. Co., London, 1959

Designs of the Year 1958, Council of Industrial Design, London, 1958

Robert Welch: Designer-Silversmith, A retrospective exhibition 1955–1995, Cheltenham Art Gallery & Museums, 1995

Robert Welch, Inspirations and Innovation, Court Barn Museum. Chipping Campden, 2014

Index

Page numbers in *italics* indicate illustrations

Adie & Nephew 212
'Aladdin's Lamp' tea set *see* Alveston range
Albany bathroom fittings 212
All India Handicraft Board 34, 45, 158
Alveston range 72
    bud and flower vases 226
    candlesticks 225
    carving set 106–7
    condiment set and dredger 226
    cutlery 26, 44, 90–91, 106
    tea set 27, 92–93
Amethyst dish 34, 136–37, 239
Ammonite cutlery (for Ginkgo)
    Flat 172
    Hollow 172, 229
Anglo Continental Clock Co. 214
Apicella, Lorenzo (Pentagram) 38
Apollo table light (for Chad Lighting) 217
architectural fittings 211, 213 *see also* Dryad; Simplan
Arden range
    bowl (for Crate & Barrel) 203
    candlesticks 183, 188, 203
    cutlery 231
    table light 217
Arström, Folke 17, 67
Arts and Crafts Movement 8, 20, 100, 162
Ashbee, Charles Robert 8, 18, 19
Ashberry, Peter 115
Ashbury Bright cutlery 230
Ashwell, Cyril (Westclox) 86
Astoria wall clock (for Westclox) 215
Avon range 122

baby's bath 211
Bäckström, Olof 142
Barnett, Samuel and Henrietta 8
Bauhaus 110, 116
Baxendale, Robert 11, 44
Beach cutlery and stand (for Yamazaki Kinzoku Kogyo) 34
Bearston, Harold 140
beer pump 211
Benita table clock (for Westclox) 214
Benney, Gerald 12, 15, 25, 171
Birmingham College of Art 11–12, 25, 44, 74, 138
Bistro cutlery 85
BOAC first-class inflight tray 212
Bobblesticks candleholders 241
Bojesen, Kay 17
Boucher, Thomas 232
Brancusi, Constantin 36
Brearley, Harry 14, 16
Breeze, George (Cheltenham Art Gallery and Museum) 173
Breeze candelabrum 173
Breuer, Marcel 36
Bridge Crystal Glass Company 118
'British Artist Craftsmen ... ' exhibition, Smithsonian Institution,
    Washington, DC, USA 25, 47, 60, 69
British Home Stores (BHS) 85
British Museum candelabra 35–36, 156–57
British Railways washbasin and lavatory 211
Brixham Pottery 34, 131
Broadway coffee set 26, 74
bronze ware 34, 35, *36*, 45, 158–59, 160
Brown, Ralph 158–59
Brunel coffee table 213
Bud cutlery 45, 200
Burford bathroom accessories 41, 198–99
Butler, John 126

CAD (computer-aided design) 41, *180–81*, 189
cake basket (for Old Hall) 116
Calibre cutlery (for Yamazaki Kinzoku Kogyo) 34, 229
Cambridge School of Art 11, 44
Campden Designs 27, *31*, 33, 37, 94–97, 104–5, 161, 214, 218–19
Campden (previously Galerie Cuisine) cookware 170
Campden tableware (for Olde Hall) 60
    candleholder 60–61
    coffee set 44, 58–59, *60*, 75
    condiment set 20, 22, 224
    cutlery 22, 44, 54–55
    tea strainer 225
    toast rack 19, *21*, 22, 44, 56–57, *60*, 224
Campden tableware (for Poole Pottery) 213
cast ware 27, 33, 34, 36
    1960s *26*, *31*, 44, 94–97, 104–5, 218–19
    1970s 130, 215, 219, 220–21, 234, 235
    1980s 160–65, 204, 221, 222
    1990s 176–77, 217, 222–23
'Casual Collection' cutlery (for Yamazaki Kinzoku Kogyo) 34
CD range (cast ware) 95, 96, 97, 104–5, 218–19
Central School of Arts and Crafts, London 20
ceramics
    1960s 80–81, 108–9, 210, 214
    1970s 34, 131, 212, 221
    1980s 213
    1990s 36, *38*, 174
ceremonial silver 240–41
Chad Lighting 37, 216, 217
Chantry, James 99
Chantry knife sharpener 98–99, 106, 186
Charlotte Jacob Prize for Silversmithing 11, 44
Cheltenham Art Gallery and Museum 173, 241
Cheltenham coffee service 241
child's cutlery 228
Chipping Campden, Gloucestershire 8, 19, 27, 190 *see also* Old Silk Mill;
    Robert Welch Studio shops
church plate (St. Mary's Church, Swansea) 76-77
Churchill College, Cambridge 240
coffee suite 82–83
claret jug 134–35
Clearcall alarm clock 215
clocks 214–15, 241 *see also* named clocks; Westclox
Clove tealight holder 194
Cockroft, Sir John 82
Comet cutlery 41, 45, 231
companion set 210
Computim digital wall/desk clocks 214
Comus canteen crockery (Meakin for Ministry of Public Building and
    Works) 108–9
Concord kitchen scissors 117
Consulate table and pendant lights (for Lumitron) 216
Contour steak knives 206
Cook, Kenneth 159
cookbook stand 161, 204 *see also under* Signature range
Copenhagen Cutlery (Danish Universal Steel Company) 17
Coper, Hans 25
Cotswold tea service 80–81
Cotswolds, Gloucestershire 8, 18, 25, 30, 67, 74, 122, 190
Council of Industrial Design 20, 22, 23, 54, 56, *57*, 86, 90, 112, 240
Courvoisier cigar box 240
'Craftsman's Art' exhibition (1973), Victoria and Albert Museum, London
    34, 47, 136
Crate & Barrel 203
Cuisine Cookware 170
Cultura covered serving dish (Persson for Silver and Stål) 17
Cutlery Allied Trades Research Association (CATRA) 186, 205
Cylinda-Line stainless steel range (A. Jacobsen) 122

Dakota cutlery 229
Danesco kettle 226
Darwin cake knife 224
Darwin, Robert 12
Davies, Cyril 76
deBretton Gordon, Kit *40*, 41, 45, 180, 192, 196, 198, 200, 201, 202, 204, 207
deBretton Gordon, Paul *40*, 41, 45, 183, 186, 195, 197, 202, 204, 205
Decorative Art yearbook (*The Studio* magazine) 19, 30, 97
Denmark 17, 30, 44, 97, 227
Dennison 236
Denovo car tyre tread (for Dunlop) 146, *147*, 213
'The Design and Production of Stainless Steel Tableware' (RW's thesis, 1955) 16–18
Design Centre Awards 44, 45, 86, 90, 140
Design in a Cotswold Workshop (1973) *26*, 45
Design magazine 14, 23, 52, 86, 88, 108, 117, 118
Designers series (BBC) 35, 45
Deta cutlery range 41
domestic silverware *13*, 16, 26, *31*, 33, 34, 41, 74–75, 100–103, 120–21, 228, 238–39
Doulton 210
Downing Street coffee set (for The Silver Trust) 36, 171
drawing compass 213
Dreyer, Paul (Prestige Group) 133
Drift jugs 45, 202
Drury, Martin 186
Dryad Metal Works 115, 162
Dryad range 37
  architectural ironmongery (Dryad 70) 115
  candlesticks 36, 162–63
  table light (for Chad Lighting) 217
  see also Simplan
Duke of Edinburgh 56, 57
Dumpy range
condiment set 239
sugar sifter 224
Dunlop 146, *147*, 213

ecclesiastical design 35, 76–77, 144–45, 234–35
Elastoplast trophy 233
Elegance cookware and kettle (for Judge) 88–89
Thomas R. Ellin 211
Edward Elwell 211
Emirates inflight service 227, 230
Ercolani, Lucien 84
Ergo knives 186

Facette (Arström for Gense) 17
Falk, Rolf (Heal's) 30
Fiddle cutlery 228
Finland 30
Firth Brown, Sheffield 16
Fiskars 142
Fleming, Margaret 236, 242 n.56
Fletcher, Alan (Fletcher Forbes Gill) 86
Flexi range lighting (for Lumitron) 124–25
Flowers in Hospital trophy 232
Focus cutlery (Arströ) 67
Foggin, Lilias (personal assistant) 22
Football Manager of the Year trophy 233
Footprint Tools screwdriver and saw 211
Forbes, Colin (Fletcher Forbes Gill) 86
4000 Series kitchen tools (for Prestige Group) 132–33
Foyle's Art Gallery, London 19–20, 50
Frink, Elisabeth 25
fruit basket (for Old Hall) 116
Furniture Makers loving cups 240

Galerie Cuisine (now Campden) cookware (for Cuisine Cookware) 170

garden spade 211
General Time Corporation 215
Geneva table clock (for Westclox) 215
Gense 15, 17, 22
Georg Jensen 17, 33
Giacometti, Alberto 36
Ginkgo 38, 172, 174
glassware
  1950s 18, 19, 50, 52–53
  1960s 84, 118–19
  1970s 134–35
Glaxo wine goblet 241
Goldsmiths' Hall 18, 25, 30, 44, 60, 74, 75, 76, 84, 154, 238, 240
  candelabra 126–27
  Surprise clock 154–55
Goodden, Robert 12, 18, 44
Grange, Kenneth 140
Guest, Patrick 14, 27–28, 242 n.11
Guild of Handicraft 8, 18, 19, 242 n.27
Guinness 211

Hackworth, Lt. Col. 239
Halliwell, Albert 20
Hallundbaek, Hans (Yamazaki Kinzoku Kogyo) 146
Hand and Machine (Welch) 18, 45
W.J. Harris 213
Harrison Fisher 36, 90, 99, 117, 140–41, 142 see also Taylor's Eye Witness
Hart family 18, 93
Heal, Ambrose 100
Heal's, Tottenham Court Road, London *31*, 33, 100
  silverware collection 30, *31*, 100–103, 239
Heneghan, Paul 126
Herløw, Erik 17
High-Tech style 115, 124
Hobart range
  candlesticks *26*, 94, *95*, 97, 218
  nutcracker 104–5
Honda trophy 232
Hughes, Graham (Goldsmiths' Hall) 25, 30, 69, 238
Hygiene Plastics 210

Ideal Standard 210
inkstand (for the City of Leicester) 84
International Ice Dancing trophy 233
International Silver Corporation competition (1959-60) 26, 72–73, 90
Interplas trophy 233
Iona Bright cutlery 231

Jacobsen, Arne 122
J.B. tea and coffee set 120–21
jewellery design 35, 36, 45, 164, 172, 236–37, 242 n.56
Jewson, Norman 33
John Lewis 198–99
Judge Holloware Ltd 88–89
Jury Holloware 210, 211

Kerala cast bronze wares 34, 35, *36*, 45, 158–59, 160
Kettle, Barry 28
King, Fred (Westclox) 86
Kitchen Devils knife range 34–35, 45, 140–41
'kitemark' (Council of Industrial Design) 23, *57*

H. E. Lauffer
  candleholder 219
  cast-iron cookware 34, 130
  kitchen utensils 213
  tableware 212
lawnmower grassbox attachment 211
Le Buffet serving utensils (for Samuel Groves & Co.) 35, 152–53
Le Corbusier 36, 84

Index

Leigh, Ray 30, 93
Liberty weighing scales 222
lighting 216–17 *see also* Chad Lighting; Lumitron
Limbrey, John 22, *24*, 28, 36, 41, *136*, *138*, *144*
career with RW
1950s 22, 25, 44, 63, 74
1960s 82, 126, 227
1970s 34, 136, 138
1980s 150, 154, 156
2000s to present 180
death 45
drawings *8*, *147*
Lindberg, Stig 14–15, 50
lost wax (*cire perdue*) casting 70, 158
Lumitron lighting 33, 36, 108–9, 124–25, 216
Lynton washbasin 210

Major, John *171*
Malvern School of Art 10, 11, 44
Manager range (for Westclox) 112
Mangiarotti, Angelo 35, 214
Mappin & Webb 67
Market Hall, Chipping Campden, Gloucestershire *8*
McFall, Donald 19, 22, 36
McMullen, Tony 120
J. & G. Meakin 108, 109
Mellor, David 12, 14, 22–23, 34, 44, 54
Melody alarm clock (for Westclox) 215
Meridian cutlery 230
Merit cutlery 228
Merlin alarm clock (for Westclox) *31*, 44, 86–87
Mies van der Rohe, Ludwig 36
Miller, Alec 18
Modernism 36, 72, 84, 93, 100, 116
Møller, Svend Erik 33
Molton candlesticks 192–93
Molton cutlery 41, 45, 201
Moody, Victor Hume 10, 44
Moore, Henry 25
Morris, William 8, 20, 122
Muir, Jean 171

Neo-Deco style 34, 36
Nest candelabrum 196
New Generation cookware 219
'New Look' style 26, 56, 58, 72, 90, 100
Nicholson, Ben 25
Nielsen, Harald 52
Norway 15, 17, 30, 44
November uplighter (for Chad Lighting) 216
nutcracker (for Old Hall) 34, 70–71, 106 *see also* Hobart range

Obelisk (Herløw for Copenhagen Cutlery) 17
Octopus pendant (for Shetland Silvercraft) *37*
The Old Silk Mill, Chipping Campden, Gloucestershire 8, 9, 18–20, *24*, 30, 41, 44, 45, *126*
'Olde Hall' (later 'Old Hall') Tableware (J. & J. Wiggin) 15, 16, 35, 44
1950s 16, 18, 20, 22–23, 25, 52, 54, 56, 58, 60, 63, 70
1960s *21*, 27, 33, 90, 92, 114, 116, 122–23
see also Bridge Crystal Glass Company; Prestige Group
1001 carpet shampooer 210
Order of St John cross and candlesticks 35, 144–45
Oriana cutlery (Mappin & Webb) *23*, 63, 66–67
Oriana tableware range (Olde Hall) 23, 25, 44, 62–65
ice bucket 225
Orient Line 23, 25, 63, 67
Owl string holder 223

Palm Bright cutlery 231
Peach, Harry 115

Pendulum cutlery 41, 231
Pentagram 38, 41, 86, 182
Permutit water softener 22, 44
Persson, Sigurd 14, 17
pestles and mortars 160, 220
Petersen, Hagbarth Skjalm 30, 33, 97, 104
Pick, William 115
Piper, John 25
Pizza Express 38–39, 45, 175
Pollock, Jackson 25, 69
Poole Pottery 213
Post-Modernism 36, 146, 169, 172, 229
Premier cutlery 41, 180, 228
Prestige Group 35, 132–33, 152, 233
Priestley, J. B. 120
Prinz range
fondue set 213
kettle 212
Pryke, Gavin 38
Public Building and Works, Ministry of
canteen crockery 108
wall clock 113
Pyment, Harold 18, 242 n.27

Qualcast 210
Quistgaard, Jens 17

Radford cutlery 41, 180–81
Raymor, New York 30, 33
Regalia cutlery (for Yamazaki Kinzoku Kogyo) 34, 146–47
Rie, Lucie 25
Ritz wall clock (for Westclox) 214
Robert Welch Designs Ltd 28, 44, 45, 60
awards 45, 186, 197, 200, 202
1990s 38–39, 97, 175, 227
2000s to present 39, 41, 45, 85, 182, 183, 188, 192, 194, 196, 206
Robert Welch Studio shops
Bath 41, 45
Chipping Campden 9, *32*, 33–34, 36, 38, *39*, 41, 44
Warwick 45
Robinson, Phil (Olde Hall) 63
rocking horse 210
rosewood 58, 82, 84, 85, *101*, 120, 145, 234
Rossetti, Dante Gabriel 8
Rourke, Brian (B. Rourke & Co.) 37, 162
Royal College of Art, London 12, 14, 16, 25, 41, 44, 45, 50, 138, 182
RSA candelabrum 241
Rushan bowls 189
Ruskin, John 8, 20
Russell, Gordon (Council of Industrial Design) 18, 20, 26, 30, 112, 240, 242 n.28
RW1 and RW2 cutlery *see* Alveston range
RW range (cast ware) 96, 160, 219, 220, 221, 222, 223

Samuel Groves & Co. 35, 152
Sarpaneva, Timo 30
sauceboat (for Old Hall) 114, 238
Scandinavian design 14–15, 16, 17, 23, 26, 50, 52, 67, 122, 135, 142, 195
Sea Drift range
candelabra 176–77, 223
cutlery (for Ginkgo) 174, 230
cutlery (for Virgin Atlantic) 38, 174
doorstop 223
Pebble vase 36, *38*
Secticon clock (Mangiarotti) 214
Serica glassware 118–19, 135
Sesame tealight holders 195
seven-branch candelabrum 25, 60, 68–69
Sheppard, Richard 82
Shetland Silvercraft 36, *37*, 45, 164

Shiner, Cyril 11, 44
ship's decanter 134–35
Signature range
cookbook and tablet stand 204
household scissors and stand 205
knives and block 41, 45, 184–87
salt and pepper mills 45, 197
storage jars 207
utensils and stand 183, 195
silver and amethyst glass condiment set 18, 52–53
Silver & Stål 17
Silver Trust coffee sets 36, 171
The Silver Wink trophy 232
silverware
1950s (student work) 13, 14, 15, 16, 18, 50
1950s 19–20, 25–26, 60, 68–69, 72–77, 232, 234, 238, 240
1960s 30, 76–77, 82–84, 100–103, 120–21, 126–27, 232, 233, 234–35,
236–37, 238–39, 241
1970s 34, 35, 134–39, 144–45, 228, 233, 234–35, 236–37, 238–39, 240–41
1980s 35, 36, 37, 41, 150–51, 154–57, 241
1990s 36, 173, 241
Simplan architectural fittings 115, 212
Society of Industrial Artists and Designers (Chartered Society of
Designers) 30
SonA kettle 27, 224
Smithsonian Institution 25, 60, 69
Sparta lighting (for Chad Lighting) 36, 168–69
Spring cutlery (Walker & Hall) 22–23, 54–55
St. Lucia coffee service 150
St. Mary's Church, Swansea silverware 76–77
Stabler, Harold 16, 17
stacking tea set 15, 16, 51
stainless steel 14, 15, 16–17, 51
stainless steel wares
1950s 15, 16, 19, 20, 21, 22–23, 44, 51, 52–67, 70–71, 224–25
1960s 23, 26–27, 76–77, 90–93, 106–7, 114, 116, 122–23, 224–25, 226–27,
228
1970s 34, 35, 132–33, 140–43, 213, 216, 226–27, 228–29
1980s 34–35, 36, 152–53, 228–29
1990s 38–39, 172, 174–75, 227, 229, 230–31
2000s to present 41, 85, 180–206, 230–31
Stanton cutlery 38–39, 45, 175
Starpacks trophy 232
'Staybrite' stainless steel (Firth Brown and 'Olde Hall') 16
Stedelijk Museum, Amsterdam 47, 106
Strong, Sir Roy (Victoria and Albert Museum) 150
The Studio magazine 19, 30, 97
Super Avon jug range (for Old Hall) 122–23
Surprise clock (for Goldsmiths' Hall) 154–55
Sutherland, Graham 25
swan-necked coffee set 26, 75
Sweden 14–15, 17, 44, 50

Tarratt, George 84
Taylor's Eye Witness scissors 34–35, 117, 142–43
teak 60, 75
Thames cutlery 229
Thebe (Arström for Gense) 17
Theodor Olsen, Bergen 14, 15
3000 Series lighting (for Lumitron) 108–9
Torben Satin cutlery 230
Tower of London goblet 35, 138–39
Trattoria cutlery 85, 230
Tree pendant (for Shetland Silvercraft) 37
trivets 36, 158, 164–65, 220
trophies (silver) 232–33

Vale cutlery 230
Viceroy cutlery 229
Victor Cast Ware 27, 97, 160, 161

Victoria and Albert Museum, London 12, 19, 34, 136, 150
candelabra 35–36, 150–51
Virgin Atlantic 38, 174, 213, 230
Vista cutlery 41, 182
Volkins, Katherine (Yamazaki Kinzoku Kogyo) 146

Walker & Hall 22–23, 54
Walters & Dobson 212
Wave cutlery (for Yamazaki Kinzoku Kogyo) 34, 228
Wejra kettle 227
Welch, Alice (daughter) 9, 27, 28, 35, 40, 44, 46, 242 n.62
Robert Welch Designs Ltd 38, 39, 41, 45, 196, 200, 207
Welch, Dorothy (née Perkins, mother) 10, 34, 46
Welch, Leonard (father) 10, 19, 46, 242 n.2
Welch, Patricia (née Hinksman, wife) 25, 27, 28, 30, 35, 37, 44, 45, 46
Welch, Robert Radford 6, 10, 24, 35, 40, 42, 46, 48, 57, 64, 171
childhood and education 10, 25, 44
death 39, 45, 175
houses 14, 19, 25, 27–28, 29, 44, 214
illnesses 19, 39, 45, 175
marriage and family 9, 25, 27, 28, 35, 37–38, 39, 41, 44, 45
MBE 35, 45
National Service 10–11, 44
at art school 10–12, 14, 15, 16–18
awards and prizes 11, 14, 18, 44, 45, 50, 54, 56, 86, 140
exhibitions 19–20, 25, 30, 33, 34, 47, 50, 56, 102, 106, 173
Indian trips 34, 35, 45, 158
Japanese trips 34–35, 45
National Diploma in Design (NDD) 11, 13, 44
Scandinavian trips 14–15, 30, 33, 44, 50, 51, 97, 122
studio/workshop 8, 9, 18–20, 24, 30, 41, 44, 45, 126
teaching and lecturing 20, 44, 90
writing 16–18, 44, 45
drawings and sketches 58, 62, 100, 118, 156, 158
design 75, 120, 135, 136, 142, 147
exhibition 86, 88
preliminary 56, 106, 150, 161
scale 90, 104, 113, 114
student 10, 11, 12, 25, 138
models 22, 25, 32, 69, 86, 114, 140, 150, 159
prototypes 15, 22, 51, 63, 70, 72–73, 81, 86, 106, 177
Welch, Rupert (son) 9, 27, 28, 35, 40, 44, 46
Robert Welch Designs Ltd 37–38, 39, 41, 45, 175, 180, 183, 186, 188, 202,
205, 207
Welch, William (son) 28, 35, 39, 41, 45, 46, 182
Westbury Bright cutlery 231
Westclox clocks 31, 33, 86–87, 112, 113, 214, 215
Weston, Ralph 242 n.56
White House, Alveston, Warwickshire 14, 25, 27–28, 29, 44, 214
J. & J. Wiggin 15–16, 18, 20, 21, 25, 44, 52, 232
Wiggin family 15, 16, 19, 23, 35
A.L. Wiggin trophy 232
Wigmore Distributors 27, 97
Williams, Ruth 41, 45, 188, 189, 190, 192, 194, 195, 203
Wilson, Sir David (British Museum) 156
Windrush range
candlesticks 41, 190–91
cutlery 228
Wirkkala, Tapio 30, 35
Woodroffe, Paul 162
Wormersley, Peter 28
Worshipful Company of Goldsmiths see Goldsmiths' Hall
Wynton Contracts ashtray 218

Yamazaki Kinzoku Kogyo 34, 35, 36, 45, 146–47
Yamazaki Serving Collection (for Yamazaki Kinzoku Kogyo) 36, 146
Yannedis & Co 210
yew 17, 235

Acknowledgements

I recall visiting Chipping Campden as a seven-year-old child and being taken to the Robert Welch studio shop, which along with the Design Centre in London's Haymarket was one of my very first encounters with 'proper' modern design. It must have had a formative influence for a few decades later, thanks to life's great meander, my husband Peter and I now find ourselves not only writing about Robert Welch, but also living in his beloved Chipping Campden – a town steeped in design history thanks to its earlier associations with the architect Charles Ashbee and his socially idealistic Guild of Handicraft. For us, therefore, this book has been a very personal project that has not only offered a fascinating voyage of discovery into the life and legacy of one of the most important British designers of the twentieth century, but also given us a truly unique insight into how modern design developed in Britain, revealing a tangible link between the Arts and Crafts Movement and postwar design, and demonstrating just how important the balancing of craft and industry was in this story.

In researching this book, we were extremely fortunate that Robert, throughout his life, was a meticulous hoarder of documents, whether it was his thesis, private letters, accounting ledgers, receipts from suppliers, magazine articles, newspaper clippings, launch invitations, product brochures, press releases or company catalogues – nothing, it would appear, had ever been thrown away. Added to this rich trove, the Robert Welch archive also possesses literally thousands of photographs, design drawings and sketchbooks, as well as hundreds of sample products, models and prototypes. Navigating this cornucopia of primary research material would have been completely impossible without the assistance of Charlotte Whitehead, Robert Welch Designs' archivist, who throughout the project has not only shared our obsessive enthusiasm for the subject, but offered countless thoughtful suggestions as well as invaluable practical help with sourcing images and fact-checking – therefore, to Charlie, we offer our most heart-felt thanks.

A big thank you must also go to Tony Muranka for his initial design concept for this book and to Andy Stammers for his exceptionally beautiful and specially commissioned new photography. Samuel Morley also deserves a very special mention for his wonderful graphic design work, as well as his good-natured perseverance with seemingly never-ending 'tweaks'. Thanks must also go to Tom Dunlop for help with sourcing addtional imagery, and to Emma Paragreen, the curator of the Sheffield Assay Office, for assisting with key hallmarking attributions. We also offer thanks to the Silver Trust, the Worshipful Company of Goldsmiths, Canterbury Cathedral and KODE Art Museums of Bergen for arranging and supplying new imagery for this book. In addition we would like to thank Angus Hyland, Peter Jones and Kim Wakefield at Laurence King Publishing for their helpful inputs, as well as Rosanna Lewis for her careful copy-editing, Lisa Cutmore and Geraldine Muranka for their exacting proofreading, and Sue Farr for her precise indexing.

And lastly, but by no means least, we are immensely grateful to Kit and Paul DeBretton Gordon for taking the time to explain how each new product is painstakingly developed 'the Robert Welch way', to Ray Leigh for imparting to us happy recollections of his long-time friend, and of course, to Pat, Alice and Rupert Welch for sharing their precious and deeply personal memories of a much-loved husband and father.

Picture Credits

All images used in this publication are from the archive of Robert Welch Designs, with the exception of the following:
p.14: KODE Art Museums of Bergen, photographer: Dan Fosse
pp. 72, 73 (both), 74 (top), 75 (top), 127, 238 (top row, left), 238 (top row, right): Worshipful Company of Goldsmiths, London, photographers: Richard Valencia, Clarissa Bruce p.171 (bottom): The Silver Trust

Please note: Any archival images credited (RW) were personally taken by Robert Welch, while all new photography from the Robert Welch archive was taken by Andy Stammers, Beata Bradford, Tony Muranka and Ivor Innes

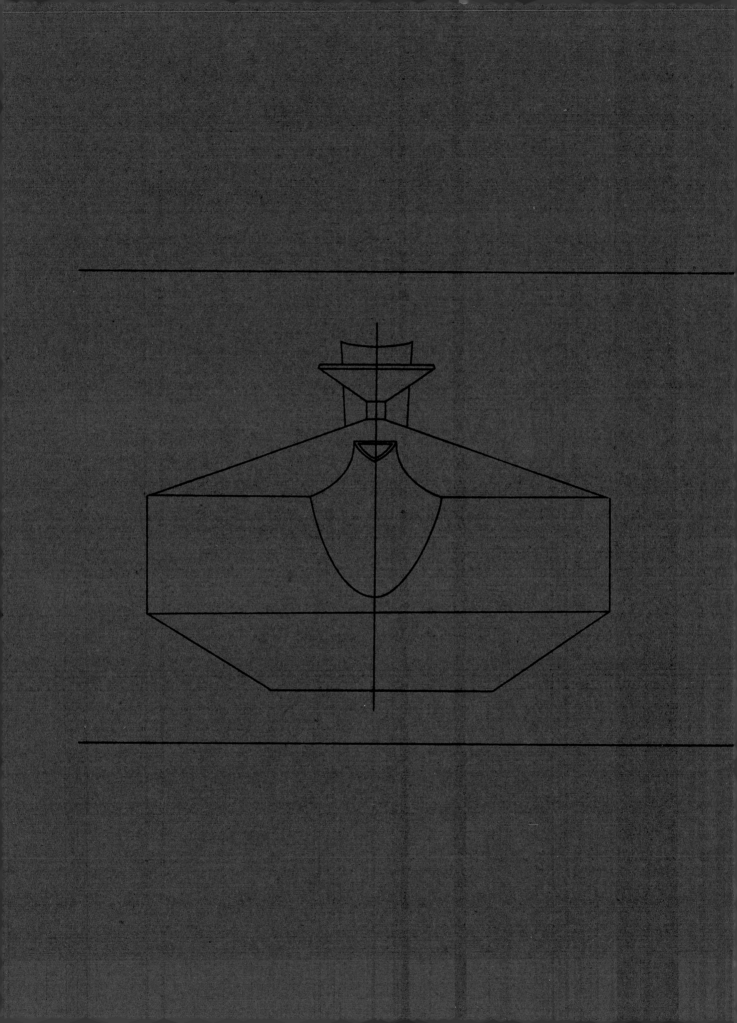